SCHAUM'S OUTLINE OF

THEORY AND PROBLEMS

OF

PUNCTUATION, CAPITALIZATION, AND SPELLING

Second Edition

EUGENE EHRLICH

*Senior Lecturer, Retired
Department of English
and Comparative Literature
School of General Studies
Columbia University*

SCHAUM'S OUTLINE SERIES
McGRAW-HILL

New York San Francisco Washington, D.C. Auckland Bogotá Caracus Lisbon
London Madrid Mexico City Milan Montreal New Dehli
San Juan Singapore Sydney Tokyo Toronto

W

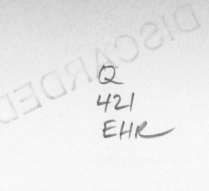

Q
421
EHR

EUGENE EHRLICH served for many years as Senior Lecturer in the Department of English and Comparative Literature, School of General Studies, Columbia University. He is the author of a number of books on language.

Schaum's Outline of Theory and Problems of
PUNCTUATION, CAPITALIZATION, AND SPELLING

4 5 6 7 8 9 10 11 12 13 14 15 16 17 18 19 20 PRS PRS 9 8 7

ISBN 0-07-019487-4

Sponsoring Editors: John Aliano, Patty Andrews
Production Supervisor: Leroy Young
Editing Supervisors: Meg Tobin, Maureen Walker

Library of Congress Cataloging-in-Publication Data

Ehrlich, Eugene H.
    Schaum's outline of theory and problems of punctuation,
capitalization, and spelling / by Eugene Ehrlich. — 2nd ed.
        p.   cm. — (Schaum's outline series)
    Includes index.
    ISBN 0-07-019487-4
    1. English language—Punctuation. 2. English language—
Capitalization. 3. English language—Orthography and spelling.
I. Title. II. Title: Theory and problems of punctuation,
capitalization, and spelling. III. Title: Punctuation,
capitalization, and spelling.
PE1450.E5 1992
421'.1—dc20   91-4108
                                                    CIP

McGraw-Hill

A Division of The McGraw-Hill Companies

Preface

Few aspects of writing trouble students more than the mechanics of punctuation, capitalization, and spelling. Professional writers keep within arms' length one or more dictionaries and reference books to check on point after point during the demanding hours of writing. No matter how experienced or how expert, few writers can write for long without having to ponder whether a comma is needed in a particular sentence, whether a certain word should be capitalized, whether this word or that is correctly spelled.

The bulk of this book is devoted to the rules of punctuation. Punctuation has only one function: that of making writing clearer for the reader. Our tendency today is to use as little punctuation as possible, but we must never forget that the inclination to omit punctuation for the sake of a clean-looking page must be weighed against the reading requirements of the intended audience. Equally important is adherence to the norms of capitalization and correct spelling, because eccentricity, deviance, inconsistency, or errors in these areas distract and confuse readers and ultimately undermine the function of any writing—the communication of a message as clearly and as efficiently as possible.

The rules and guidelines presented here are based on current practices of good writers and editors. Some of these rules will never change. Others are followed in the United States but not in Canada and other countries where English is spoken. Some are in the process of change because our language is always changing and particularly because newspaper practice, which tends to be imprecise, plays a large role in shaping our linguistic habits. Regardless of these factors, you will not be mistaken if you follow the rules and guidelines presented here. If you elect to disregard any of them, you should do so only on the basis of conscious choice for stylistic reasons.

As you do the work presented in this book, you will learn to reduce the number of times you must consult your trusted reference sources. Your writing will match more closely the requirements of good style in your first drafts of themes and papers. As you edit and revise your work, you will be able to recognize errors that have slipped by you initially. Even better, you will understand such things as why you must use a comma here and a semicolon there, why you must italicize one title and enclose another in quotation marks, why you must use brackets for one purpose and parentheses for another. You can also expect writing to become easier for you as you develop greater mastery of mechanics.

This book provides the useful rules of punctuation, capitalization, and spelling. In addition it offers exercises and answers to every exercise to give you the practice you need and the immediate feedback that will reinforce learning. You may work through the book from beginning to end or elect to start with those topics that you need immediately.

A brief appendix has been included, indicating the current conventions for punctuating footnotes, bibliographies, and personal and business letters. In addition, you will find the table of contents and index helpful in locating specific assistance that you need.

EUGENE EHRLICH

Contents

The Period, the Question Mark, and the Exclamation Point

THE PERIOD

The period has only two uses: to end most sentences and to indicate abbreviations. Much of the discussion that follows concerns the combined use of periods with other marks of punctuation.

At the End of a Sentence

A period is used to indicate the end of a declarative sentence, an imperative sentence, and certain sentence fragments.

A *declarative* sentence is one that makes a statement:

All the girls decided to cooperate fully with their leader.

An *imperative* sentence is one that states a command:

Cooperate or leave the group.

A *sentence fragment* is an incomplete sentence that is punctuated as though it were a sentence:

Who is to blame for the difficulties nations have in reaching international agreements? The nations themselves.   (*The nations themselves* lacks a predicate—a complete verb—and so it is considered a sentence fragment. But what does the reader understand from this fragment? *The nations themselves are to blame*. Although the fragment does not meet the full definition of a sentence, it functions as a sentence and is therefore punctuated as a sentence.)

Note that fragments may be punctuated with question marks and exclamation points when necessary.

Who?
They!
Really?
What a day!

1. Insert the correct punctuation in the following sentences, as shown in the examples below.

    All their encounters were pleasant.
    Be sure to complete your work by early afternoon and then close the office.
    Not if you are unwilling.

    1. We were amazed to find the judge so willing to hear our explanation
    2. Do four laps before you stop
    3. Only six of them may stay
    4. The theater will be dark this season if we do not convince the unions to work for the same money they earn now
    5. No answer
    6. Common sense dictates that caution is needed in that part of town
    7. Read your novel aloud

8.   You will find happiness in your work if you apply yourself to the full extent of your ability

9.   Hugh's project will keep him busy for many years

10.   Please take your seats now

In Abbreviations

A period is used to indicate an abbreviation. With few exceptions abbreviations must be marked by periods:

> Ms. Adams will chair the afternoon session.
>
> Alice was awarded the Ph.D. degree after seven years of study.   (Notice that no extra space is needed after the period following Ph.)
>
> We will be ready at seven a.m. Thursday.   (The abbreviation a.m. can also be written A.M.)

Acronyms are abbreviations that are pronounced as words. They are not punctuated:

> radar   (acronym for [ra]dio [d]etecting [a]nd [r]anging)
>
> UNESCO   (acronym for [U]nited [N]ations [E]ducational, [S]cientific, and [C]ultural [O]rganization)

A sentence ending in an abbreviation that is followed by a period does not require a second period:

> Her card calls attention to the fact that she is Margo Wykeham, D.D.S.

A sentence that requires a question mark or an exclamation point must have the appropriate mark even if the sentence ends in an abbreviation followed by a period:

> Where did Jonas Salk receive his M.D.?
>
> What an opportunity for someone without a Ph.D.!

Many abbreviations that once were punctuated with periods no longer are. This is a matter of taste and current practice. Government agencies, for example, tend to omit the period:

> TVA   (Tennessee Valley Authority, once known as T.V.A.)
>
> CIA   (Central Intelligence Agency, once known as C.I.A.)

Radio and television stations do not use periods for their call letters:

> WETA, WPIX, WNYC

Scholarly abbreviations still employ periods:

> l. (line)
>
> ll. (lines)
>
> op. cit.   (*opere citato*, in the work cited)
>
> viz.   (*videlicet*, namely)

Units of measurement do not use periods when abbreviated:

> mph   (miles per hour)
>
> rpm   (revolutions per minute)

2.   Insert periods and other marks of punctuation in the following sentences, taking care to close up words and letters that should not be given extra spacing. See the examples below.

> Josephine earned the **M.S.** degree in one academic year.
>
> He left a call for six **a.m.** in hope of arriving at the airport in time for his eight **a.m.** flight.

1.   Mrs Lewis will soon receive a B S degree and then go on to work toward an R N
2.   Cicero is believed to have been born in 106 B C and died in 43 B C
3.   She was a W A C during World War II and later became an instructor at U C L A
4.   Has Dr Wells arrived yet
5.   Do you think you will be able to offer that salary and attract a Ph D
6.   In the history of the college, she is the youngest person who ever received the B A degree
7.   The S E C is investigating the possibility of stock fraud in many Wall Street firms
8.   Why use *i e* when you can write its English equivalent, *that is*
9.   Acceleration due to gravity is 32 f p s p s
10. Which law school awarded that incompetent person a J D

Quotations

When a sentence ends in a quotation but requires quotation marks, a single period serves the quotation and the sentence. Required periods are placed *inside* final quotation marks.

Asked to name the most pressing problem facing the world at present, the Prime Minister said, "We simply have too many mouths to feed for the amount of food we can raise."

Last year they read one of Joseph Conrad's best stories, "Youth."

When a sentence ends in a quotation but requires a final question mark, no period is used. (See pages 77–79 for placement of question marks inside and outside quotation marks.)

Did the judge really say, "We will do nothing for the defendant"?

Can you recall the plot of Heinrich Böll's "The Death of Elsa Baskoleit"?

When a quotation at the end of a sentence requires a question mark, no final period is used.

Mr. Churchill then went on to ask, "Is England asleep at this fateful moment in history?"

The poem begins, "What is it to grow old?"

When a sentence ends in a quotation but requires a final exclamation point, no final period is used.

What a terrible mess was made by "the people's choice"!

When a quotation at the end of a sentence requires an exclamation point, no final period is used.

By now we are all familiar with the real truth of "Read my lips!"

3.   Insert periods, questions marks, and exclamation points where appropriate in the following sentences. Close up words and marks that should not be given extra spacing.

I refer you to Graves and Hodge, *The Reader Over Your Shoulder*, Chapter Two, "The Present Confusion of English Prose."

"Easter 1916" is one of her favorite poems.

Can you recite any lines from Auden's "In Praise of Limestone"**?**

1.   The chilling phrase he used at the close of his speech to the Congress was ''the threat of extinction ''
2.   In which great oration did Lincoln use the expression ''A house divided against itself ''
3.   To hell with his boring ''Idylls of the King ''
4.   The poor boy looked miserable as he struggled heroically with ''Why Did I Laugh Tonight ''
5.   We were all in the dark by the time Macbeth got around to exclaiming, ''Out, out, brief candle ''

6. Without a moment's hesitation the loyal minister replied, ''The Queen is always right ''

7. Are you certain that the witness said, ''I was entirely to blame and will accept full responsibility ''

8. We are going to the auction next week to see whether we can purchase the manuscript of Dorothy Parker's ''Big Blond ''

9. In 1 Timothy, Paul wisely warns, ''The love of money is the root of all evil ''

10. Can you tell me the source of ''A work that aspires, however humbly, to the condition of art should carry its justification in every line ''

With Parentheses

Depending on the context, periods are placed inside or outside the parentheses.

A parenthetical element may appear within a sentence and require no period within the parentheses.

> Johnson's three-month journey to the Hebrides in 1773 (see John Wain, *Samuel Johnson*, Chapter 25) was not without peril.

> Johnson's three-month journey to the Hebrides in 1773 was not without peril (see John Wain, *Samuel Johnson*, Chapter 25).

A parenthetical element may stand as a sentence and require a period.

> Johnson's three-month journey to the Hebrides in 1773 was not without peril. (See John Wain, *Samuel Johnson*, Chapter 25.)

Notice that only the last example has a period within parentheses. This is because the writer has chosen to treat the material as a complete sentence. In the first two examples, the periods punctuate the sentences, not the parenthetical elements, and so periods are not used within the parentheses.

4. Insert periods where appropriate in the following sentences. Close up words and marks that should not be given extra spacing.

> The young men were not willing to go to war for lack of principle (conditioning throughout their lives prevented such action) nor were they willing to go to war for principles they did not hold.

> I do not agree with certain modern stylists (Strunk and White, Stone and Bell, and Porter G. Perrin) on many aspects of sentence structure.

1. There was little left for the old Queen to do but die gracefully (Elizabeth Jenkins, *Elizabeth the Great*, pages 322 to 324)

2. Many so-called underdeveloped nations (they are actually resource-rich nations that have not yet exploited their mineral riches) form a potent bloc within many United Nations organizations

3. Now we will turn our attention to the career of Martin Luther (German theologian born in 1483)

4. Sen Barry Goldwater (Republican from Arizona) retired from the Senate after many years of service to his country (and his party)

5. The last witness of the day took the stand and was sworn (She was later to prove the most important witness the defense had in the case)

6. Three types of dogs (collies, Weimaraners, and German shepherds) are not suitable pets for people living in small city apartments

7. Many still remember Sam Rayburn with great affection for his firm performances in the chair at Democratic Party conventions (the Speaker was permanent chairman many times)

8. I hope to bring this matter to the floor (my health permitting) when the National Council on Women's Rights meets again

9. Many students forget that there are several coordinate conjunctions besides *and* (for example *but, for, or,* and *nor*) and thus lose opportunities to write forcefully

10. This approach to education has many of the virtues (and the faults) of all other systems I have studied (I hope we have seen the last of such proposals for a while)

With Commas

When a sentence includes an abbreviation that immediately precedes a comma, the period required in the abbreviation is retained.

> We will welcome Ellen Schneider, M.A., to the laboratory at a coffee hour next week.
>
> I had the easier task of playing against Charles Commager, Sr., while my doubles partner had to face last year's champion, Bill Whitcraft.

5. Insert periods where appropriate in the following sentences. Close up words and marks that do not need extra spacing.

> We were scheduled to leave at seven p.m., but our plane did not arrive until eight.
>
> The toastmaster will be Leonard Quinn, M.D., and the featured speaker will be Margaret Fraser, M.D.

1. Father Hans Gropius, S J , has written a marvelous new book on ethics
2. Whether you want to sit next to Ned, Jr , or not, you will be obliged to, since the dinner is being arranged by Mrs Ned, Jr , and you know how insistent she is on having her own way
3. He took his complaint to Francisco Ortiz, D D , the one man in the entire seminary who would receive such a complaint
4. Tamara Morgan, Ph D , will never offer a course again in this department
5. Mr Barnum Jeffreys, Esq , will serve as Master of the Hunt

THE QUESTION MARK

Direct Questions

A question mark is used after a direct question. A *direct question* is one that is quoted verbatim or is addressed directly to the reader. It is easy to understand why question marks are needed after the following sentences:

> "Shall I compare thee to a summer's day?"
>
> Has anybody here seen Kelly?
>
> By that stage of the war, who could have failed to understand that our country had made yet another tragic mistake?   (This thought is addressed to the reader as a rhetorical question, a question for which no answer is expected.)

A question mark is used for a question phrased as a declarative sentence but spoken with the rising intonation of a question.

> There is a bird in the house?   (Someone has stated that there is a bird in the house. The writer of this sentence replies incredulously with a repetition of the sentence, but intends it as a question.)
>
> You really are six years old?   (Another question in the form of a declarative sentence.)

6. Insert a question mark or period where appropriate in the following sentences. Extra space is provided for your convenience in writing.

Have you ever seen a rainbow?

"The election was won by the weaker candidate."

"The weaker candidate?"

1. Can you help me find an inexpensive hotel room in Florence

2. "The hardest knife ill-used doth lose his edge "—Shakespeare

3. "Today I shall help you with your homework."
   "Why today Won't tomorrow do just as well "

4. I shall ask Jane that question when I see her

5. Questions, questions; nothing but questions

6. Whom would you like to invite for dinner

7. Can you find your way by yourself

8. "Marine drill instructors never have been the kindliest of men "
   "Never "
   "Never "

9. What you call a mistake is what I call a deliberate evasion of duty

10. "Is this your book " he asked

11. *Hamlet*: There's another Why may not that be the skull of a lawyer Where be his quiddities now, his quillities, his cases, his tenures, and his tricks Why does he suffer this mad knave now to knock him about the sconce with a dirty shovel, and will not tell him of his action of battery Hum!

12. *Hamlet*: Alas, poor Yorick! I knew him, Horatio, a fellow of infinite jest, of most excellent fancy He hath borne me on his back a thousand times And now how abhorred in my imagination it is! My gorge rises at it Here hung those lips that I have kissed I know not how oft Where be your gibes now Your gambols, your songs, your flashes of merriment that were wont to set the table on a roar Not one now to mock your own grinning Quite chapfallen Now get you to my lady's chamber, and tell her, let her paint an inch thick, to this favor she must come Make her laugh at that Prithee, Horatio, tell me one thing
    Horatio: What's that, my lord
    Hamlet: Dost thou think Alexander looked o' this fashion i' th'earth

13. I ask you only one question: The petty amount of money this old man had in his pocket was enough to make you commit such a crime

14. The attorney asked me whether I had any interest in the estate

15. I wonder if you understand what a terrible act you committed

Indirect Questions

An *indirect* question is a question that is not quoted verbatim or addressed directly to the reader. It is written as a subordinate element of a sentence and does not require a question mark or quotation marks.

They asked me whether I could help their son find a job.

The detective questioned me about where I was on the night of the crime.

While direct questions are followed by question marks, indirect questions are not.

7. Insert question marks or periods where appropriate in the following sentences.

Are you going to the office tomorrow?

I want to know whether you are going to the office tomorrow.

1. The policeman said once more, "Do you remember stopping at a bar on your way home from the party "

2. I have repeatedly asked myself the most important question of all: Is this the man with whom I want to spend the rest of my life

3. Jerome tormented himself with questions concerning the universality of temptation

4. The director finally asked, ''You are certain you want to take this position ''

5. I would like to know how much you care about my daughter

6. Do you care for her enough to think of her happiness before yours

7. Are you certain you followed all reasonable leads in your research

8. You must make sure you ask the right questions of your witnesses

9. Do you really know what you want to do with the rest of your life

10. Has anyone ever asked you whether you know what you want to do with the rest of your life

Polite Requests

In the desire to phrase requests politely, speakers and writers may use a word order that usually is employed for questions.

Will you please check to see whether you have all the necessary forms before you leave the room.

May I hear a round of applause for this excellent speaker.

Notice that these sentences do not require question marks. They are not questions. The first one is a polite request, and the second one may be thought of as a polite command. The audiences for both sentences are expected to comply rather than reply.

8. Insert periods and question marks where appropriate after the following sentences.

Will Jimmy please stop smiling for just one moment.

Can you understand what Gerry is trying to say?

1. May I hear from you soon

2. Is there any chance you will be visiting our city sometime this year

3. Will you please send me two pounds of your best coffee

4. Will you please stop your bickering

5. Is there any way I can convince you of my good intentions

6. Can you please help me cross the street

7. Is there any way out of this incredible mess

8. May we show you the correct solution now

9. Is there any cream for the coffee

10. Will you please deliver the flowers I ordered

Questions within a Sentence

Question marks are used after questions within a sentence. Writers occasionally construct sentences containing a series of questions. These questions can all be punctuated by question marks to emphasize the individual questions. Because the questions are all part of a single sentence, the first word of each question is not capitalized.

The attorney asked the witness where he was born? where he grew up? how much formal education he had? where he worked? whether he was married or single? where he lived? and how long he had known the accused?

Such questions can also be punctuated with commas. Notice that if the sentence itself is not a question, then the final punctuation is a period. If the sentence itself is a question, the final punctuation is a question mark.

The attorney asked the witness where he was born, where he grew up, how much formal education he had, where he worked, whether he was married or single, where he lived, and how long he had known the accused.

Did the attorney ask the witness where he was born, where he grew up, how much formal education he had, where he worked, whether he was married or single, where he lived, and how long he had known the accused?

The questions in the above sentences are not direct quotations. In the following sentence, the questions are quoted directly.

The attorney submitted a series of written questions to the witness: "Where were you born?" "Where did you grow up?" "How much formal education have you had?" "Are you married or single?" "Where do you live?" "How long have you known the accused?"

Writers also construct sentences that include questions placed parenthetically within the sentence. (See pages 77–79.) A question mark is needed after such questions.

They insisted they knew nothing of the affair—where were they while so much was going on?—and should be permitted to go home without further interrogation.

9. The following sentences contain series of questions, series of statements, and parenthetical questions and statements. Where appropriate, replace commas with question marks between elements of the series, and insert question marks where appropriate in parenthetical elements.

Can you say what you did with the license plate, the tool box, the automobile registration, and the spare tire?

Can you say what you did with the license plate? the tool box? the automobile registration? the spare tire?

He searched and searched until he was weary—was there no end to his search—and then searched some more.

He searched and searched until he was weary—was there no end to his search?—and then searched some more.

1. Why were they so interested in his locker, his school bag, his lunch box, his desk.

2. I cannot go on this way—do you understand—because no good can come of so much deceit, lying, and treachery.

3. Can you repair washing machines, television sets, small appliances?

4. We are going to undertake a comprehensive study of American purchasing habits, voting patterns, and family structure.

5. Have you wondered why many city families now own dogs, why sales of locks and window bars have increased dramatically, why burglar alarm companies are mushrooming?

Uncertain Information

A question mark enclosed in parentheses shows that information is open to question. When the best available sources cannot supply a date, a number, or any other asserted fact with full certainty, the writer indicates this by inserting a question mark enclosed in parentheses after the item open to question. This does not mean that the writer can simply hazard a guess and then fall back on the question mark enclosed in parentheses.

Geoffrey Chaucer was born in 1340(?) and died in 1400.   (The best scholarship indicates Chaucer was born in 1340 but no one is certain of the date.)

Theodoric, 454(?)–526, was king of the Ostrogoths and ruler of Italy from 493 until his death.

If the uncertain item is placed inside parentheses, the question mark is not enclosed in its own parentheses.

Geoffrey Chaucer (1340?–1400) was the author of the *Canterbury Tales, Troylus and Crysede, The Parlement of Foules,* and other works still read today.

Johann Gutenberg (1398?–1468) was the inventor of movable printing types.

Question Marks Not Used to Indicate Irony

A question mark cannot do more than indicate a question or a doubt. Amateurs mistakenly use the question mark enclosed in parentheses to indicate to their readers that a word or expression in a particular sentence is not intended in the usual sense.

Wrong   The actor showed a grasp of pathos(?) in the second act that left us laughing uncontrollably. The question mark is intended to show that the writer did not want us to take *pathos* seriously. The rest of the sentence should make this clear without the mark.)

Right   The actor showed an inept grasp of pathos in the second act that left us laughing uncontrollably.

Wrong   She showed her charity(?) in everything she did.   (The writer obviously wants us not to take *charity* in the literal sense. The question mark leaves it up to the readers to find this out.)

Right   She showed her lack of charity in everything she did.

Right   She betrayed her lack of charity in everything she did.

Right   Everything she did betrayed her lack of charity.

If a word is intended by a writer to be taken in other than its usual meaning, the writer has to construct the rest of the sentence in a manner that will not leave the reader in doubt. At most, the writer may use the expression *so-called* before the intended irony. Inserting a question mark is a poor substitute for clear writing.

10.   Insert question marks enclosed in parentheses within the following sentences wherever they are appropriate. Where they are not, rewrite the sentences.

Ramses I, 1324(?)–1258 B.C., was a king of ancient Egypt.

The general hilarity that followed was proof of his ineptness as a comedian.

The general, forced hilarity that followed was proof of his ineptness as a comedian.

1.   Late in his term of office, the president still showed the same sparkling wit that had dulled his early years in office.

2.   The realistic portrayal of life in Japan that marks Gilbert and Sullivan's *The Mikado* represented the only impression many Europeans of that time had of the Orient.

3. That certainly was a good brand of tobacco he had in his little cigarette.

---

4. Saint Wenceslaus, 903 –935 A.D., was duke of Bohemia in the last seven years of his life.

---

5. Shakespeare's earliest work as a dramatist, *Henry VI*, written in 1591 , is not often acted today.

Inside or Outside Quotation Marks?

When question marks are combined with quotation marks, a little thought is needed: Is the question part of the quote? Then the question mark goes inside the final quotation mark. Is the sentence itself a question? Then the question mark goes outside the final quotation mark. (See pages 77–79 for the rules covering the combination of question marks and other punctuation.)

Right   Did he really say, "I would rather be dead than hungry"?   (The sentence is a question, not the quoted material.)

Right   She asked, "Are you so hungry that you cannot wait another minute or so for dinner?" (The quotation is the question.)

When a question mark is used after a quotation at the end of a sentence, a question mark is not needed after the final quotation mark even though the sentence enclosing the quotation is itself a question.

Wrong   Did she really ask, "Are you so hungry that you cannot wait another minute for dinner?"? (We never have two question marks consecutively.)

Right   Did she really ask, "Are you so hungry that you cannot wait another minute for dinner?" (Notice that the entire sentence is a question and that the quotation is a question. The single question mark for the quotation is enough.)

Notice also that a sentence that ends in a question mark does not require a final period, nor is a comma needed when a question mark appears.

Wrong   My mother said, "Is Alice coming to dinner tonight?".

Right   My mother said, "Is Alice coming to dinner tonight?"

Wrong   "Is Alice coming to dinner?," my mother asked.

Right   "Is Alice coming to dinner?" my mother asked.

11. Insert periods and question marks where appropriate in the following sentences. Extra space is provided before and after quotation marks for your convenience.

> The fireman said, "Have the police been here yet?" as he jumped from his truck.
> Does he always ask, "Can you spare three dollars?"

1. Do you know that Anne's favorite story from *Dubliners* is "Araby "
2. "Have you mailed the package yet, Jon " his teacher asked
3. The child kept pestering his mother with one nagging question, "When will Daddy be home " until she burst into tears
4. Do they always say "please " every time they ask for something
5. Can you remember his saying, "I will get what I want or you won't see me again "
6. "Did the choir sing well " the minister asked

7. Is your mother the kind who always says, "Why do you want the car tonight "

8. I am not sure he really said, "One more word like that, and I'll blow your head off. Do you understand "

9. "Have you ever seen a more beautiful sunset in your life " the guide asked.

10. The worst news came at the end of the examination, when Dr. Alpert asked in his most innocent manner, "Have you ever had root canal therapy "

THE EXCLAMATION POINT

Emphatic Interjections

An exclamation point is used after an emphatic interjection. Interjections are words and phrases that express emotion. Some of the most common are *ah, gosh, ha, hello, no, oh,* and *yes.* All these interjections can be expressed with great emphasis or with little emphasis, depending on the feelings of the speaker or writer. When little emphasis is intended, the appropriate punctuation is a period.

"Oh. I didn't know you wanted me to call back."

If the interjection is made part of a sentence and little emphasis is intended, a comma is appropriate.

"Oh, I didn't know you wanted me to call back."

When the interjection is intended to show great emphasis, an exclamation point is used.

"No! No! I will never submit!"
"Hello! I'm so happy you called!"

12. Rewrite the following sentences to heighten the emphasis of the interjections.

Hold on, you do not understand what I'm trying to say.
Hold on! You do not understand what I'm trying to say.

Wait, you dropped your purse.
Wait! You dropped your purse.

1. Please, let the child explain what she means.

    _____

2. Gosh, that meal was the best I have ever eaten.

    _____

3. Lord, I've made a mistake.

    _____

4. Ah, that wine has such a delicate bouquet.

    _____

5. Ha, you are trapped and will never get away!

    _____

6. O, my offense is rank; it smells to heaven. (Shakespeare)

    _____

7. Lo, thy dread empire Chaos is restored. (Pope)

    _____

8. Ouch, this needle really hurts!

    _____

9.   Yes, I will do whatever you want.

_____

10.   No, you cannot have any more cake.

_____

Exclamatory Phrases, Clauses, and Sentences

An exclamation point is used after any truly exclamatory sentence or sentence element. The exclamation point is a trap for the unskilled writer who tries to convey strong feeling by punctuating sentence after sentence with exclamation points; having exhausted exclamation points in this way, such a writer may have to go to double and then triple exclamation points for emphasis.

Unfortunately, one exclamation point is all that is allowed under the rules of punctuation. Doubling signals that the writer lacks words needed to express strong feeling. The rule calls for an exclamation point after any *truly exclamatory* sentence element, and you must decide what is worthy of this mark, keeping in mind that every exclamation point used may rob the following one of effectiveness.

Typical correct uses include sentences containing *what* or *how* and used as exclamations.

What a beautiful child!

How I suffered!

Curses and blessings:

Damn you!

May your life be happy!

Accusations and characterizations:

Thief! Cheat!

You cowardly liar!

It is obvious from these examples that most writing does not require exclamation points, even when strong emotions are being conveyed. Consider, for example, this passage from a radio speech of Winston Churchill on July 14, 1940, when England was threatened with invasion.

We shall defend every village, every town, and every street. The vast mass of London itself, fought street by street, could easily devour an entire hostile army; and we would rather see London laid in ruins and ashes than that it should be tamely and abjectly enslaved.

Not a single exclamation point is needed. The vigor of the language supplies the desired strength.

13.   Insert exclamation points or other punctuation where appropriate in the following sentences.

How lovely a view!

May you live a thousand years!

1.   What a mess I'm in
2.   What time is it
3.   I would say he was rich—he has much more than one million—even by today's standards
4.   May the devil take them
5.   May I have a glass of water
6.   A fine husband you are
7.   Not another minute
8.   You marvelous child
9.   The greatest in all the world
10.   How she worried

Forceful Commands

An exclamation point is used after forceful commands. Here, the use of the exclamation point is a direct attempt to convey the urgency with which a command is issued. If a command is less than forceful, no exclamation point is needed. Using an exclamation point in less than forceful commands is an error of punctuation.

Wrong   Send in your application today!   (While the writer is telling the reader to do something, you can be sure that the writer only hopes the reader will do so. How can a writer command a reader to comply?)

Right   Send in your application today.

Right   Put down your gun!   (A forceful command and enforceable too!)

Right   Follow that car!   (The most famous command of Hollywood movies.)

You must differentiate between forceful commands and mere requests. The former require exclamation points, the latter only periods.

14.   Insert an exclamation point or other mark of punctuation where appropriate in the following sentences.

> Get out of my sight!
> Mind your manners.

1. Stop running through the halls
2. Stop smoking if you want to live a long life
3. Stand back
4. Be quiet
5. Have another glass of wine
6. The little boy cried, ''Run for your lives ''
7. Gather ye rosebuds while ye may,
       Old Time is still a-flying,
    And this same flower that smiles today
       Tomorrow will be dying
8. Sell everything you own and run away with me
9. Drink milk for health
10. Get out as quickly as you can

Inside or Outside Quotation Marks?

If an exclamation is part of a quotation, the exclamation point goes inside the final quotation mark. If the sentence itself is the exclamation, rather than the quotation, the exclamation point goes outside the final quotation mark. Again, there are a few details that need discussion, but the general rule is firm.

Right   The young officer waited the required three minutes and then cried, "Charge!"   (The quotation is the exclamation.)

Right   How extraordinary that she has never read "The Wasteland"!   (The sentence is the exclamation.)

When an exclamation point is used after a quotation at the end of a sentence, an exclamation point is not needed after the final quotation mark even though the sentence enclosing the quotation is itself an exclamation as well.

Right   What greater joy than to read Lee Strout White's "Farewell, My Lovely!"   (The exclamation point is part of the title of White's essay. Even though the sentence is itself an exclamation, the single exclamation point is sufficient.)

Wrong   Don't ever yell "Fire!"!   (We never have two exclamation points consecutively.)

Right   Don't ever yell "Fire!"

Notice also that a sentence that ends in an exclamation point does not require a final period, nor is a comma ever used with an exclamation point.

Wrong   The police officer yelled, "Drop your gun or I'll fire!".

Right   The police officer yelled, "Drop your gun or I'll fire!"

Wrong   "May he live a long and happy life!", an old woman said.

Right   "May he live a long and happy life!" an old woman said.

15.   Insert periods and exclamation points where appropriate in the following sentences. Extra space is provided before and after quotation marks for your convenience.

> Don't ever again forget to say "sir"!
>
> "Ship it C.O.D.!" said my supervisor.

1. Henry Baldridge—damn him!—shouted, "Help "
2. How marvelous are the opening lines of "Tintern Abbey "
3. "If you have nothing more to say," she answered, "get out of here "
4. The bride's mother toasted the new couple: "May the new husband and wife live happily together May their children enjoy a good family life May the children's grandparents enjoy fifty more years "
5. What a great song is "Happy Days Are Here Again "
6. The sergeant bellowed, "Rookie, get here P.D.Q. "
7. How I love Ernest Hemingway's story "Fifty Grand "
8. "How nice to see you again after all these years " she exclaimed
9. Stop saying "England expects that every man will do his duty "
10. All she could say was "Oh "

Chapter 2

The Comma

Like all the other marks of punctuation, the comma functions to help readers understand readily what a sentence means. At various times the comma may join, enclose, or separate the various parts of a sentence.

Items in a Series

Commas are used to separate items in a series. The items in a series may be words, phrases, or clauses. The last item is usually preceded by a conjunction, such as *and* or *or*. When no conjunction is used to connect the last item in a series, the last item is still separated by a comma: *a, b, c.*

Words in Series

Breakfast, lunch, dinner, and *supper* are still my favorite occasions between snacks.

Our city manager will not recommend *inexperienced, unreliable,* or *nonunion* contractors for work on public housing projects.

We arrived at the concert *exhausted, hungry, ill-tempered.*

Phrases in Series

Plenty of strong tobacco, a well-seasoned pipe, and *a shelf of good books* saw the old professor through his lonely winters.

Out of funds, unlucky in love, afraid to face the future alone, the young man decided to return to his parents' farm.   (The comma after *alone* is explained on pages 21–24.)

Clauses in Series

Emma wrote newspaper releases, Richard wrote copy for radio broadcasts, and *the rest of us helped the candidate prepare her speeches.*

My company is ready to hire fifty more factory hands, other companies have announced plans for expansion, the new shopping center needs many additional sales clerks, yet *our town still has a high rate of unemployment.*

1. In the following sentences insert commas where appropriate to separate items in series.

    Bill could not manage a job, a family, and college at the same time.

    Every morning began in the same way: out of bed, a hurried breakfast, children off to school, a quick clean-up, off to work.

    Many dental assistants prepare amalgam, sterilize instruments, clean patients' teeth, assist in operations, and keep all records of treatment.

    1. The size and effectiveness of your vocabulary affect your writing speaking and reading throughout your life.
    2. Norma has not yet decided whether she will continue in her present job work only half-time or give up work completely.
    3. Some of us are not aware of the expense the anxiety the inconvenience encountered in living outside great cities.

15

4. Strauss found himself burdened by heavy debt seriously hampered by poor health yet gloriously happy in his general acclaim.

5. In our European travels we found ourselves received everywhere with warmth hospitality and generosity.

6. Most of the merchandise the store offered for sale was shabby overpriced or old-fashioned.

7. They were equally fond of swimming dancing hiking and riding.

8. The oldest daughter took up nursing the next prepared for college teaching but the youngest gave no thought to the future.

9. Daisy was able to find her food eat it and hide the empty dish no matter how we tried to fool her.

10. Evergreen trees make a splendid hedge are easy to maintain and have long lives.

The Final Comma in a Series

Some writers omit the comma before the conjunction in a series, and many teachers sanction the omission by telling students the final comma is optional. In fact, the final comma is a small mark that provides insurance against misreading.

Unclear   My favorite breakfast is juice, toast, crunchy granola and maple syrup and coffee.   (Imagine eating a dish of *crunchy granola and maple syrup and coffee!* Just one more comma would do wonders for that breakfast.)

Clear   My favorite breakfast is juice, toast, crunchy granola and maple syrup, and coffee.

Some sentences leave readers uncertain over whether the modifier of the next-to-last item in a series carries over to the last item. This can often happen without the final comma before the *and*.

Unclear   All the children in the family agreed they would need bicycles, motorized bikes and scooters. (Are the *scooters motorized* as well as the *bikes?*)

Clear   All the children in the family agreed they would need bicycles, motorized bikes, and scooters.   (The scooters are not *motorized*.)

Clear   All the children in the family agreed they would need bicycles, motorized bikes, and motorized scooters.   (The *bikes* and *scooters* are *motorized*. Repeating the modifier *motorized* does the trick, and the comma before *and* does no harm.)

Clear   All the children in the family agreed they would need bicycles, scooters, and motorized bikes.   (Rearranging the items in the series helps clarify the sentence, and the final comma does its share toward ensuring clarity.)

2. Insert commas where appropriate in the following sentences.

> Emily bought two magazines, a quart of milk, and honey.
>
> We all need a pleasant environment, good company, and self-respect.

1. Wherever he went, Sam carried his tape recorder typewriter notebook dictionary and thesaurus.

2. The angry landlord told my son to clean the apartment pay the rent and get out.

3. "Coffee tea or milk?" was all I heard on the long trip across the country.

4. Keats Shelley Byron Coleridge and Wordsworth are usually studied in a single college English course.

5. During their long holidays together, Mickey and Margie concentrated on rest good eating and relaxed conversation.

6. The children sat still all though the enforced recess and regretted their unruly behavior.

7. The young bride took no interest in the conversation of her women neighbors the men her husband invited home or the daily telephone call from her doting mother.

8. Unemployment statistics do not reflect accurately the number of people who are no longer looking for work the underemployed and all the unfortunate college graduates who have not yet found their first jobs.

9. The tired author was still writing new material correcting first drafts and reading the initial galleys.

10. Many things adults do without thinking about them are difficult tasks for the young the disabled and the mentally handicapped.

The Bacon-and-Eggs Mistake

Paired words or phrases in series are correctly treated as single items. Careless writers sometimes treat members of a pair as individual items, inserting a comma where none is needed. This is called the bacon-and-eggs mistake. Consider the following sentence.

Right   You may order anything you want at my diner as long as you order sausage and eggs, ham and eggs, or bacon and eggs.

This sentence contains a series of three items: *sausage and eggs, ham and eggs,* and *bacon and eggs.* Each item in the series consists of a pair of nouns connected by *and.* Commas are used to separate the items in the series. To break up any of the paired nouns with a comma or any other mark of punctuation is to destroy the intended meaning.

Commas are not used to break up happily paired words or phrases.

Right   The chef said he needed sausage, ham, bacon, and eggs.

This sentence contains a series with no paired words or phrases. The chef needs four items: *sausage, ham, bacon,* and *eggs.* He may use them for any number of dishes in addition to his breakfast specialties.

Wrong   I resent paying so much for dinner and having to implore the waiter for a napkin, water, bread, and butter.

We always think of *bread and butter* as an inseparable pair at the dining table. To break up the pair by use of a comma is a mistake. If we want readers to understand that *bread and butter* are separate items, we must rewrite the sentence. If we want readers to understand *bread and butter* as a single item, we must eliminate one comma and supply another *and.*

Right   I resent paying so much for dinner and having to beg the waiter for a napkin, water, butter, and bread.   (This sentence tells us that I had to ask for *butter* alone at least once and for *bread* alone at least once.)

Right   I resent paying so much for dinner and having to beg the waiter for a napkin, water, and bread and butter.   (The waiter neglected to provide *bread and butter*, and I had to ask for it.)

3. Insert commas where appropriate in the following sentences.

Tom is willing to pay for transportation, room and board, and out-of-pocket expenses.

My favorite stationery store maintains adequate supplies of paper and ink, carbon paper, and typewriter ribbons.

1. The rebel army soon found itself without fuel and electricity medical supplies food and water able-bodied troops and officers and the will to fight.

2. Nations of the world are now concerned with potential shortages of grain and fodder vital minerals and fuels and food for growing populations.

3. Medical researchers maintain constant surveillance of epidemic and pandemic disease new viral and bacterial strains and water and air pollutants.

4. Bread and jam peanuts and popcorn and candy bars and soft drinks cannot be counted on to nourish growing children.

5. Trick knees and athlete's foot are not the exclusive property of athletes.

6. The dancer moved rapidly across the stage turned and leapt and then dropped gracefully to her knees.

7. Communities often find that city administrators will usually listen to complaints promise attention and relief during elections and continue to ignore people's needs.

8. He learned patience from his father and thrift from his mother.

9. Soldiers and sailors school teachers and construction workers and physicians and nurses marched together in the demonstration for better health care.

10. The building tilted dangerously during renovation appeared to straighten and settle and then suddenly collapsed completely.

Independent Clauses

A comma is used to separate independent clauses joined by a coordinating conjunction. Independent clauses can stand alone as sentences:

> *She fought for the rights of the homeless for many years. Her younger sister showed no interest in the seemingly endless struggle.*

Independent clauses can also be joined to form compound sentences:

> *She fought for the rights of the homeless for many years, but her younger sister showed no interest in the seemingly endless struggle.*

To form a compound sentence of two or more independent clauses, a coordinating conjunction—*and, but, for, nor, or, so,* or *yet*—is usually used before the final independent clause. A comma precedes the conjunction. (For exceptions in the use of a comma in this construction, see the following pages.

The following sentences show how important this comma is:

> With his remaining strength Larry fought the powerful sailor, and a military policeman who was passing by came finally to his aid.   (Without the comma after *sailor*, readers may think *Larry fought* the *military policeman* as well as the *sailor*.)

> We must do all we can to protect the environment, or the vitality of natural forces may prove inadequate to sustain life in a few more decades.   (Without the comma after *environment*, readers may think we must protect the *vitality of natural forces* as well as the *environment*.)

With two brief independent clauses, the comma is not used as long as there is no risk of misleading readers.

> Debbie left for home early but Ronald stayed all evening.

> The bird flew to the feeding station and the cat prepared to spring.

With more than two independent clauses, the rule for use of commas for items in series applies.

> The wind howled, the rain fell steadily, but we kept warm before the welcome fire.

> A sinister man walked slowly through the shop, the detective followed him closely, and an innocent-looking young woman snatched the necklace and slipped quickly into the street.

4. In the following sentences insert commas where appropriate to separate independent clauses.

> The auditor spent many hours searching the company books without success, yet the junior accountant was able to find the irregularity in a few minutes.

Caesar delivered his speech with great feeling and everyone cheered.

Birds entertain the invalid, dogs comfort their owners, but gerbils and hamsters just eat and reproduce.

1. We have learned much about mistakes made throughout history but our leaders do not seem to have profited much from those mistakes.

2. The islands still held strong attraction for Juan and José and they could not become accustomed to life on the mainland.

3. Children are permitted to play baseball but football is forbidden.

4. One couple wanted to rent a large apartment another wanted to rent a house and the rest could not make up their minds.

5. A typewritten term paper makes a good impression but the most important factor in earning good grades is the quality of thought and writing.

6. The cities are gradually facing up to the need for improving public housing but sufficient funds are not easy to obtain in times of recession and inflation.

7. Sycamores shed much of their bark almost every summer yet these shade trees do much to improve the appearance of streets in our neighborhood.

8. Prices of most commonly used foods seem to rise continually and so frugal shoppers must select carefully when buying food for family meals.

9. Her laboratory assistant could find no reason for the death of the animals in the sterile room nor could the consulting pathologist.

10. Roofing materials have not changed much over the years but the average homeowner still has not mastered the art of putting a roof down perfectly.

11. Children were always welcomed by the lonely old couple for they missed the sound of young voices in their home.

12. Drug users have little opportunity to find useful employment and so they frequently resort to crime to gain the money needed to support their habits.

13. Inner-city problems will have to be solved by federal authorities or municipal governments will soon find themselves bankrupt.

14. Graduate students in many universities find themselves unable to go on with their studies or embark on new careers.

15. They completed preparations for the trip and retired early.

Introductory Phrases and Clauses

A comma is used to separate a long introductory phrase or subordinate clause from the rest of the sentence. The comma is not used when there is no risk of misleading readers. This rule is open to interpretation of the word *long*. The following discussion presents two interpretations to give you the background for selecting the practice you wish to adopt.

Many sentences begin with introductory phrases or subordinate clauses. A *phrase* is defined as a grammatical unit of two or more words that does not contain a verb. A *verbal phrase*, which will be discussed later, is one that contains a verbal. A *subordinate clause* differs from an independent clause in that it cannot stand alone as a sentence. The next two sentences show a phrase and a subordinate clause used as introductory sentence elements.

Phrase:

For many hours after midnight, the husband and wife sat and wondered why their oldest son had not yet returned from his date.

Subordinate Clause:

> *While his two passengers waited impatiently,* the chauffeur worked as hard as he could to start the limousine again and drive the couple to the airport.

Recall the wording of the comma rule for introductory phrases and clauses. It speaks of *long* introductory phrases and subordinate clauses. Are the phrase and clause in the two sentences above short or long? The phrase has five words, and the clause has six. Who is to say whether they are short or long? Any judgment of length is merely a judgment. Notice, however, that both the phrase and the clause are followed by commas that separate them from the rest of their respective sentences. If we remove the commas, we find that the sentences read well. Would readers have any difficulty interpreting these sentences?

> *For many hours after midnight* the husband and wife sat and wondered why their oldest son had not yet returned from his date.

> *While his passengers waited impatiently* the chauffeur worked as hard as he could to start his limousine again and drive the couple to the airport.

These sentences are clear without the commas. The reason is that the introductory element in each sentence is closely related to the sense of the main clause. Only when an introductory element is not related to the sense of the main clause is there a chance of misinterpretation. Yet many writers adopt an arbitrary rule for using commas after introductory phrases and subordinate clauses.

Writers who like foolproof rules adopt the following rule: *Use a comma after every introductory sentence element.* This approach avoids misleading readers and requires little thought. The drawback is that the rule may require more commas than most writers like to use.

Writers who prefer to use as little punctuation as possible and are willing to do a little extra thinking adopt a more liberal approach: (1) *Use a comma after introductory phrases and subordinate clauses of more than five words;* (2) *omit the comma after introductory phrases and subordinate clauses only when there is no chance of misleading readers.* With this approach the writer must count the words in introductory elements—a small task—and evaluate the risk of misleading readers—a larger task. The following sentences will illustrate the considerations involved.

Unclear   *Without a doubt* in a carload you will have more potatoes than you ever dreamed possible. (*Without a doubt* or *Without a doubt in a carload*? Doubts do not normally come in carload quantities, but why let readers wonder what is meant?)

Clear   *Without a doubt,* in a carload you will have more potatoes than you ever dreamed possible.

Notice that when the introductory phrase *Without a doubt* is removed from the sentence, a second introductory phrase *in a carload* remains. When *in a carload* serves as the introductory phrase of the sentence, readers cannot misinterpret even if the phrase is not followed by a comma.

Clear   *In a carload* you will have more potatoes than you ever dreamed possible.

Clear   *In a carload,* you will have more potatoes than you ever dreamed possible.

Unclear   *When the opportunity for changing lanes* passed our car remained stuck in the long line of stalled cars.   (Did the *opportunity pass* or did the *opportunity pass our car*? We know that cars cannot have opportunities, yet readers can be misled by the absence of a comma after *passed*. This sentence demands a comma under either the foolproof rule or the more liberal rule, since the introductory element has more than five words, but it illustrates the confusion that can be avoided by use of a comma after an introductory subordinate clause.)

Clear   *When the opportunity for changing lanes passed,* our car remained stuck in the long line of stalled cars.

Unclear   *After he left* the house never seemed the same again.   (Here is an introductory subordinate clause of only three words. The reader will think at first that the sentence begins with *After he left the house* rather than *After he left.*)

Clear   *After he left,* the house never seemed the same again.

In the examples of unclear sentences, the introductory elements are not closely related to the main clauses of the sentences: *Without a doubt* has little to do with *in a carload you will have more potatoes than you ever dreamed possible*. The same is true for *When the opportunity for changing lanes had passed* and *After he left* in the other sentences. This is not to say that these introductory elements do not belong in the sentences in which they are found. But *In a carload* bears much more directly on the rest of the sentence it introduces: *In a carload you will have more potatoes than you ever dreamed possible*. So do *For many hours after midnight* and *While his passengers waited impatiently*. All three are closely related to the main clauses of their respective sentences.

You must decide whether to follow the foolproof rule of *using a comma after every introductory element* or to take the approach of *omitting commas after introductory elements of five words or less when there is no risk of misleading readers*. (The writer of the book you now are reading follows the more liberal rule and takes pains to determine whether absence of a comma after an introductory element will disturb his readers.)

Verbal Phrases

A comma is used to separate an introductory verbal phrase from the rest of a sentence. *Verbal phrases* are phrases that contain verbals, that is, infinitives, gerunds, and participles.

- infinitives: (*to*) *teach*, (*to*) *work*
- gerunds: *teaching, working* used as nouns
- participles: *teaching, working* used as adjectives

Infinitive Phrase:

> *To be sure,* all the delegates decided to wait until the chair announced her ruling.

Gerund Phrase:

> *In reaching the unpopular decision,* the city council appeared to ignore justifiable complaints of people from all parts of the community.

Participial Phrase:

> *Finding himself completely alone in his position on the matter,* Cicero decided to give in to his opponents.
>
> *Exhausted by many hours of swimming,* Gertrude Ederle showed remarkable courage as she was assisted from the waters of the English Channel.

In the following two exercises, practice punctuating introductory phrases and subordinate clauses. In the first exercise follow the foolproof rule for use of a comma after these elements. In the second exercise follow the more liberal rule as well as the rule for commas after verbal phrases.

5. Insert commas in the following sentences after every introductory phrase and subordinate clause.

> For all we know, we will never see the likes of her again.
>
> During intermission, we met in the theater lobby to decide whether or not to stay for the second act.

1. From middle age on my aunt enjoyed far better health than ever before in her life.
2. Walking slowly through the park she peered about constantly to see whether she could find the person who had snatched her purse.
3. In hope of eventual restoration of his pension Joseph spent every penny he could find on lawyers.
4. In the end Cynthia decided to return to her position on the faculty.

5. Escorted by her sons the old woman walked proudly down the church aisle and took her place in the front pew.

6. With nothing left to lose the gambler left the casino and walked slowly back to his lonely room.

7. Minus its tail the old dog no longer looked the fierce fighter it once had been.

8. In the aftermath of the cyclone all the town could do was start the long clean-up operation and attempt to bring life back to normal.

9. Unless more people volunteer we will have too many supervisors and not enough workers.

10. As the clock began to strike the entire crowd held its breath in anticipation of the impending announcement.

6. Insert commas in the following sentences in accordance with these rules: (1) Use a comma after introductory phrases and subordinate clauses of more than five words. (2) Omit a comma after introductory phrases and subordinate clauses of five words or less only when there is no chance of misleading readers. (3) Use a comma after introductory phrases of any length when the phrases contain a verbal.

Long after the final date for applications, the registrar was still receiving inquiries concerning admissions.

Before the first game the team showed signs of nervousness at the thought of playing baseball in league competition.

Defeated at last, the army withdrew toward France.

1. With no money left to spend the couple agreed it was time to return home.

2. Improperly treated even a minor illness can have serious consequences.

3. Just as before the injured ankle prevented full enjoyment of the afternoon's outing.

4. In good times Hazel and Harry gave no thought to budgeting.

5. Across the square the crowd gathered in angry protest against what seemed to have been an inequitable decision by the court.

6. Straining to be heard the street singer quickly wore himself out and left the neighborhood.

7. To find the girl all able-bodied people of the neighborhood banded together under the minister's leadership.

8. In seeking to grasp the poet's meaning the careful reader goes over and over every word of the poem in question.

9. In the end there was nothing left to do but tear the building down and start all over again.

10. Before starting a fire make certain that all the wood is dry.

11. Before lighting a candle one might reflect for a moment on what the act of lighting the candle signifies.

12. According to our map the towns are at least twelve miles apart.

13. If you arrive early open the windows and sweep out the meeting room.

14. If you want to you may take a place on the platform and have a few minutes to address the group.

15. Standing apart the stranger made most of us uneasy.

16. From middle age on my uncle saw his health decline gradually.

17. Walking slowly from the park she peered about constantly to see whether she could find the men who had snatched her purse.

18. In hope of eventual restoration of his pension Joseph spent every penny he could find on lawyers.

19. In the end Annette decided to return to her teaching position in the college.

20. Escorted by her sons the old woman walked proudly down the church aisle and took her place in the first pew.

21. With nothing left to lose the gambler quit the game and walked back to his lonely room.

22. Minus its tail the old dog no longer looked the fierce fighter it once had been.

23. In the aftermath of the cyclone all the town could do was start the long clean-up operation and attempt to bring life back to normal.

24. Unless more people volunteer we will have too many supervisors and not enough workers.

25. As the clock began to strike the crowd held its breath in anticipation of the impending announcement.

Coordinate Adjectives

A comma is used to separate coordinate adjectives that appear before a noun and are not joined by *and*. Two or more adjectives that independently modify the same noun can be joined by *and*. Such adjectives, often describing age, color, education, or number, are classified as coordinate. The problem for writers is to determine when to use commas between adjectives when *and* does not appear: *fresh fruit flavors* or *fresh, fruit flavors? Long spiral pass* or *long, spiral pass*?

Every writer uses the *and* test to determine whether adjectives are coordinate. When *and* can be used between adjectives, the adjectives are coordinate, and a comma can replace the *and*. When *and* cannot be used between adjectives, the adjectives are not coordinate, and a comma cannot be used.

Here are examples of phrases consisting of nouns and coordinate adjectives:

with *and*:	*and* replaced by comma:
dark and blustery nights	dark, blustery nights
healthy and intelligent children	healthy, intelligent children
hot and humid summers	hot, humid summers

Notice that the adjectives in these phrases are independent of one another. They modify only the noun following. The adjectives *dark* and *blustery* modify *nights; dark* does not modify *blustery nights*. The adjectives *healthy* and *intelligent* modify *children; healthy* does not modify *intelligent children*. The adjectives *hot* and *humid* modify *summers; hot* does not modify *humid summers*. Coordinate adjectives independently modify the noun that follows.

Here are examples of phrases consisting of nouns and adjectives that are not coordinate:

six dark nights

many intelligent children

expensive chrome furniture

corrupt local governments

small white hat

economical sports cars

Apply the *and* test to determine whether commas are needed between the pairs of adjectives in these phrases. Can you say *six and dark nights, many and intelligent children, expensive and chrome furniture, corrupt and local governments, small and white hat*, or *economical and sports cars*? Not if you wish to make good sense. The phrases in this list have failed the *and* test. They do not contain coordinate adjectives, and commas must not be used between the adjectives.

Which is correct: *fresh fruit flavors* or *fresh, fruit flavors*? Can you say *fresh and fruit flavors*? Not if you wish to make good sense. *Fresh fruit flavors* is correct. How about *long spiral pass* and *long, spiral pass*? Can you say that *a quarterback has thrown a long and spiral pass*? Not a chance.

7. In the following sentences, apply the *and* test to insert commas where appropriate.

> Many people I know are fond of expensive antique chairs and tables.
> Six fresh clams are his favorite appetizer when I am paying the bill.
> Nights at the lake contrasted sharply with the hot, muggy nights at home.

1. The same bold spirit that took her through the life-threatening illness will see her through the present emergency.
2. Decrepit old Mrs. Lang no longer seems to get much pleasure from life.
3. Blue denim slacks command a high price in countries that do not produce such clothing.
4. Send me a dozen red roses and six white gardenias.
5. Four long hard years lie ahead for any newly elected President of the United States.
6. Heavily grained red morocco cannot be genuine.
7. Twelve interested jurors followed every word spoken by the impassioned young prosecutor.
8. That dusty rutted road leads to the shack my friends rented in a rash moment.
9. A clean well-lighted supermarket attracts shoppers eager to spend their few hard-earned dollars.
10. Six happy minutes flew by during the transatlantic call.
11. Chinese red paint is not what I had in mind for my quiet comfortable study.
12. New dormer windows are difficult to install without a strong aluminum or magnesium ladder.
13. Crisp fresh salad greens are essential if you are going to tempt me to eat anything on a hot August night.
14. Beautiful Marilyn Monroe died a tragic premature death.
15. The exciting pennant race was not settled until the leaves had turned deep red.

Splitting the Unsplittable

A final modifier and the element it modifies are unsplittable. Writers intent on using commas correctly to separate items in a series sometimes get carried away. When they punctuate a series of adjectives, they may insert a comma after the final one, splitting it off from the word or words it modifies. This must never be done.

Wrong   Sven found he could not concentrate yesterday, even though he usually likes to work on warm, dry, days.   (The mistake is the comma between *dry* and *days*.)

Right   Sven found he could not concentrate yesterday, even though he usually likes to work on warm, dry days.   (Remember why a comma is used before *even*? See page 31 if you do not. Remember why a comma is used between the adjectives *warm* and *dry*? See pages 23–24 if you do not.)

Wrong   The most valuable, reliable, volume in any student's library is a good dictionary.   (The comma after *reliable* must go.)

Right   The most valuable, reliable volume in any student's library is a good dictionary.

Wrong   The great, uncharacteristic, speed the legislature showed in moving the bill through committee was evidence that a deal had been made between certain members of Congress and the oil lobby.

Right   The great, uncharacteristic speed the legislature showed in moving the bill through committee was evidence that a deal had been made between certain members of Congress and
the oil lobby.

8.   In the following sentences insert commas where they are needed and remove commas that are inappropriate.

Fitzgerald wrote in an unhurried, disciplined manner even when he was in debt.
All their pets were overfed, pampered, pesky animals.

1.   Margie especially admired graceful, controlled, dancers who appeared to know and
love music.
2.   Rich, pungent, tobaccos made his afternoons especially rewarding.
3.   Some, very, old, people are able to talk amusingly even with the extremely young.
4.   We found his speech long-winded and boring, and so we left the committee meeting
as soon as we could.
5.   Henrietta played the long, demanding, part as well as it could be played.
6.   They seemed always to be searching for their long, lost, youth.
7.   Can you tell me where I can find a succulent tomato-rich dripping-with-cheese pizza
in this neighborhood?
8.   One expensive, excellent, meal is worth sixty take-out, Chinese, deep-fat, disappointments.
9.   Young, Prince Hamlet walked slowly about the darkened stage, reading from a small
volume of poetry.
10. The long cold Arctic nights do not bother David too much.

Introductory Modifiers

A comma is used to set off all introductory modifiers. Adjectives, adverbs, participles, and participial
phrases—all modifiers—often are placed at the beginning of a sentence to give them special emphasis. In some
cases these words or phrases modify the entire sentence. In other cases they modify a particular element of the
sentence. No matter what they modify, they are set off from the rest of the sentence by a comma. This rule
holds true even for single-word modifiers.

Introductory Modifier—Adjective:

Victorious, the army withdrew a thousand meters and encamped for the night.
Alive, beef cattle are worth a great deal of money.

Introductory Modifier—Adverb:

Socially, she was completely at ease even in trying circumstances.
Legally, neither candidate had any right to hold public office.

Introductory Modifier—Participle:

Singing, Rick went quickly through the apartment to put it in order for the dinner party.
Defeated, the boxer stretched out on his dressing table in complete silence.

Introductory Modifier—Participial Phrase:

Seeking interesting employment, the young couple drove their camper westward.
Threatened by the rising waters of the river, the residents of the town hurriedly abandoned
their homes and fled to high ground.

9. Insert commas where appropriate in the following sentences.

Drained by the events of the week, Emily and Duke took to eating their meals in silence.

Surely, they will take solace in the fact that they are not the only ones to have made such a mess of things.

Ashamed, the little boy left his seat and hid in the cloakroom.

1. Electrified the audience arose as one person and applauded wildly for an orator who had treated important themes in clear and concise language.
2. Spent the pony walked slowly along behind the cowboy who had roped it so expertly.
3. Ironically we are willing to entrust to our politicians sweeping powers we dare not employ ourselves.
4. Smiling broadly the entertainer rose to her feet once more to accept the generous ovation given her final performance.
5. Awakened at last to the need for action the legislature unanimously agreed to vote full power to the military junta.
6. Interestingly there was little basic difference between their points of view.
7. Obviously we must move to provide decent housing and health care for the under-privileged among us.
8. Saddled with so much responsibility at the age of fifteen the young woman managed to make something of herself and go on to contribute remarkably to the good of the nation.
9. Finally the family found a way to support all their relatives until economic recovery enabled them to stand on their own.
10. First Alice and Bob decided to establish a self-sufficient life on a small farm.

Nonrestrictive Phrases and Clauses

Commas are used to set off nonrestrictive phrases and clauses. Modifiers are either restrictive or nonrestrictive. Restrictive modifiers *are not* set off by punctuation; nonrestrictive modifiers *are* set off.

A *restrictive* modifier identifies, defines, or limits the term it modifies. A restrictive modifier *cannot* be removed from the sentence in which it appears without significantly changing, even destroying the intended meaning of the sentence.

A *nonrestrictive* modifier adds information concerning a term already identified, defined, or limited. A nonrestrictive modifier *can* be removed from the sentence in which it appears without changing the intended meaning of the sentence.

It may be helpful to understand the origin of the terms *restrictive* and *nonrestrictive*. A restrictive modifier restricts a class of items or individuals to a particular item or individual. A nonrestrictive modifier does not.

Restrictive Phrases: NO COMMAS

Henry *the Eighth* ruled England from 1509 to 1547.   (Without the restrictive modifier *the Eighth* this sentence would not identify the particular English monarch intended. No commas around *the Eighth*.)

The couch *in our dining room* came from a Salvation Army store.   (Without *in our dining room* this sentence would not identify the couch under discussion. No commas around *in our dining room*.)

Nonrestrictive Phrases: COMMAS

Pooch, *almost seventeen years old*, is no longer in good health.   (Pooch is already identified by name. Omitting *almost seventeen years old* would not change the intended meaning of the sentence. Commas around *almost seventeen years old*.)

Any unabridged dictionary, *whether current or not*, provides useful information and should never be discarded. (The *dictionary* is already limited by *Any unabridged.* Omitting *whether current or not* would not change the essential meaning of the sentence. Commas around *whether current or not.*)

Restrictive Clauses: NO COMMAS

Carl and his wife are interested in buying only paintings *that will impress their friends.* (Without the restrictive modifier *that will impress their friends* this sentence would have an entirely different meaning: *He and his wife are interested in buying only paintings.* No comma before *that will impress their friends.*)

Warren is seen at first as a person *who is a great deal smarter than anyone near him.* (Without the restrictive modifier this sentence would have a strange meaning: *Warren is seen at first as a person.* No comma before *who is a great deal smarter than anyone near him.*)

I need a kitchen *that makes cooking easier* and I will find one somehow. (Without the restrictive modifier this sentence would have an entirely different meaning: *I need a kitchen and I will find one somehow.* No commas around *that makes cooking easier.*)

Nonrestrictive Clauses: COMMAS

Lord Herries, *who was Mary's ambassador to Elizabeth*, demanded that England supply an army to restore Mary to the throne of Scotland. (*Lord Herries* is sufficiently identified by his name. The modifying clause is not needed for the sense of the sentence: *Lord Herries demanded that England supply an army to restore Mary to the throne of Scotland.* Commas around *who was Mary's ambassador to Elizabeth.*)

Thousands of Vermont cows, *which feed all summer on ample supplies of grass,* supply milk for many Bostonians. (The *cows* are already identified by *Thousands of Vermont.* The modifying clause is not needed for the sense of the sentence: *Thousands of Vermont cows supply milk for many Bostonians.* Commas around *which feed all summer on ample supplies of grass.*)

Caesar and Cleopatra, which was first shown in England and met a poor critical reception, did well at the box office when it opened in the United States. (The film is sufficiently identified by its title. The modifying clause is not needed to convey the sense of the sentence: *Caesar and Cleopatra did well at the box office when it opened in the United States.* Commas around *which was first shown in England and met a poor critical reception.* Notice that there is also a restrictive modifying clause in the sentence: *when it opened in the United States.* Without this clause the sentence would change meaning: *Caesar and Cleopatra, which was first shown in England and met a poor critical reception, did well at the box office.* Where? The sentence no longer says. We know that it *did well at the box office when it opened in the United States.* No comma before *when it opened in the United States.*)

To test whether a modifying phrase or clause is restrictive or nonrestrictive, read the entire sentence. Ask yourself whether the phrase or clause can be omitted without endangering the sense of the sentence. If it cannot, the modifier is restrictive and requires no punctuation. If it can be omitted, the modifier is nonrestrictive and must be set off by commas.

10. Insert commas where appropriate in the following sentences to set off nonrestrictive phrases and clauses.

Only the people at our party who enjoy an evening of classical music are having a good time.

That tree, which I have watered and fertilized carefully all spring, shows signs of dying.

The row of seats at the back of the hall is reserved for members of the clergy.

Tim's display of courage, whether intentional or not, impressed all the members of the party in power.

1. Ethel who ordinarily is extremely quiet at parties went about and talked with anyone who appeared interested in talking with an intelligent woman.

2. The ballplayer with the highest batting average in the league was not selected for the All-Star Game.

3. Plants that have finished bearing fruit should be cut back to save nutrients in the soil for plants that are still bearing.

4. Many imported wines that are heavily advertised are not nearly as good as domestic wines which are usually the product of small vineyards.

5. My reliable automobile which I bought second-hand three years ago still takes me back and forth every day between my home and office.

6. The compositions Anne wrote as a child still give me pleasure.

7. A book as interesting as that one will always find readers among those who have a taste for fine literature.

8. Animals in our local zoo are perishing for lack of food and water which are the responsibility of an overworked and underpaid staff.

9. Fruits and vegetables sold in supermarkets sometimes are not as high in quality as those sold by greengrocers.

10. Leaves that have turned yellow should be pruned and carted away to a compost heap which will turn them into valuable sources of food for other plants.

11. We always donate all our old clothes to organizations that will repair them and see that deserving people receive them.

12. The Kennedy years which saw the hopes of young Americans raised came too quickly to an end.

13. Pictures in our family for years were lost when our house burned down.

14. The circus which still gladdens the hearts of young and old will be coming to town next week to give five performances under the big tent.

15. Most people who take pleasure in attending the theater like to live near a city that offers serious playgoers the chance to see good productions.

11. The following sentences contain restrictive and nonrestrictive modifiers. Some of the modifiers are incorrectly punctuated. Mark every sentence *Correct* or *Incorrect*. Correct the punctuation wherever necessary.

> Dan and Eileen have gone off to Ireland this week to complete the work they started last summer.   *Correct*
> A restaurant as fine as that one ought to hire a chef who knows how to cook.   Incorrect

1. The Vietnam War shameful as it was in so many people's minds is forgotten now by all except those who bear its wounds. _____

2. I received a telephone call that shook me thoroughly and sent me back to my study unable to work for the rest of the day. _____

3. Our youngest son wants to settle in California which is so far from home, that we will not be able to see him except on summer holidays. _____

4. Infectious diseases, which often spread because of poor sanitation are not easily controlled in countries that do not have adequate medical facilities. _____

5. Many women, who have been elected to positions of major importance in their own countries, still find themselves treated badly when they travel to other countries. _____

6. Instead of the warm reception that he expected on his return home, Alfred was greeted coldly by all his sisters and brothers. _____

7. Those of us, who are willing to cooperate, expect to be given some help by the others.
   _____

8. Some of the articles that appear in *Playboy*, are worth reading. _____

9. Any man or woman who consults no one before undertaking a job, as big as that one, takes undue risks. _____

10. That metaphor which I have read a dozen times is as inappropriate now as it was the first time I read it. _____

11. Rather than try immediately to look up every word, that troubles you, keep a list of such words and set some time aside for dictionary work each evening. _____

12. Universities that capitulate to every demand made by the students, will surely regret doing so.
    _____

13. Encyclopedias which are expensive to buy and bulky to store are valuable tools for families with several children in school. _____

14. The more time, a man spends on himself, the less time he has for others. _____

15. Old people who are lucky enough to live independently are usually happier than those who are confined to nursing homes or live with resentful relatives. _____

Appositives

Commas are used to set off nonrestrictive appositives. Appositives are sometimes described as noun repeaters. They point out or identify the nouns with which they are in apposition. Like modifying clauses and phrases, appositives are either restrictive or nonrestrictive.

Appositives are usually nouns, noun phrases, or noun clauses.

Appositive—Noun

My brother *Tom* spent two years in the Peace Corps.   (The noun *Tom* is in apposition with *brother*.)

Appositive—Noun Phrase

We look forward each year to eating MacIntosh apples, *the most delicious fruit available in autumn.*   (The noun phrase *the most delicious fruit available in autumn* is in apposition with *MacIntosh apples*.)

Appositive—Noun Clause

The Secretary of State's declaration *that force will be met with force* caused young men all over the world to wonder whether they were about to be told to go to war.   (The noun clause *that force will be met with force* is in apposition with *declaration*.)

Gerund phrases can also be used as appositives:

Mary's principal interest, *learning all she can about urban problems,* absorbs all her waking hours.   (The gerund phrase *learning all she can about urban problems* is in apposition with *interest*.)

As in the case of modifiers, *restrictive appositives* cannot be omitted from a sentence without severely altering the meaning of the sentence, while *nonrestrictive appositives* can be omitted. The rule is the same as for modifiers—restrictive appositives, no commas; nonrestrictive appositives, commas. (See pages 81–82 for the use of dashes to punctuate certain nonrestrictive appositives.) In each of the following examples, consider whether the italicized appositives can be omitted without altering the intended meaning.

Restrictive

My brother *Tom* spent two years in the Peace Corps.   (The implication is that I have more than one brother. Without the appositive *Tom*, the reader cannot tell which brother I am discussing.)

Nonrestrictive

My oldest sister, *Peggy*, will take her vacation early this year.   (I have only one oldest sister. The appositive *Peggy* can be omitted from the sentence without damaging its meaning.)

Restrictive

The Secretary of State's declaration *that force will be met with force* caused young men all over the world to wonder whether they were about to be told to go to war.   (The Secretary of State makes many declarations. This is just one of them. Without the appositive, the reader does not know which declaration is causing young men to wonder, and so the appositive is restrictive.)

Nonrestrictive

Lincoln's Secretary of State, *William H. Seward*, was an adroit politician as well as an exceptional diplomat.   (Lincoln had only one Secretary of State. The appositive can be omitted from this sentence without damaging its meaning.)

Nonrestrictive

We look forward each summer to eating MacIntosh apples, *the most delicious fruit available in autumn.*   (MacIntosh apples are MacIntosh apples whether or not they are the most delicious fruit available in autumn. The appositive can be omitted from this sentence without damaging its meaning.)

Nonrestrictive

Kenyon's cheese cake, *the richest and smoothest cake I have ever tasted,* is known throughout the neighborhood.   (*Kenyon's cheese cake* is sufficiently identified without the appositive. The appositive can be omitted without damaging the meaning of the sentence.)

In all the sentences above, nonrestrictive appositives were set off by commas. Restrictive appositives were not.

Notice that *or* sometimes introduces an appositive. In such cases the appositive is nonrestrictive and requires commas. Do not confuse the use of *or* in other constructions with *or* used with appositives.

Appositives

Carol's administrative assistant, or *executive secretary*, will not be back in her office until next Monday.   (The *administrative assistant* and *executive secretary* are the same person.)

The newly married couple were looking for a courting chair, *or love seat*, for their apartment. (*Courting chair* and *love seat* both are names for the same item of furniture.)

Not Appositives

Carol's administrative assistant *or copy editor* will take charge of the manuscript.   (Two different individuals.)

The young couple would like to move from their small apartment to a ranch house *or split-level.*   (Two different styles of homes.)

12.   Use commas where appropriate in the following sentences to set off nonrestrictive appositives.

I am especially troubled by his habitual lateness, a habit that consistently delays completion of his work until the last possible moment.

The English critic John Ruskin did more to advance the appreciation of painting than any other person before him.

The German shepherd, or police dog, has a devoted following among frightened apartment dwellers in northeastern cities.

1. Alexander Solzhenitsyn poet and novelist went into exile to protest conditions in the Soviet Union.
2. The book *All the President's Men* remained on the best-seller list for many months.
3. Her uncle Ralph always took her fishing when she was a child.
4. Vermont the Green Mountain State has a long history of independent thought and action.
5. Ms. Atkins our school bus driver can be relied on in bad weather as well as good.
6. Honey a delicious and nutritious food is produced by bees.
7. Jane's first choice graduate study in English proved an unwise selection for the job market of her day.
8. My earliest memory seeing my grandfather sicken and die affected me throughout my early life.
9. Arlene's career dancer and singer was cut short by her inability to face large audiences.
10. The feeling that something dreadful is about to happen is a common complaint of neurotics.
11. Rare earth elements closely related metallic elements of atomic number 57 to 71 find many uses in high-technology applications.
12. Subway cars covered with graffiti the artistic decorations that express a yearning for recognition used to be commonplace in New York.
13. The short story ''A Little Cloud'' remains one of my favorites.
14. *PM* a newspaper that accepted no advertising made a place for itself in journalistic history.
15. Her oldest brother Fred was unable to find work for three years after high school.
16. Anachronisms or chronological errors throughout the otherwise-serious film made most of the audience laugh and sickened the director.
17. College football no longer performs its primary function raising enough money to finance the entire college physical education program.
18. Coniferous trees or evergreens supply most of the vast quantity of pulpwood needed for newspapers.
19. The most expensive office machine the digital computer creates enormous amounts of useless information while wasting paper and manpower.
20. *War and Peace* Tolstoy's greatest novel is read by every generation of lovers of literature.

Subordinate Clause after Independent Clause

A comma is used before a subordinate clause that follows an independent clause—but only if the thoughts of the two clauses are not closely related. Unlike independent clauses, subordinate clauses cannot stand alone as sentences. A sentence that contains an independent clause and one or more subordinate clauses is called a complex sentence. Commas are sometimes used in complex sentences to separate an independent clause from a subordinate clause that follows.

Subordinate clauses are recognized by the words that introduce them: subordinating conjunctions and relative pronouns.

Subordinating Conjunctions

after	before	so that	where
although	how	though	wherever
as	if	till	while
as if	in order that	unless	why
as long as	since	until	yet
because	so	when	

Notice that *so* and *yet* function both as subordinating and coordinating conjunctions, but *so* is usually a subordinating conjunction.

Relative Pronouns

     that   what   which   who

A change of subject from the independent clause to the subordinate clause is usually a clear indication that the thoughts of the two clauses are not closely related.

Right   The police searched for the escaped convict throughout the dense woods, *where* witnesses had last seen the missing man.   (The subordinating conjunction is *where*. The subject of the independent clause is *police*. The subject of the subordinate clause is *witnesses*. The two clauses are not closely related in thought, and so a comma is needed before *where*.)

When the subject of the independent clause is the same as that of the subordinate clause, the two clauses are usually closely related in thought.

Right   Gordon decided to buy the expensive ballet tickets *though* he could scarcely afford to pay his rent that week.   (The subordinating conjunction is *though*. The subject of the independent clause is *Gordon*. The subject of the subordinate clause is *he*, a pronoun replacing *Gordon*. The two clauses are closely related in thought and should not be separated by a comma.)

Examine the following sentences closely to determine whether they require commas before the subordinate clauses following independent clauses. The subordinating conjunctions are italicized.

Right   Make your bed *before* you leave home in the morning *so that* you will be free of the chore later in the day.   (This sentence has two subordinate clauses after an independent clause, *Make your bed*. The subject of *Make your bed* is *you* understood. The subjects of the subordinate clauses are *you* and *you*. The subordinate clauses are closely related to the independent clause, and so no comma is needed.)

Wrong   Trees shed their leaves prematurely during a drought *when* farmers cannot supply sufficient water to maintain normal growth.   (The independent clause is *Trees shed their leaves prematurely during a drought*. Its subject is *Trees*. The subject of the subordinate clause is *farmers*. The thoughts of the two clauses are not closely related, and so a comma is needed: Trees shed their leaves prematurely during a drought, *when* farmers cannot supply sufficient water for normal growth.)

Wrong   Mother always did the cooking for us *while* Father looked after marketing, laundry, and other chores.   (The two clauses are not related, even though a quick examination might suggest that the subordinate clause tells when *Mother did the cooking*. In this case, *while* does not mean *when*. The subjects of the two clauses are different. A comma is needed: Mother always did the cooking for us, *while* Father looked after marketing, laundry, and other chores.)

Right   The Sandborns are willing to attend the party *as long as* they are invited.   (Subject of independent clause, *Sandborns*; subject of subordinate clause, *they*, meaning *Sandborns*. No comma before *as long as*.)

Wrong   We all yearn for increased leisure time *although* most of us do not know how to use it. (Different subjects in the two clauses. Comma is needed: We all yearn for increased leisure time, *although* most of us do not know how to use it.)

Right   I shall never know *how* she accomplished so much in so short a time.   (Close relationship between clauses, with subordinate clause acting as object of verb *shall know* in independent clause. No comma.)

Right   I have admired them *since* they were children.   (Close relationship between clauses, with subordinate clause acting as modifier of main clause. No comma.)

Right   Rent a car and drive upstate *until* you reach the Finger Lakes.   (Same subject, *you* understood, in both independent clauses and *you* in subordinate clause. No comma.)

Wrong   President Kennedy's inaugural address caused many young hearts to beat faster *though* older people generally were unmoved by his words.   (Different subjects in the two clauses. Thoughts not closely related. A comma is needed: President Kennedy's inaugural address caused many young hearts to beat faster, *though* older people generally were unmoved by his words.)

There is room for interpretation in deciding whether the thoughts of two clauses are closely related, but experienced writers show remarkable agreement in their judgments.

13.   Insert commas where appropriate before subordinate clauses in the following sentences.

> A drug rehabilitation center will be located in our neighborhood, unless most of the residents object strongly.
>
> She promised to meet me near the County Center, where the Bronx River Parkway crosses a small stream.
>
> Many of the ballplayers meet after each game to eat and drink together unless they have lost by an overwhelming margin.

1. Doris managed to keep her wits about her when the man jumped in front of her and demanded her purse.

2. The City Council will meet twice next week when the bill for revision of the charter comes up for its final vote.

3. Smoking is considered bad for the health although pipe smoking is said to be less harmful than cigarette smoking.

4. The entire family decided to go to the movies together although no film appealed to everybody equally.

5. I will not take a long airplane flight as long as you refuse to go along with me.

6. John asked to have a window fan installed in his office because the hot weather was causing him to lose much time during the day.

7. The death of a family pet comes as a shock to everyone if it is not anticipated.

8. She walked down the street as if she owned everything she saw.

9. The Accounting Department will not send a representative to the meeting since the meeting does not concern finances.

10. Ambiguity crops up wherever people gather because no one is willing to take the time to think clearly or speak clearly.

11. He believed that things would turn out all right since everyone in the group professed interest in the general welfare.

12. Candidates for public office will promise anything while having no intention to deliver on their promises since promises are essential in winning elections.

13. Harriet would not say why she had made the decision until most of us grew tired of wondering about her motives.

14. I promise that you will meet courteous people wherever you travel in the United States.

15. Wait until you are at least twenty-one when maturity is a little closer.

Interrupters

Commas are used to set off interrupters. An *interrupter*, also known as an interrupting element and as a parenthetic element, is a word, phrase, or clause that breaks into the expected movement of a sentence, often interrupting the logical flow. For this reason an interrupter must be set off by commas. When an interrupter is very long, it is set off by dashes. The question of how long is *very long* becomes a matter of individual taste. The writer of this book uses dashes only for an interrupter that can stand logically and grammatically as a sentence or for an interrupter that is internally punctuated. (See pages 81–82.)

Conjunctive adverbs are one category of single-word interrupters. The most frequently encountered conjunctive adverbs are:

accordingly	furthermore	instead	notwithstanding
also	hence	likewise	otherwise
anyhow	henceforth	meanwhile	still
besides	however	moreover	therefore
consequently	indeed	nevertheless	thus

Notice that conjunctive adverbs can function either as adverbs or as conjunctions. When they function as adverbs, they require no punctuation. When they function as conjunctions, they must be set off by commas. (When conjunctive adverbs are used to join clauses, they are preceded by a semicolon and followed by a comma.) (See pages 49–51.)

Adverb

However earnest the poor child is, we cannot afford to take the time to deal with her constant complaints.   (The adverb *However* modifies *earnest* and must not be punctuated.)

Still responding to the eloquence of the candidate's lengthy address, we found ourselves unwilling to leave the hall.   (The adverb *Still* modifies *responding*. No punctuation.)

Conjunction

A hyperactive boy may be a constant source of annoyance, *however*, and create ever greater disturbances as he grows taller and stronger.   (The conjunctive adverb, coming between the compound verbs *may be* and *create*, interrupts the movement of the sentence. Commas must be used.)

The union agreement specified, *moreover*, that employees would not work overtime when other union members were unemployed.   (The conjunctive adverb stands between the verb *specified* and the object of the verb, the following clause. Commas must be used.)

Expressions of direct address are interrupters and require commas. Many expressions are used in direct address. A few are cited here to illustrate the variety of expressions of direct address.

Doctor	my friends	sir
ladies and gentlemen	no	well
madam	please	yes
Mr. Jones		

I tell you, *man*, not to go on this way if you want to stay out of prison.   (The flow of the sentence is interrupted by the expression of direct address. Commas are needed.)

Please, *John*, help me with my calculus homework so that I can pass my examination.   (*John* interrupts the flow of the sentence. It must be set off by commas.)

Can you, *dear friend*, find a way to solve your problem without involving me or the other members of the group?

Phrases of various types act as interrupters and require commas.

Joe, *despite my repeated warnings*, left the house too late to board his train and missed another day's pay.   (The interrupter breaks into the movement of the sentence, coming between the subject, *Joe*, and the first of a pair of compound verbs, *left*. It must be set off by commas.)

Governmental institutions, *acting in a long tradition of ignoring human needs*, seem oblivious to the tide of events as they grow fatter and slower year by year.   (The interrupter comes between the subject, *institutions*, and its verb, *seem*. It must be set off by commas.)

Inhumane treatment of pets, *to cite one example*, must be dealt with in the next meeting of the town council.   (Another interrupter of the logical flow of a sentence. Commas must be used.)

Clauses act as interrupters and require commas.

The bill introduced by the minority party, *I can assure you*, will never be passed in its present form.   (The interrupter breaks into the movement of the sentence, appearing between the subject, *bill*, and the verb, *will be passed*. It must be set off by commas.)

Richard, *as he had done so many times in the past*, paid his friend's debts and never mentioned the kind deed to anyone.   (The interrupter comes between the subject and verb. Commas are needed.)

There are many ways, *you see*, of overcoming the reluctance of people to submit to arbitrary regulations.

14. Insert commas where appropriate in the following sentences to set off interrupting elements.

The best means, of course, is to stop all new expenditures until the family budget reaches a realistic level.

We do not deny that he is otherwise acceptable for membership in the group.

You will, therefore, appear within the hour to present your side of the dispute.

1. My business affairs I tell you gladly are in better condition today than they have been for fifteen years.
2. There is more than one way to deal with the problem of drugs and street crime you know and you must remain flexible.
3. They go on nevertheless dealing in marijuana and risking arrest despite their otherwise clean records.
4. Anne and Bob as a matter of course arrive late at every party they attend.
5. The child lay still and pretended to sleep all through the evening.
6. I must fight for my liberty you will grant above all other considerations if I am to remain true to my political convictions.
7. Most of the people in the company furthermore do so little work that one cannot understand how it remains a successful organization.
8. Air conditioners are accepted as a necessary item of office furniture by many who are willing to put up with high temperatures at home.
9. You will please think the matter over carefully before you make your decision.
10. Reference books dictionaries included are becoming so expensive that we must think a long time before deciding to purchase a volume we really need.
11. If we take much longer to pay the bill you see the company may decide to cut off our credit.
12. Taxes will never go down in our community as long as the taxable buildings keep disappearing and businesses maintain their resistance to staying in the inner city.

13. Rosa acting against her better judgment went along with the other girls that day and managed to get into serious trouble.

14. We cannot as we have told you so many times continue the present arrangement unless you agree to make important changes.

15. The lunch went badly as I predicted it would because both husbands insisted on dominating the conversation and totally overlooking their wives' interests.

16. I must you understand give my full attention to this report until I have finished it.

17. Will you finally madam cease interrupting until I have completed my full presentation of the evidence?

18. The opposing position will therefore not be supported unless a majority indicates sufficient interest to warrant a complete explanation.

19. Many members of the committee will consequently withhold their votes in deference to the wishes of the chair.

20. Oh well you cannot expect him to capitulate right after he has expressed himself so forcefully against the popular opinion.

I, Love, You.

The principal elements of the English sentence are subject, verb, and object. A single comma is not used between subject and verb. A single comma is not used between verb and object. We do not write *I, love, you.*

When an interrupter (see pages 34–36) makes punctuation necessary, use a pair of commas around the interrupter. (See also pages 80–85 for uses of the dash.)

Wrong   The boy without informing his parents stopped off at his friend's house before returning from the museum.   (The interrupting element *without informing his parents* is nonrestrictive and must be set off by commas.)

Wrong   The boy without informing his parents, stopped off at his friend's house before returning from the museum.   (A single comma serves only to break the flow of the sentence from subject *boy* to verb *stopped.*)

Wrong   The boy, without informing his parents stopped off at his friend's house before returning from the museum.   (Same fault.)

Right   The boy, without informing his parents, stopped off at his friend's house before returning from the museum.   (The nonrestrictive element is set off properly by commas.)

Wrong   The offer by French authorities made to tell the truth new enemies among the inhabitants of the tiny Atlantic island.   (The interrupter *to tell the truth* creates serious confusion. It requires punctuation.)

Wrong   The offer by French authorities made, to tell the truth new enemies among the inhabitants of the tiny Atlantic island.   (The single comma breaks the flow between verb *made* and object *enemies.*)

Wrong   The offer by French authorities made to tell the truth, new enemies among the inhabitants of the tiny Atlantic island.   (Same fault.)

Right   The offer by French authorities made, to tell the truth, new enemies among the inhabitants of the tiny Atlantic island.   (The interrupter is properly set off. Confusion is banished.)

To repeat the message once more: use a pair of commas around interrupters appearing between subject and verb or between verb and object. Never use a single comma.

15. Some of the following sentences are correctly punctuated; others are not. Mark each sentence *Correct* or *Incorrect.* Correct the punctuation wherever necessary.

Dolores and Juanita decided to return to Chicago once the heat wave had ended.
Correct

People call the first ten amendments to the United States Constitution the Bill of Rights.
__Correct__

The new hotel caters to the rich and the expense-account crowd.   __Incorrect__

1. Anne's ability to diagnose rare diseases without relying on laboratory tests, impresses all her teachers. _____

2. Those of us who wish to live productive lives, should eat sensibly and drink only in moderation. _____

3. The citizens' group announced that, there will be no further building on the street until the Landmark Commission reveals its decision. _____

4. The varsity soccer team is so pleased with attendance at its games, that three additional games will be scheduled. _____

5. We finally decided we would stay until after the first frost. _____

6. What I find hard to accept, is her unmatched obstinacy. _____

7. Omar's obvious popularity, apparently made him the object of unremitting envy by many other men. _____

8. The woman with blond hair, spent many hours each week, at the beauty parlor.

    _____

9. Many people, for all we know, take great pleasure in listening to music they profess to despise. _____

10. Have you never read, *For Whom the Bell Tolls?* _____

11. The brave fire fighter carried two women, and one child, from the burning house.

    _____

12. Many students will back democratic principles up to the point at which their own interests begin to suffer. _____

13. Those who gamble, on their lives, are admired only by the immature and the bloodthirsty.

    _____

14. The name I find hardest to remember, is Myron. _____

15. The helicopter began to depart from the airport without all the people who had bought tickets.

    _____

Absolute Phrases

Commas are used to set off absolute phrases. An absolute phrase consists of a subject and a modifier, which is often a participle. An absolute phrase modifies the entire sentence in which it occurs and lacks grammatical connection to any single element of the sentence. Like other phrases, an absolute phrase does not contain a verb. Unlike other phrases, an absolute phrase expresses a full idea. For stylistic reasons absolute phrases generally are placed at the beginning or end of a sentence.

All our work completed, we settled down to an evening of television.

They left the room unhappy over their performance on the examination, *a passing grade being no more than a remote possibility.*

The party over, the couple began to wash a sinkful of dishes.

Absolute phrases must be set off by commas because they are not connected to other sentence elements.

16. Insert commas where appropriate in the following sentence to set off absolute phrases.

His first love affair unhappily ended, the young poet set out to drown his sorrows in beer and verse.

Gertrude wanted to have the opportunity to return to school, housework and baby-sitting having proven an unending bore.

1. Their best efforts entirely fruitless the three sisters decided to abandon the idea of going into business.
2. Stockbrokers recall a certain day in November many years ago when the New York Stock Exchange experienced a tremendous drop in prices the efforts of a few banks notwithstanding.
3. Sailors leaving port exult in the freedom of the seas all cares and concerns of land-locked existence behind them.
4. The novels of Ernest Hemingway are universally admired their freshness of language and innovations in style resembling nothing that went before.
5. All the oats and barley safely in the barn farmers can turn their attention to much-needed repair of equipment and tools.
6. Taxi cabs are finding well-educated drivers these days the time of great employment opportunities being past for college graduates.
7. All regular business being concluded the party leader turned the attention of the faithful to the need for finding promising candidates for the next year's election.
8. Fred decided to return home there being no chance to find full-time employment in the city.
9. Any chance for a reprieve ended the unhappy prisoner turned his thoughts to making his peace with God.
10. The herd moved to lower pastures early the upper fields having shown no sign of producing sufficient grass for its needs.

Quotations

Commas are used to set off expressions that indicate direct quotation. Direct quotations repeat the exact words used by a writer or speaker. Direct quotations are enclosed in quotation marks. (See pages 64–66.)

Indirect quotations are accounts of the thoughts expressed by a writer or speaker, but not in the same words originally used. Indirect quotations are not enclosed in quotation marks.

Direct Quotation

"Leave the room!"

Indirect Quotation

She told us to leave the room.

Expressions such as *he said, she said*, and *they said* are commonly used to identify the speaker or writer quoted in a direct quotation. The expressions can be placed before or after the quotation or somewhere within the quotation.

We asked, "Will you ever stop talking?"

"Tell the truth when you go before the grand jury," *the attorney advised*, "and you will have nothing to fear."

"Mind your own business," *the plumber replied.*

When a sentence supplying a direct quotation contains such an expression, commas must be used to set off the expression.

When the expression falls between two independent clauses that are not connected by a conjunction, a period or semicolon replaces the second comma.

"I will not be bullied," *the young instructor insisted.* "This opportunity means too much to me."

"I will not be bullied," *the young instructor insisted*; "this opportunity means too much to me."

"I will not be bullied," *the young instructor insisted*, "for this opportunity means too much to me."   (This version of the direct quotation is correct only if the person quoted actually used the word *for*.)

When a direct quotation is punctuated with a question mark or exclamation point, no comma is used before the expression indicating direct quotation.

"How can you neglect your own child?" *the social worker asked*.

"Will you be able to work tomorrow?" *Lisa asked*. "I think we can complete the project in just one more day."

"What an outrage!" *the chairman said*.

"You are guilty of giving up the fight for better housing for the poor of this district!" *the speaker went on*. "We must not allow people to go on living this way."

17. Insert the missing punctuation in the following sentences. Commas, semicolons, periods, question marks, and exclamation points may be required. To make the exercise challenging, quotation marks have been omitted. Supply quotation marks for all direct quotations.

"Why bother with an elaborate dinner?" she said. "Meat and potatoes will suit those boys."

The candidate declined to answer the question and said that he would do so after the election.

"Violent exercise is not advised for cardiac patients," the physician said, "who wish to live out their normal life spans."

"Go to the devil!" she added. "You will be in good company."

1. They were cautioned against sailing out of the harbor that day and assured us they would not do so.

2. Is this really the way it happened Mother asked Did you know that you were going to have to repair the car before starting out on the trip?

3. My parents said they wanted to stay at home with us to celebrate our first wedding anniversary.

4. The child then added The man asked me to go to the movies with him to eat popcorn and have a good time.

5. Instead of advising us to relax and enjoy life, they keep telling us Exercise Work Eat less Stop drinking Stop smoking I answer Why bother with that routine? There is no point in living that way.

6. Can you really take so much pleasure in misleading the gullible she asked me.

7. The conductor told the tuba player that sounds coming out of her instrument sounded more like bleats than music.

8. Books are meant to be read the librarian said they are not meant to be destroyed.

9. Certain corrections are needed in the score the composer said but I can accomplish them within the week.

10. Can you imagine such behavior the old woman said In all my eighty-five years I have never seen anything like it.

11. A horn was sounded to signal the arrival of a new shipment for auction the historian wrote and all tobacco merchants in the town assembled on the waterfront.

12. Ms. Prentiss insisted she would get to the bottom of the mess before long and asked us to grant her a few more days.

13. Are there any cookies in the house the child asked My friends are hungry.

14. The foreman said that no overtime would be needed until after Labor Day.

15. You can be sure that I will do my best for you and you can bet I will get you the appointment you want the instructor told the student.

Dates

Familiar ways of punctuating dates are beginning to give way to new practices, but the formal use of commas is still most widely followed. At the same time new practices are appearing that are recommended. In formal writing it is wise to follow formal practice. In business and technical writing, above all in informal writing, the newer practices can be adopted. Consistency in a single piece of writing is the essential element.

Formal Punctuation

Use a comma to separate a day from a month:

Tuesday, August 5   Thursday, June 6

Use a comma to separate a date from a year:

November 11, 1918   December 7, 1941

Use commas around a year following a date:

July 4, 1776, was the date chosen to celebrate the birth of a new country.

Use no comma between a month and a year:

February 1879   November 1922

Less Formal Punctuation

Use a comma to separate a day from a month:

Sunday, April 6   (or Sunday, 6 April)
Friday, October 30   (or Friday, 30 October)

Reverse the order of date and month and use no comma:

6 September   12 March

Reverse the order of date, month, and year and use no comma:

This bill was sent 15 October 1976.

Use no comma between a month and a year:

April 1881   January 1916

Notice that in the following sentence no commas are needed around *1977*, because it is a restrictive appositive. (See pages 29–31.)

The year 1977 is considered by some historians to have presaged the beginning of marked social unrest in Africa.

18. Insert commas where appropriate in the following sentences. Follow the rules for formal punctuation in the first five sentences. Follow the rules for less formal punctuation in the next five.

Formal   The baby was delivered early on Saturday, July 28, 1990.
Less Formal   The baby was delivered on Saturday, 28 July 1990.

1. We have chosen June 21 as the best day on which to hold the dog show.
2. Saturdays in August are all reserved for band concerts on the village green.
3. It is difficult to believe she will be seventy years old on July 4 1994.

4. She was looking forward to Sunday June 15 her wedding date.
5. April 1 is April Fools' Day.
6. I expect that January 1994 will be a good month for selling snow shovels.
7. He was discharged from the Marine Corps on 12 July 1945.
8. The fiscal year used to begin 1 July each year.
9. New orders will not be taken at these prices after 6 September 1991.
10. The new sales manager will take over on Monday 10 March.

Addresses and Place Names

Commas are used to separate a name from a street address, a street address from a city, a city from a state, and a state from a country. A comma is not used to separate a state from a zip code or, in the case of a foreign address, a city from the zip code equivalent.

Addresses written in sentence form require commas to separate all their elements.

They were fortunate in finding inexpensive furniture that suited their taste at Lyman's Antique Shop, 157 Mamaroneck Avenue, Mamaroneck, New York 10543.

You can forward her mail care of Dean of Students, Roanoke College, Salem, Virginia 24153.

I believe Dick's address is 45 Falkland Road, London NW5, England.

Place names written in sentence form also require commas to separate individual elements.

Bradford, Vermont, is a center of commercial life for much of the area between Hanover, New Hampshire, and St. Johnsbury, Vermont.

19. Insert commas where appropriate in the following sentences.

You can obtain the tourist information you need by writing to the California State Chamber of Commerce, Suite 300, 455 Capital Mall, Sacramento, California 95814.

Salem, Massachusetts, and Salem, Illinois, share little beyond their names.

1. He has written to the Director of Personnel McGraw-Hill, Inc. 1221 Avenue of the Americas New York New York 10020.
2. For a long time they lived in Branford Connecticut.
3. They have their offices at 795 Peachtree Street N.E. Atlanta Georgia 30308.
4. I am looking forward to retiring to my parents' home in Siena Italy.
5. She has rented Post Office Box 56 Metis Beach Quebec Canada.
6. You will be impressed by the Cathedral of Notre Dame in Paris France.
7. Palermo Italy was the scene of bloody fighting during World War II.
8. For a long time he maintained an office at 502 Park Avenue New York New York 10022.
9. The famous *Librairie Larousse* is located at 17 rue du Montparnasse Paris VIe France.
10. Lawrence has decided to leave North Collins New York and try for a new life in Scarborough Ontario Canada.

Titles and Degrees

Commas are used to set off titles and degrees that are used as appositives.

As discussed in pages 29–31, nonrestrictive appositives are set off by commas. See the examples below:

Our Chairman of the Board, Arthur B. Gross, will be retiring soon, after half a century of service to the organization.   (*Arthur B. Gross* is in apposition with *Chairman of the Board*.)

I am proud to honor the late Dr. Abraham Jacobson, a *distinguished physician*, for his contributions to medical science.   (Notice that *Dr.* precedes *Abraham Jacobson* and is not separated by a comma.)

Newly appointed Provost Jacques Vorst will serve also as Dean of Faculties.   (*Jacques Vorst* is not in apposition to *Provost*.)

Titles and degrees used as appositives are set off by commas when they follow a name, since they are nonrestrictive.

Arthur B. Gross, Chairman of the Board, is retiring this year after half a century of service to the organization.   (*Chairman of the Board* is in apposition with *Arthur B. Gross*.)

I am proud to honor the late Abraham Jacobson, M.D., for his contributions to medical science.   (*M.D.* is in apposition with *Abraham Jacobson*.)

Alice Duchin, Professor of Romance Languages, will give a paper on the novels of Stendhal.

The surgical team no longer will be assisted by Gloria Esterbrook, Ph.D.

Henry Arkwright, M.A., is undertaking a study of contributions to political candidates.

Notice that Jr. and Sr. are often used as appositives and must be set off by commas, since they are always nonrestrictive.

I would prefer that Martin Edgeworth, Sr., not be considered for that position.

A Roman numeral that is part of a name is a restrictive appositive and is not set off by commas:

George III was the reigning English monarch during the American Revolution.   (Without *III* we would not know which *George* was being discussed.)

Prince Carl of Denmark was known as *Haakon VII* when he was King of Norway.

Siebrand H. Nieuwenhous III will not appear at the ball this year.

20.   Insert commas where appropriate in the following sentences.

Karl Otto Helmholtz, Professor of Linguistics, has been appointed to the Faculty Council.

Mr. William Healy, Jr., Army Marketing Manager, will direct the Asteroid Project during the coming year.

1. Chairman Godfrey Helms has appointed a committee that is expected to raise the profits of the factory.
2. Ramses II reigned during the second millennium before the birth of Christ.
3. The child was given the imposing name of Mark Eldridge Satterthwaite IV.
4. One of the junior partners was appropriately named David Forsythe Jr.
5. Henri Lachaise Chairman of the Department of French holds two Ph.D. degrees.
6. Adrian Longworth Ph.D. has been Visiting Professor of Classical Languages at Smith College.
7. Pharmacologists often hold the Ph.D. degree as well as the M.S. and B.S. degrees.
8. The young man decided that an A.A. degree would be sufficient for any job he had in mind.
9. Robert Aldington B.A. has been designated departmental expediter.
10. Expo II was nowhere near as successful as Expo.

Omitted Words

Commas are used to indicate omitted words. To achieve a desired stylistic effect, writers may choose to omit certain words from a sentence. Unless these words are omitted at the end of a sentence, the omission is marked by insertion of a comma.

You take great risks in committing crime; in obeying the law, none at all.   (The words *you take* have been replaced by a comma: You take great risks in committing crime; in obeying the law *you take* none at all.)

In a pipe smoker the immature once saw great wisdom and good judgment; in a cigar smoker, maturity and signs of wealth; in a cigarette smoker, only furtiveness and insecurity.   (The words *the immature once saw* have been omitted after *cigar smoker* and after *cigarette smoker*.)

Colleges award degrees to their graduates, but high schools do not.   (The words *award degrees to their graduates* have been omitted after *high schools do not*. No comma is used, because the omission occurs at the end of the sentence.)

(The omissions for stylistic reasons that have been discussed are often referred to as *elliptical constructions*. In shortening quotations, writers employ the mark of punctuation known as *ellipsis*.) (See pages 102–104.)

21. Insert commas where appropriate in the following sentences.

Coming upon a mountain stream for the first time is a great event; for the second time, merely a delight.

In California such events are commonplace; in other parts of the country, rare indeed.

1. Falling in love for the first time is like seeing the sun rise after the long Arctic night; falling out of love like seeing your favorite team lose the seventh game of a World Series.

2. In San Francisco a level street is an occasional treat; in Kansas City a steady diet.

3. A floppy hat suits the candidate best; a pillbox not at all.

4. Bryan finds books his best companions and television his worst enemy, but Mary cannot find time for either.

5. We expect that Jon will be home in time for dinner, ready to eat as soon as he walks in the door; we are certain Henry will be late for dinner and ready to eat whenever he walks in.

6. Meeting her the first time was an experience unforgettable; seeing her the last time an ordeal insupportable.

7. Barney's suit was a miracle of synthetic delight; his shirt and tie crumpled visions of once-proud long-staple cotton.

8. Giving him the bad news that his employment with us was over was no problem for me; watching his reaction a painful incident.

9. All of us decided to leave on Monday morning; the rest on Monday night.

10. Jane began to forget she had ever known him; Charles to remember how lovely their life together had been.

Replacing *and*

A comma can be used in place of *and* before the second element of a pair. To achieve emphasis, writers will often omit *and* between elements of a pair. The effect is to emphasize the second element of the pair, and a comma is needed to show the omission.

We want a new house, a new life.   (Which is more important in the reader's mind, the *new house* or the *new life*? Does *a new life* overshadow *a new house*, even though one is a necessary part of the other? Compare your response to this sentence with your response to the same sentence with the *and* included: We want a new house *and* a new life. The two elements of the pair appear equal in value. Replacing *and* with a comma gives greater emphasis to the second element.)

The greater my involvement, the deeper my feelings, the less they seem to care.   (The omission of *and* after *involvement* increases the importance of *the deeper my feelings*.)

The longer they went on, the harder we listened, the less we understood.   (Compare this sentence with one containing the *and*: The longer they went on *and* the harder we listened, the less we understood. Replacing *and* with a comma calls the reader's attention to the second of the two elements.)

22.   The following sentences include some that have the word *and* between pairs of elements. Replace the *and* with a comma. Others have neither comma nor *and*. Insert commas where appropriate.

> They told their stories whenever they had an audience, ~~and~~ whenever they had none.
>
> The hungry child ate quickly when she liked her food, quicker when she disliked it.

1.   Many of the workers appeared enthusiastic when interviewed on television and disgruntled when they spoke with friends.
2.   Liberal arts students often speak openly against varsity sports and privately in favor of them.
3.   I am willing to buy second-hand furniture eager to purchase fine antiques.
4.   Much of his time is spent in idleness and little in productive work.
5.   Hunting for a job is difficult when times are good and impossible when times are bad.
6.   How can a person keep calm when confronted with a situation so demanding and so confining?
7.   Barbara told her sad story many times and told it even when no one could bear to hear it again.
8.   She persisted in her search when others would have relaxed and would have abandoned their efforts.
9.   Felice was an avid reader and an even more avid teller of stories.
10. Cities find themselves unable to provide desirable services for their citizens and unable even to provide essential services.

Clarity, the Overriding Requirement

Commas should be used wherever needed to ensure clarity. Writers should keep in mind that chances are that *anything that can be misunderstood by readers will be misunderstood by readers*. If any construction can possibly be misconstrued by readers, a remedy is needed. Complete rewriting may be the only remedy in some cases. In others insertion of a single comma may make the difference between misunderstanding and understanding, between hesitation and confidence, between ambiguity and clarity.

In all the sentences that follow, one or more of the comma rules presented in this chapter are violated. Your job is to test your perception of the sentences without selecting a rule to apply. A finely developed sense of clarity will tell you that something is wrong. If it does not, then you must go back and review the rules. If you have mastered the rules, you will know at once what is wrong and how to repair each sentence.

Wrong   Before cleaning and dyeing the garment must be inspected for damage.

Right   Before cleaning and dyeing, the garment must be inspected for damage.

Wrong   Outside the tent appeared perfectly rainproof.

Right   Outside, the tent appeared perfectly rainproof.

Wrong   Long after the village had not yet recovered from the shock of the terrible accident.

Right   Long after, the village had not yet recovered from the shock of the terrible accident.

Wrong   The police did not leave for the mob showed no signs of dispersing.

Right   The police did not leave, for the mob showed no signs of dispersing.

Wrong	After the American Legion members left the disease began to make its presence felt.
Right	After the American Legion members left, the disease began to make its presence felt.
Wrong	Thousands of happy ticket holders went to their seats inside and outside thousands of others clamored for admission to the auditorium.
Right	Thousands of happy ticket holders went to their seats inside, and outside thousands of others clamored for admission to the auditorium.
Wrong	Whatever Robert does does not involve me.
Right	Whatever Robert does, does not involve me.
Wrong	In place of Janet Smith appeared.
Right	In place of Janet, Smith appeared.
Wrong	Inside the dog a Dalmatian barked noisily to show its affection.
Right	Inside, the dog, a Dalmatian, barked noisily to show its affection.
Wrong	The last forty-six pages of *Ulysses* present the uninterrupted flow of Molly Bloom's thoughts and yearnings and inspiration for writers employing interior monologue.
Right	The last forty-six pages of *Ulysses* present the uninterrupted flow of Molly Bloom's thoughts and yearnings, and inspiration for writers employing interior monologue.
Wrong	Kennings characteristically found in Old English poetry are stereotyped synonyms or compound words and phrases and are infrequently found in modern poetry.
Right	Kennings, characteristically found in Old English poetry, are stereotyped synonyms or compound words and phrases, and are infrequently found in modern poetry.
Wrong	Farmers find they can get exceptional crop yields by avoiding insecticides and chemical fertilizers and carefully practicing organic farming principles.
Right	Farmers find they can get exceptional crop yields by avoiding insecticides and chemical fertilizers, and carefully practicing organic farming principles.

23. Insert commas where appropriate in the following sentences to assure clarity.

What Philip makes, makes no difference to me.

As the surgeon cut in, the medical students gasped.

1. Rather than Billy let us try Bob again.
2. Once read the book proved useful in all respects.
3. Most of the people lingered for the afternoon showing was not ending on time.
4. Before leaving the department store clerks had to process their full receipts.
5. Above all apple trees must be carefully pruned.
6. Once we had eaten the cat demanded its own food.
7. Because Luis could hit his coach insisted on starting him.
8. To encourage the assistant manager to leave the manager offered a two-week vacation instead of just one.
9. After she had eaten the woman left without leaving a tip.
10. Several times in the past weeks would go by without their exchanging a civil word.
11. Al thought his job was a great way of making a living for his days on unemployment insurance had shown him the value of steady work.
12. Prompt payment of bills is essential for good credit is built upon it.
13. Without exaggerating thousands of errors are found each month in departmental calculations.
14. Terry couldn't tell the time for his watch had been stolen.

15. They searched the entire forest and the child still had not been found.

16. We now can forget about finding a good place to eat for five dollars will buy only a bad meal.

17. Immediately after I fired the superintendent of police came upon me.

18. If the band does not play there is no chance anyone sober will be left at the party.

19. Even though Father spent many hours scraping and priming Dick found plenty of painting left to do.

20. A poor job of finishing Mother insists will mean an entire job to do all over again.

21. All the corn kernels were golden and green beans lent their bright color to the dish.

22. My sister is interested in decorating and painting is a task my brother detests.

23. Once you have studied Sam Johnson's interpretation of what words mean Noah Webster can be appreciated more.

24. I was paid lower wages for my sister-in-law was the store manager.

25. When you finally finish painting Bill will give you other work to do.

26. June was pleased with her catch for the tuna weighed more than one hundred pounds.

27. Everyone was there but one of the team members was ill.

28. To shut the window great strength is needed.

29. After this one mistake will cost you dearly.

30. When old cows give little milk.

31. Radio would be much more enjoyable if we could tune out noisy commercials and talkative disc jockeys.

32. Television can be as effective in influencing voters as strong-arm methods and chicanery once were.

33. The Boy Scout troop had difficulty in attracting new members that year and meeting its budget and had to disband.

34. My sister is delighted with the new job she has found and with the additional income it brings.

35. The illness that ruined her final year of life made conditions difficult for the family in many ways and drained family resources.

36. Our community asks constantly for autonomy and lower tax rates.

37. Family medicine no longer is practiced by most physicians in the belief that specialized services promote greater efficiency and better quality of medical care.

38. Clothbound books have the advantage of longer life compared with many paperbound books and pamphlets.

39. The child found himself faced with decisions and responsibilities too difficult for one so young with no adult to consult.

40. Many rulers in earlier centuries looked with disfavor on demands by their subjects for freedom and suffrage and reacted with increased oppressiveness.

With Quotation Marks

When commas are used with quotation marks, one comma is placed before the first quotation mark and one before the second quotation mark.

When a quotation is introduced by an expression such as *he said* or *she said*, a comma is needed before the initial quotation mark. (See Chapter 5 for the rule governing the use of quotation marks to indicate a direct quotation.)

Frieda said, "I am eager to finish my work and go out tonight."

When any other sentence element before a quotation requires a comma, the comma is placed before the quotation mark.

According to Professor Kronish, "Economic theory does not explain all recent experiences in the international money market."

When a quotation is run into a sentence without an introductory expression, the comma is not used.

The witness testified that the union's real purpose was to "annoy management" in hope of instigating a lockout.

When a quotation is followed by an expression identifying the source of the quotation, a comma is needed before the final quotation mark.

"Help yourself to another cup of coffee," the host said.

When a comma is needed for any other purpose after a quotation, the comma is placed before the final quotation mark.

Yesterday he said, "I will never agree to what you want," but today he is as agreeable as anyone can be.

24.   Insert commas where appropriate in the following sentences.

My exact words were "gratuities not encouraged."

As Orwell wrote, "How could the rich, the strong, the elegant, the fashionable, the powerful be in the wrong?"

1. "There's little to be done for those left homeless by the flood " the sheriff said.
2. O. Henry was at his satirical best when he wrote "The Man Higher Up."
3. He vowed to campaign in all the cities of the state as well as in "the tiniest hamlets you can name."
4. The old man sat back in his chair and calmly said "I am ready to die."
5. First came an asthmatic wheeze and then his fateful words "I am ready to die and want all efforts to save my life discontinued."
6. The client wanted her full legal rights and "any money I can collect " for the injury had left her completely disabled.
7. Golfers teeing off are advised to shout "Fore " just before they address the ball.
8. Arthur exclaimed "Have you no mercy for one so young?"
9. Who can forget " 'Twas brillig, and the slithy toves / Did gyre and gimble in the wabe"?
10. We cannot put up with "unintentional" violence and "unpremeditated assault " any longer.

(For further uses of commas, see the Appendix: Punctuation of Footnotes, Bibliographies, and Letters, pages 145–147).

Chapter 3

The Semicolon and the Colon

THE SEMICOLON

The semicolon is seldom used by many writers, who prefer short, simple sentences and carefully avoid the kind of complexity that requires semicolons. Nevertheless, some sentences require semicolons, and they can be useful punctuation marks. On the other hand, prose that requires frequent use of semicolons may be heavy and dull. Writing that employs many semicolons should be reexamined to see whether some cutting is in order.

With Independent Clauses

A semicolon is used to separate independent clauses that are not connected by a coordinating conjunction.

A comma is used between independent clauses connected by a coordinating conjunction; *and*, *or*, *for*, *but*, etc. When a coordinating conjunction is not present, a semicolon must be used. The semicolon can also be thought of as replacing the period that would be used if the two independent clauses stood as separate sentences.

> Doris went to work, but Jon stayed home to rest.
> Doris went to work. Jon stayed home to rest.
> Doris went to work; Jon stayed home to rest.

A semicolon is not ordinarily used in a sentence as simple as the last example, although it is correct. Semicolons are considered a mark of formal style, so many writers avoid them altogether or use them sparingly. Some editors have a rule of thumb—*one semicolon to a chapter*. Yet semicolons have their uses, and one of them is separation of independent clauses not connected by a coordinating conjunction. In this capacity the semicolon says to the reader that the independent clauses on either side have equal value.

> "While there is a lower class, I am in it; while there is a criminal element, I am of it; while there is a soul in prison, I am not free."   (This famous sentence, attributed to Eugene V. Debs, has three independent clauses plus three dependent clauses. Semicolons are needed because no coordinating conjunctions are present.)

> "The only guide to a man is his conscience; the only shield to his memory is the rectitude and sincerity of his actions."   (In this sentence Prime Minister Winston Churchill was paying tribute to his predecessor in office. The semicolon heightens the effectiveness of the two closely related thoughts.)

The key to this use of the semicolon, then, is to ask whether the thoughts in independent clauses are so closely related that they must stand in a single sentence and whether a semicolon is more effective than a coordinating conjunction plus a comma.

1. In the following sentences, some independent clauses are connected by coordinating conjunctions but lack commas. Others lack conjunctions and commas. Change every sentence by inserting a semicolon in the appropriate position and removing conjunctions no longer needed.

> Prefabricated homes have many advantages; they also have so many disadvantages that potential buyers are well advised to think a long time before buying one.
> Baseball usually lacks the physical contact so often seen in football; football is much harder to follow than baseball and demands that the viewer be willing to sit for more than two hours in a cold stadium.

1. Both candidates lacked the qualities that excite potential supporters, and neither appeared to have solid support as the campaign drew to a close in November.

2. The many new nations of Africa find the United Nations an excellent platform for political propaganda the older nations sense that the day is coming when they will be in the minority in that world forum.

3. The Representative from New York grew more and more disturbed she could see that the problems of her beloved city were going to be ignored.

4. Many children have the advantage of a home life filled with love, but too many others never experience the warmth and tenderness of parents who care for them.

5. The state of Ohio boasts a great tradition of independent liberal arts colleges, and students from all parts of the United States flock there to take advantage of the fine education offered.

6. I can remember a time when all politicians were admired by their constituents almost nobody holds them in high regard today.

7. The collapse of the Teton Dam has caused many of us to wonder whether public projects are planned carefully, and it is no surprise that environmentalists are gaining new support.

8. At first colleges lacked adequate dormitory space for upper classmen and upper classwomen the rapid building program of recent years has created the problem of excess capacity.

9. Corporate officers too often ignore the welfare of their employees the result is that worker morale falls and absenteeism increases.

10. All applications for admission must be filed by the third week in November, but late applications will be processed upon payment of a penalty fee.

With Conjunctive Adverbs

A semicolon is used before a conjunctive adverb that connects two independent clauses. The most common conjunctive adverbs are *however*, *therefore*, and *thus*. They serve to connect independent clauses, just as coordinating conjunctions do. The relationship they imply between the clauses is different from that implied by the coordinating conjunctions. (See pages 34–36 for the explanation of when commas are used with conjunctive adverbs.)

> Several European countries established colonies in the New World during the sixteenth century; *however*, by the middle of the present century, the influence of these countries all but disappeared.

> Funding for many worthwhile projects was abruptly terminated by officials who consciously sought to reduce expenditures; *therefore*, day care centers for the children of working mothers were forced to institute higher fees or close their doors.   (Notice that the first independent clause is followed by a dependent clause, *who consciously sought to reduce expenditures*.)

In both these sentences the conjunctive adverbs are followed by commas. Some writers are beginning to drop the comma after a conjunctive adverb, but careful writers retain it. If the comma is dropped, there is the risk of confusing readers, who may not notice that the conjunctive adverb is functioning as a conjunction rather than as an adverb. This risk is greatest with *however*.

Wrong   The American League voted to retain the designated hitter; *however* many fans voiced their disapproval of the practice.   (Readers may think *however* modifies *many*.)

Right   The American League voted to retain the designated hitter; *however*, many fans voiced their disapproval of the practice.

It is best to preserve the comma after a conjunctive adverb that connects two independent clauses.

2. The following pairs of sentences include conjunctive adverbs. Make a single sentence of each pair and punctuate properly. You may have to move the conjunctive adverb in some cases. For your convenience, the conjunctive adverbs are italicized.

We opposed every bill that came up for consideration during the opening session of the legislature. We insisted, *moreover*, that the executive branch was guilty of failing to consult the bar association on judicial appointments.

We opposed every bill that came up for consideration during the opening session of the legislature; moreover, we insisted that the executive branch was guilty of failing to consult the bar association on judicial appointments.

Our debts far exceeded our cash reserves and anticipated income. *Thus*, there was nothing for us to do but declare bankruptcy.

Our debts far exceeded our cash reserves and anticipated income; thus, there was nothing for us to do but declare bankruptcy.

1. Shirley's first experience in graduate school was far from satisfactory. *Nevertheless*, she returned for a second semester with her confidence unimpaired.

2. We were no longer welcome in Enrico's pizzeria. For the next several weeks, *instead*, we patronized his competitor across the street.

3. Our regular veterinarian was unable to board our old hound on short notice. *Consequently*, we began to leave him at a kennel that had a poor reputation for cleanliness.

4. The closing date for applications had already passed. We decided, *nevertheless*, to send in the papers and hope for the best.

5. Some attorneys manage to antagonize their clients. Notwithstanding, when this happens, the attorneys have no option but to exert their best efforts in their clients' behalf.

6. The labor organizer compiled an excellent record during her first year in the field. She was declared, *indeed*, the most successful negotiator in the union's history.

7. I shall return next week for another attempt at the record. I intend, *meanwhile*, to spend all my spare time practicing turns and jumps.

8. This past season has been the worst in the orchestra's recent history. The budget deficit, *consequently*, is at a dangerous level.

9. Margaret Mitchell found herself unable to sell *Gone with the Wind* to publisher after publisher. She felt, *consequently*, that no one would ever publish the book that had consumed so many years of her life.

_____

_____

_____

10. Katherine applied to several medical schools before finding one that would accept her. *Furthermore*, many of them never even acknowledged receipt of her application.

_____

_____

_____

With Internally Punctuated Series

Semicolons are used between elements in a series when any of the elements have internal commas. Ordinarily, commas are used between elements in a series: *Many countries of Europe export grain*, *dairy products*, *and vegetables*. The series can be separated by commas because the elements of the series are themselves not punctuated internally: *grain*, *dairy products*, *and vegetables*. When the elements of a series are internally punctuated, however, semicolons are needed between the elements to prevent confusion.

> Three of the best sources of information on mythology are *The New Golden Bough*, Sir James George Frazer; *Funk & Wagnalls Standard Dictionary of Folklore, Mythology and Legend*, Maria Leach; and *The Mentor Dictionary of Mythology and the Bible*, Richard J. Daigle and Frederick R. Lapides.

> The four most common metrical feet in English poetry are the iamb, which consists of an unstressed syllable followed by a stressed syllable; the trochee, which consists of a stressed syllable followed by an unstressed syllable; the anapest, which consists of two unstressed syllables followed by a stressed syllable; and the dactyl, which consists of a stressed syllable followed by two unstressed syllables.

> My favorite small cities are Albany, New York; Cairo, Illinois; Duluth, Minnesota; and Fresno, California.

3. Supply semicolons where appropriate in the following sentences. Extra space is provided for your convenience in writing.

> Three geneticists made important contributions to the understanding of mutations and natural selection: R. A. Fisher, an Englishman; Sewall Wright, an American; and J. B. S. Haldane, an Englishman.

> For thorough treatment of ecology, the reader is advised to consult *Our Living World of Nature*, the first set of books to treat natural history from an ecological perspective; *Erosion and Sediment Pollution*, a practical work for conservationists; and *Wastewater Engineering: Collection-Treatment-Disposal*, a clear introduction to water conservation.

1. Students of language will find much valuable information in Wentworth and Flexner's *Dictionary of American Slang*, which is periodically revised Partridge's *A Dictionary of Slang and Unconventional English*, a favorite of those who admire good writing and Mencken's classic *The American Language*.

2. I enjoy several types of films westerns primarily because I love simple stories that always end happily romances which take me out of the real world for ninety minutes and detective mysteries because I never can guess who the guilty person is.

3. They all were gourmets my mother who never did learn how to cook properly my father, who cared little about food and my oldest brother, who would eat anything put in front of him.

4. My natural inclination to judge horses on the basis of beauty led me to lose all three races the first which had a beautiful but spavined little mare running against five fast geldings the second in which my roan dazzler never even left the starting gate and the third in which the ugliest seven-year old on the card won by nine lengths over a field of equine beauty contest winners.

5. The candidates this year include Jay Tolliver a successful fast food merchant Irwin Gordon a sometimes seller of worthless municipal bonds Les Page once a high school guidance counselor and Mary McGraw executive secretary to a traveling salesman.

As Comma Substitute

A semicolon is used wherever a comma is inadequate. The previous rule governs the use of the semicolon between elements of an internally punctuated series. The reasoning behind the rule is that commas are ordinarily used between elements of a series, but when commas are used within the elements of a series, a stronger mark of punctuation is needed to ensure comprehension by readers. That rule is a special case of the present rule, which prescribes use of a semicolon wherever a comma is inadequate.

Some voters, though conscientious about going to the polls, frequently find themselves at a loss when confronted by a long, complex, closely printed paper ballot; yet others, with no more education or experience, can work their way intelligently down such a ballot, hardly ever making an error.　(This sentence consists of two independent clauses: *Some voters . . . ballot* and *others . . . error*. Ordinarily a comma is sufficient between two independent clauses (see page 18.) The sentence, however, has seven other commas. Merely using a comma before *yet*, where a semicolon now appears, would risk misleading readers. For this reason a semicolon is required.)

During the course of his long career in the military, thirty-five years of exceptional devotion, even heroism on several occasions, General Dyer was recognized as a leader in aviation, artillery tactics, and strategic planning; but outside the military this exceptional man, always modest in his behavior, goes unnoticed by his fellow citizens, who take pains to ignore all achievements but those directed toward accumulation of wealth, prestige, and power. (Again a sentence with two independent clauses plus considerable complexity and ten commas. A comma before the coordinating conjunction *but* would be inadequate for readers. A semicolon must be used.)

4. The following sentences are printed to provide extra space wherever a comma or semicolon is needed. Insert the appropriate marks.

A few of the children lacked adequate clothing, many lacked sufficient food, and most lacked both; but the program administrators, comfortable in their elegant offices, saw nothing, did nothing, and went on collecting their generous salaries.

The miserable slaves found themselves auctioned off to the highest bidder, separated from their families, and driven mercilessly; and they wondered why slaves fortunate enough to work on nearby plantations could speak happily of generous, humane, even kindly treatment.

1. In her first visit to the leper colony   the young physician was appalled by the lack of care sanitary facilities   and adequate diet   but on returning the next year   she was encouraged by the general improvement in health   morale   and living conditions of the afflicted people.

2. After many attempts to identify the gene   the researcher decided that he had overlooked the source of his materials   the temperature at which they had been stored before shipment   and the preparation of instruments for the delicate process   yet he was still far from solution of the problem   as it turned out   since there were many more variables to control in the demanding process.

3. Successful businesses require dedicated   capable employees who are willing to exert their best efforts in support of an enterprise that yields rewards only to the group that controls it   finances

      it   and establishes policy   but many people   accustomed to hard work under any conditions   do their best even when they see no chance   ultimately   of gaining adequate reward.

4.   Plato suggested   according to some interpretations   that the loftiest occupation is the study of philosophy   but such a pursuit would not be possible for men and women forced by the demands of living to spend all their time seeking food   protecting themselves against attack by wild animals   and keeping warm in a harsh environment.

5.   Once the convention was over   the delegates filed out   thoroughly confused   terribly disturbed by what they had seen   wondering whether they had really participated in a democratic process   and many of them still wondered about their roles when they went home the next day to be questioned by those who had elected them believing that every delegate would represent the people back home wisely   confidently   and carefully.

6.   The individuals to watch as the events began to unfold   he said   were not Edwards   Pulham and Godfrey   they were already too involved   by self-interest   by past actions   and by personal commitments to the goals of the organization.

7.   On the economic question   to tell the truth   there was little to be done   little to be gained   and the harsh realities of the political situation   too long ignored   demanded either a policy of total and immediate commitment   since all parties were involved   or total absence of action.

8.   Hazel intended   as well as she understood her intentions   to become a full participant in all activities of the program   including housing and public welfare   so that she could achieve what she had set out to achieve   Sam   for his part   had every intention of doing nothing   since he had become thoroughly disillusioned by what he had seen already.

9.   By the middle of his second term   as a result of many months of hard work   Warren knew he would be unable to complete his thesis or his course work no matter how much time   effort   and dedication he put into his work   the only attitude he could adopt   therefore   was one of complete resignation to the failure that was on its way.

10.   The committee   it appeared   credited him fully insofar as his research was concerned   but no one in the department   it was also clear   saw him as performing his teaching duties outstandingly   even acceptably.

THE COLON

The colon is a mark that is helpful in certain conventional uses, primarily in introducing enumerations and lists. Beyond these uses the colon is seen infrequently. In certain sentences, it is used as an alternative to the semicolon when providing explanatory material.

With Enumerations and Lists

A colon introduces an enumeration or list. When the word preceding an enumeration or list is either a verb or a preposition, a colon is not needed. The enumeration or list is either the object or complement of the verb, or the object of the preposition. When an enumeration or list is preceded by a noun or noun phrase, a colon is needed. The enumeration or list in that case is in apposition with the element preceding the colon.

Enumerations

> The Pentateuch consists of five books: Genesis, Exodus, Leviticus, Numbers, and Deuteronomy.   (The titles of the books are in apposition to *books*.)

> The Furies are terrible goddesses of Greek and Roman mythology: Alecto, Megaera, and Tisiphone.   (The names of the Furies are in apposition to *goddesses*.)

When an enumeration follows a verb, the enumeration is the object or complement of the verb and must not be separated from the verb by punctuation.

Wrong   The three guiding qualities of his life are: faith, hope, and charity.

Right   The three guiding qualities of his life are faith, hope, and charity.

Right   His life reflects three guiding qualities: faith, hope, and charity.   (The words *faith*, *hope*, and *charity* are in apposition with *qualities*.)

When an enumeration follows a preposition, the enumeration is the object of the preposition and must not be separated from the preposition by punctuation.

Wrong   Before going to school each day, he was required to: make all the beds in the house, wash the breakfast dishes, and tidy the house.

Right   Before going to school each day, he was required to make all the beds in the house, wash the breakfast dishes, and tidy the house.

Right   Before going to school each day, he was required to perform three chores: make all the beds in the house, wash the breakfast dishes, and tidy the house.   (All the work cited is in apposition with *chores*.)

Lists

The requirements for a colon before lists are the same as those for enumerations: A colon is not used after a verb when introducing a list; a colon is not used after a preposition when introducing a list.

Wrong   His company manufactures:
               automobiles
               helicopters
               trucks

Right   His company manufactures all types of vehicles:
               automobiles
               helicopters
               trucks

Right   His company manufactures
               automobiles
               helicopters
               trucks

Wrong   The vehicles his company manufactures are used in:
               commercial applications
               industrial applications
               military applications

Right   The vehicles his company manufactures are used in the following:
               commercial application
               industrial applications
               military applications

Right   The vehicles his company manufactures are used in
               commercial applications
               industrial applications
               military applications

Many business writers disregard the requirement of apposition and use a colon indiscriminately to introduce any list. This practice, like many others, has the sanction that comes from frequent misuse by the uninformed over a long period of time. In formal writing the requirement of apposition is never violated.

   5. Insert colons where appropriate in the following sentences.

               My favorite dessert is a compote of four fruits: apples, pears, peaches, and plums.

               I have trouble spelling certain words:

accidentally
laboratory
literature
occasionally

1. I am sending my applications to four schools Williams, Cal Tech, Vanderbilt, and Case.
2. Bill can always get work as a nurse, social worker, or teacher.
3. Our club has four standing committees Budget, Ceremonies, Personnel, and Awards.
4. The Chamber of Commerce represents the interests of all the businesses in our area, including companies in the following industries

   metallurgy
   chemicals
   aerospace
   office equipment
5. My favorite authors are Dos Passos, Dreiser, Mann, and Galsworthy.
6. Leading companies in the United States automobile industry are General Motors, Ford, and Chrysler.
7. Lincoln Center, in the heart of New York City, each year produces excellent ballet, drama, and music for the general public.
8. The New England states include Maine, New Hampshire, Vermont, and Massachusetts; Rhode Island is so small that we are inclined to overlook it.
9. Some of the following are suspected of containing carcinogenic substances

   tobacco
   fish
   pork
   beef
   chicken
   Can you identify the suspect substances?
10. Emma soon became known for the quality of her work in the following media needlepoint, batik, tie-dye, and macramé.

With Formal Statements, Quotations, Questions

A colon sets off expressions that introduce formal statements, quotations, and questions. As a rule introductory expressions before direct quotations are set off by commas. Now we are dealing with the punctuation of introductory expressions that occur before formal statements.

A formal statement is defined by the setting in which it is made, for example, a meeting of a professional group, campaign address, published book or article; or by the status of the person being quoted: a public official, important person, distinguished scholar, and the like.

The statement may be a direct quotation or a paraphrase. It may take the form of a question. Notice that in all these cases the first word after the colon is capitalized.

This is the issue on which her campaign is based: "All people must be housed with dignity, suitably employed, and educated to the extent of their ability. Nothing less than this will do for a nation as wealthy as ours."

As Rousseau said in *The Social Contract:* "As soon as public service ceases to be the chief business of the citizens, and they would rather serve with their money than with their persons, the State is not far from its fall."

The Detection Club, Miss Sayers reported, asks this question in its membership oath: "Do you promise that your Detectives shall well and truly detect the Crimes presented to them, using those Wits which it shall please you to bestow upon them and not placing reliance upon, nor making use of, Divine Revelation, Feminine Intuition, Mumbo-Jumbo, Jiggery-Pokery, Coincidence, or the Act of God?"

I am interested in only two questions: Is the club membership prepared to oust all officers who betray their official trust? Is the membership prepared to act promptly on submittal of conclusive evidence?

The Dean concluded her lengthy remarks by forcefully restating her position: The College was organized to educate. Conditions on campus are making education impossible. Unless conditions change quickly, there will be no alternative to shutting it down.

6. Insert a colon or a comma after the introductory expressions in the following sentences.

> The child said, "I don't want a tuna fish sandwich."
>
> Maeterlinck took this melancholy view: "All our knowledge merely helps us to die a more painful death than the animals that know nothing. A day will come when science will turn upon its error and no longer hesitate to shorten our woes."

1. The departmental chairman rose to his feet and began   "Not one of the distinguished members of this university has addressed the root question even though we all have heard opinions on every aspect of our peripheral functions. What I ask is whether we do ourselves more harm than good by refusing to face what is really troubling all of us."

2. The child's nurse answered   "I have always done my level best to raise the boy the way a boy should be raised."

3. At the conclusion of the service, the minister left the pulpit and walked to the floor of the church   "I must speak to you on the matter of your responsibilities as citizens in deciding which of the two candidates for President you prefer. For my own part I say that no one in the clergy has any right to instruct you in such temporal matters."

4. Their position was stated plainly by their leader in these unforgettable words   "I am going to make you an offer you cannot refuse. Either you return the cash immediately and see your family again or you die right now."

5. Nietzsche said of the mind of the vain man   "It resembles a well stocked and ever renewed store that attracts buyers of every class. They can find almost everything, have almost everything, provided they bring with them to right kind of money—admiration."

6. The old man looked at his wife and said   "I shall not live much longer, I know, but I do not want to make out a will just yet."

7. Thomas Mann, in *The Magic Mountain*, had this to say of time   "Time has no divisions to mark its passage; there is never a thunderstorm or blare of trumpets to announce the beginning of a new month or year. Even when a new century begins, it is only we mortals who ring bells and fire pistols."

8. Helen replied   "There is no reason for buying a house just yet, since we are getting along well enough in this apartment."

9. I still recall words spoken by Elmer Davis after World War II   "Atomic warfare is bad enough; biological warfare would be worse; but there is something that is worse than either. The French can tell you what it is; or the Czechs, or the Greeks, or the Norwegians, or the Filipinos; it is subjection to an alien oppressor."

10. Let us all consider this thought   If we do not ensure a decent life for all our people, then none of us will rest easy again.

With Independent Clauses

A colon separates two independent clauses when no conjunction is used and the second clause explains, amplifies, or illustrates the first clause. A semicolon is used to separate two independent clauses when no conjunction is used. With a semicolon, the clauses are considered to have approximately equal value.

When a colon is used between two independent clauses, the reader is signaled that a special relationship exists between the two clauses: the second clause explains the meaning of the first clause or expands or illustrates its meaning. Notice that some of the following sentences are compound-complex, consisting of two or more independent clauses plus any dependent clauses. The rule still holds.

> The married couples had no intention of going to the party: they were bored by such affairs and preferred staying home.

> The language spoken in Korea shares a characteristic with Japanese and Chinese: it has no inflections for plurals or tense.

> San Francisco attracts many visitors each year: cable cars are fun to ride and watch, the waterfront brings fishing boats rich with fresh sea life, and Chinatown beguiles the gourmet tourist and collector of *objets d'art*.

The special relationships between opening clauses and what follows are apparent in these three examples. To punctuate them with semicolons would not constitute errors, but would be something less than fully effective.

7.   Insert a colon or semicolon where most appropriate in the following sentences.

> Annette's true motives never surfaced: not even her immediate family understood why she refused to accept early retirement.

> The storekeeper shook his head and pointed grimly to the sign above the cash register: "In God We Trust. All Others Pay Cash."

1. The war in Vietnam had an impact on the people at home unlike that of any other recent American war   people seemed torn between a deeply engrained patriotism and a suspicion that a terrible mistake had been made.

2. World War I ended for the United States in a little over a year   World War II lasted almost four full years.

3. Familiarity breeds contempt   if peoples everywhere got to know one another better, the world would be torn apart.

4. The pleasures of marriage are not understood by the unmarried   they think only of emotions and passions remote from the contentment of the happily married state.

5. The museums of New York City are rich in art treasures   the night life is unsurpassed anywhere.

6. The dying man said he would not want even one extra hour of life   how could he pretend that his life had been enjoyable?

7. Without great art, life would be less human   the work of the masters dignifies and enriches our existence.

8. Thoughts of suicide console the desperate   they help many of us get through especially bad nights.

9. A good critic tries to see the world through the eyes of the playwright whose work he evaluates   can it really be this way, are people capable of such actions, is life really that good or that bad?

10. Fear of being caught prevents many honest people from committing crime   desire to be caught prevents many criminals from living honest lives.

Miscellaneous Uses of the Colon

1.   A colon is used between hours and minutes in expressions of time:

> 12:45 p.m.   1:10 a.m.

2. A colon is used after the speaker's name in a play:

> Iago: Sir, would she give you so much of her lips
> As of her tongue she oft bestows on me,
> You would have enough.
> Desdemona: Alas, she has no speech!
> Iago: In faith, too much.

A Semicolon Is Not a Colon

Perhaps because of the similarity of the marks, the most frequent error made by beginning writers is confusion of the semicolon with the colon. The rules governing both marks are clear. Review them if you care to before undertaking the next exercise.

8. Each of the following sentences is fully punctuated except for a semicolon or colon. Insert the required marks in each sentence.

> I am interested in acquiring works of the following composers: Mozart, Haydn, and Beethoven.
>
> The golf course has now closed for the winter; the country club, of course, remains open year round.

1. Several counties were severely affected by the recent hurricane   Westchester, Suffolk, Putnam, and Nassau.

2. Our group will meet on Monday night if a quorum is present   otherwise, the next meeting will be delayed one month.

3. When the store reopens for business, certain managers will no longer be working there   Ms. Chadwick, Mrs. Taylor, and Mr. Forsythe.

4. I would be pleased to have your comments regarding Arlene, who led the chorus last week   my supervisor is considering her for promotion to leader of the combined chorus and has asked me to collect whatever information is available on her musicianship, leadership qualities, and reliability.

5. The prospectus left many questions unanswered   Are the archives complete? Are the documents well preserved? Are scholars encouraged to use the facility?

6. Kentucky and Tennessee burley tobaccos were carefully cultivated, harvested, selected, and aged to give the coolest smoke possible   yet, despite the best efforts of the company to control all aspects of distribution, careless packaging ruined thousands of pounds of the prize mixture.

7. We are interested in obtaining one copy of each of the following
   > John T. Gause, *The Complete Word Hunter*
   > Alfred H. Holt, *Phrase and Word Origins*
   > C. C. Bombaugh, *Oddities and Curiosities of Words and Literature*

8. Can you define the following terms   feminine rhyme, masculine rhyme, double rhyme, triple rhyme, end rhyme, and internal rhyme?

9. Chiasmus is defined as the use of phrases that are syntactically parallel but have their elements reversed, as in this line from Pope   "Works without show, and without pomp presides."

10. We all admire her wizardry with words   her difficulty in dealing with people destroys whatever effectiveness she otherwise has.

(For further uses of the colon, see the Appendix: The Punctuation of Footnotes, Bibliographies, and Letters, pages 145–147. Placement of the colon and semicolon in relation to quotation marks is discussed in Chapter 5, pages 64–66.)

Chapter 4

Parentheses and Brackets

PARENTHESES

Parentheses are used within sentences, around entire sentences, and even around entire paragraphs. Parentheses are used most often to set off elements that interrupt the grammatical and logical flow of a sentence.

When are parentheses preferred over commas and dashes to set off parenthetic elements? Parentheses are used when the elements to be set off are too relevant to omit but are not part of the sentences or paragraphs in which they are found. Readers see material enclosed in parentheses as less important, at least for the moment, than material enclosed in dashes or commas. They consider material enclosed in dashes and, to an even greater extent, material enclosed in commas as true parts of the sentence they are reading.

The greatest users of parentheses are scholars who want to tell their readers everything they know about a subject and to supply readers with as much related information as their editors will permit. Most writing, however, requires parentheses only occasionally, primarily for such conventional uses as enclosing numerals and letters in an enumeration. Parentheses are used often in this book to set off discussions from sentences used as illustrations. This is a convention of textbook publishing. The other principal use in this book is to set off cross references for the reader's convenience.

With Relevant but Not Vital Information

Parentheses are used to set off material that is too relevant to omit but is not truly part of the sentence or paragraph in which it appears. Somewhat like the actor in a Shakespearean play who addresses asides to the audience, abruptly leaving off speaking with the other actors to communicate confidentially with the audience, a writer may wish to refer to something that is not central to the topic under discussion. Knowing that the reader deserves an explanation for the sudden interruption, the writer encloses the interrupting material in parentheses. Material within parentheses is usually illustration, definition, explanation, or reference to other writing.

> Theodore Dreiser's novels are no longer popular (even though a film made of *An American Tragedy* enjoyed great commercial success some years ago), but some critics rank Dreiser among the best American novelists and anticipate a revival of interest in his work.

You can see that the reference to the film is relevant to the sentence but not truly part of it. The claim for Dreiser's ability has little to do with the film made of one of his novels. The material is worthy of inclusion in the sentence only because the subject of Dreiser's popularity was introduced. Parentheses are the correct mark to use in setting off the parenthetic element.

> Many of the early colonists fled their homes to avoid the fighting that erupted in New England (and later in other areas as well).

This material is enclosed in parentheses because the principal discussion concerns events that occurred at a particular time and place. What happened elsewhere is not of immediate concern, but the writer wishes to call attention to the fact that colonists also fled their homes in other areas. Parentheses are the correct mark. Notice that the period comes outside the final parenthesis because the parenthetical material is not a complete sentence.

> Television journalists enjoy great personal reputations and extremely high salaries. (Walter Cronkite even today is mentioned in lists of most-admired and most-trusted Americans.) Their counterparts in print journalism remain relatively unknown by the general public and are paid substantially less than the TV news people.

Introducing Cronkite's name gives us an interesting bit of information that is insufficient to offer as proof of the claim made in the first sentence. The writer knows this and offers the sentence enclosed in parentheses as relevant information but not truly a part of the paragraph.

When parentheses include only part of a sentence, the punctuation of the sentence is not affected by the parentheses.

> All the information on substantial lawsuits outstanding is included in the company's annual report (reproduced here as Appendix A).

> The composer refuses to state where she was born (three countries claim her as a native), but birth records indicate she was born on October 4, 1946, in Brooklyn, New York.

> Funding for the program falls far short of what was anticipated (newspaper accounts suggest the original amount exceeded $2,000,000); every indication at present is that the program will terminate in this coming fiscal year.

In these three sentences the final parenthesis falls inside the regular sentence punctuation. In the first sentence a period is needed to end the sentence. In the second a comma is needed before the conjunction *but*, which connects the two independent clauses. In the third a semicolon is needed between the two independent clauses.

> Dramatic expressionism is a term applied to plays that emphasize emotional content, subjective reactions of characters, and symbolic representations of reality. (O'Neill's *The Emperor Jones* is an excellent example of this genre.) In painting, expressionism suggests exaggeration and distortion of forms derived from nature combined with the intensification of color to express emotion. Thus, while the relationship of the two forms of expressionism can be perceived, the terms have differing meanings that must be explored fully for complete understanding.

> Collage employs materials classical artists would have thought alien to art. (What use would Rubens or Rembrandt have made of old newspapers and bottle caps?) Yet the principles of composition and the appreciation of color relationships in the best collages retain their resemblance to the composition and color of the older art.

These two examples show punctuation internal to parenthetic material. In the first case the parentheses set off an entire sentence punctuated by a period. In the second the parentheses set off a question. An exclamatory sentence can also be set off by parentheses. In all complete parenthetical sentences, the final parenthesis follows the period, the question mark, or the exclamation point. Notice that no period is needed after the parenthesis.

1. Insert parentheses and other marks of punctuation where appropriate in the following sentences. Extra space is provided for your convenience in writing.

> Statisticians frequently employ graphs, tables, and charts to present their data **(see Table 1 as an example)**.

> Who can fail to enjoy Fowler **(***A Dictionary of Modern English Usage* by H. W. Fowler**)** when he holds forth on the subject of tautologies**?**

1. Hemingway's novels have delighted generations of readers   promoters of bullfights appreciate them too since 1926 when *The Sun Also Rises* was published

2. In *haiku* the poet writes in three lines totaling seventeen or nineteen syllables   what would the great sonneteers have done with so little room in which to work   *haiku* employs allusions and comparisons primarily

3. Chapman once remarked that readers in years to come would not be able to tell   Hawthorne is the obvious exception here   that people in America were of two sexes

4. Modern critics are not always masters of English prose   I am not speaking of Hugh Kenner and Edmund Wilson   we can say the same of earlier critics as well

5. Earlier works in accounting pointed out erroneously that capital gains were to be treated as ordinary income   what a tax liability the unwary incurred   but later works corrected this error

6. The student writer is always passionate   whether intending to be so or not   in presenting ideas to readers   can a student writer really be said to have more than one reader   the seasoned professional reserves passion for the occasional story or essay

7. Many other stones are quite large   the heaviest ones weigh fifty tons and more   and are the remains of a cap of sandstone that once covered the entire area

8. According to Leon D. Adams   writing in a popular magazine   road signs create hazards for drivers   are you one of them   rather than advance the cause of traffic safety

9. Stephen Dedalus   *A Portrait of the Artist as a Young Man*   moves from childhood through boyhood into maturity   Salinger's protagonists never quite make it

10. I remember well the lessons my father tried to teach me   His favorite text was thoroughness in work   a lesson I never learned too well   What I remember best of all was not the subject of any particular lesson but the manner in which the teaching proceeded   I had first to stand before him while he slowly took off his awesome leather belt   While I waited in full anticipation of that dreadful first blow he would sit down and holding the strap in both his hands would stare hard at me until I could return his gaze no longer   Finally he would say and how I loved that moment "Well?" I quickly responded "I'll never do it again Pa   " "Never?" "I'm sure I'll never do it again Pa   " To my knowledge   I don't tell my own children this   he never once hit me with his strap   I am certain I would remember if he had

Miscellaneous Uses

Parentheses are used to set off numerals and letters used in enumerations and in numerical figures that confirm a spelled-out number.

> To qualify for bidding, a defense contractor is required to show evidence of (1) financial stability, (2) technical competence, (3) qualified personnel in adequate numbers, and (4) full understanding of the problem.

> Before undertaking the doctoral examinations, students must be certain they can demonstrate (a) reading knowledge of one classical and two modern languages in addition to English, (b) broad competence in American and English literature, and (c) thorough knowledge of the centuries in which they will specialize.

> The check must be made out in the amount of fifty dollars ($50.00) and must be certified by the bank on which it is drawn.   (This use of parentheses goes back to a time when transactions were recorded in pen and ink. The purpose was to clarify what often was indecipherable handwriting. With the advent of the typewriter, the convention lost its purpose.)

2. Insert parentheses and other punctuation marks where appropriate in the following sentences. Extra space is provided for your convenience in writing.

> I am expected to remit sixty-three dollars ($63.00).

> My husband expects me to **(a)** cook his meals, **(b)** wash the dishes, **(c)** clean the apartment, and **(d)** contribute to support of the household by holding down a full-time job.

1. Nuclear energy has not yet fulfilled its promise   a   nuclear power plants are often shut for repairs   b   nuclear fuel is far more expensive than fossil fuel and   c   nuclear plants cost much more to construct than we originally were led to believe

2. A Rembrandt painting was auctioned off for ten million dollars $10,000,000.00   and promptly resold for half again as much

3. The Department of Welfare cut off funds from the family because   1   the father managed to find a part-time job   2   two of the children left home   and   3   the couple could produce no marriage certificate

4. To gain a liberal arts degree at our college, students must take at least one elective course in a mathematics b science c history and d Latin, in addition to fulfilling elective requirements in a major field

5. The terminal marks of punctuation are 1 the period 2 the question mark and 3 the exclamation point

BRACKETS

Just as writers use parentheses to set off explanations or comments within their own sentences, they use brackets to set off explanations, corrections, or comments they wish to make in material they are quoting. In this latter situation writers act as editors of words spoken or written by someone else. Brackets are also used to set off parenthetic material within parenthetic material already enclosed in parentheses. We see such punctuation primarily in legal documents, footnotes, and complex bibliographic entries, infrequently in other writing.

Editorial Changes and Comments

Brackets are used to set off explanations, corrections, expansions, and comments inserted in quoted material. A quotation introduced into an essay may require slight alteration before it can be used in the sentence or paragraph for which it is intended. The writer using the quoted material is free to make any change necessary as long as the change does not alter the intended meaning of the quoted material, but the readers must know that changes have been made. Brackets around the changes are the conventional means of informing readers of the changes. These changes may take the form of explanations, corrections, expansions, or comments.

"F. Scott Fitzgerald wrote amusing lyrics for *Safety First* [the Princeton 1916–1917 Triangle show] as well as for two other operettas."   (The writer using this quotation thinks it important to supply proper identification of *Safety First*, something the writer being quoted did not choose to do.)

"The process of disentanglement from art is clearly final when *Malone Dies* [Samuel Beckett's novel, published as *Malone meurt* in 1948] ends."   (The writer using this quotation identifies *Malone Dies* for the convenience of readers.)

"Is it [Kafka's 'The Metamorphosis'] the whine of an irretrievable neurotic or is it a beautiful lament?"   (The pronoun *it* is explained by the writer using this quotation.)

"From the day the Korean War began [June 25, 1950] until the day it ended [July 27, 1953], there was substantial opposition to the operation within important segments of the press."   (The writer identifies the dates for the convenience of readers.)

"Critical acclaim came quickly for the poet from all sides [one notable exception was Diana Trilling] and with the acclaim a measure of financial security."   (The writer inserts a correction in the quotation.)

As Alexander Pope put it: "Authors are partial to their wit, 'tis true/But are not critics [partial] to their judgment too?"   (The writer quoting Pope has added *partial* to clarify the thought for readers.)

Sophocles warns against excessive self-pride in these words: "Wisdom is the supreme part of happiness; and reverence toward the gods must be inviolate. *Great words of prideful men are ever punished with great blows* and, in old age, teach the chastened to be wise." [Emphasis is author's, not Sophocles'.]   (The writer explains the use of italics lest readers think the original text of the opening clause of the second sentence appeared in italics.)

As you can see, a writer has considerable leeway in amplifying and correcting quotations. The intention of the original must not be altered, however, and readers must be shown clearly that the changes made are not those of the writer being quoted.

Another use of brackets is different from the uses described previously. It is commonly used and often misunderstood. The Latin word *sic* means *thus*. It appears in brackets when it is used as an editorial comment.

It is italicized because it is a foreign word. *Sic* in brackets after an apparent mistake in a quotation indicates that the mistake is not the fault of the writer who uses the quotation, but an error or deviation from standard practice in the text being quoted.

> The letter from the kidnaper consisted of one sentence: "You better git [*sic*] the money $250,000 dollars rite [*sic*] away and hide it ware [*sic*] I tell you soon."   (Misspellings in the letter are explained as the kidnaper's mistakes, not the writer's.)

> "I don't know where you're from, but I'm from Brooklyn, Vermont, [*sic*] and damned proud of it."   (The brackets indicate that the quotation is accurate.)

3. Insert parentheses or brackets where appropriate in the following sentences. Extra space is provided for your convenience in writing.

> Election Day **(**November 2**)** was as cold and rainy as any incumbent could wish.

> "The definitive edition of *The Trial* **[**translated by Willa and Edwin Muir**]** was published in New York by Alfred Knopf."

1.   "Can you imagine a better use for it   water   than saving the life of a child?"
2.   Can you find it   I assume you want to   without disturbing everything else in the room?
3.   "I'm a Noo Yawkuh   *sic*   and willing to suffer the consequences," he wrote in a letter to his mother.
4.   "That book   *The Great Gatsby*   showed Fitzgerald at the top of his form."
5.   Willa Cather's great novel   *My Antonia*   continues to fascinate readers.
6.   In replying to the two women, Lincoln wrote: "*The religion that sets men to rebel and fight against their Government*, because, as they think, that Government does not sufficiently help some men to eat their bread in the sweat of other men's faces, is not the sort of religion upon which people can get to heaven."   Author's emphasis.
7.   "Empathy is the projection of one's feelings into a perceived situation, an *Einfühlung* literally a feeling into—Ed.   , in which the viewer merges his own emotion with the situation."
8.   A trope   also known as a figure of speech   must be highly evocative to be effective; a trope that is not significant or moving is commonplace, not worthy of the name.
9.   Irony of fate   Fowler says this phrase is hackneyed   describes the view that God finds amusement in manipulating human beings.
10.   "Gothic novels still find readers today   the first was Walpole's *Castle of Otranto*, 1764   , and many writers earn a good living by turning such romances out as rapidly as they can to satisfy a growing audience for paperback tales designed to chill the willingly chillable."

Parenthetic Material within Parenthetic Material

Brackets are used instead of parentheses to set off parenthetic material that occurs within material already enclosed in parentheses. A difficult rule to read, this one is rarely applied except by lawyers or scholars.

> The party of the first part (in this case the lessor [the lessee is the party of the second part] unless the lessor is a corporation) is responsible for delivering to the party of the second part a building in good operating condition.

> [1]For fuller discussion, see Perrin's article on *echo phrases* (Porter G. Perrin, *Writer's Guide and Index to English* [Chicago, 1942]).

(For additional uses of parentheses and brackets, see the Appendix: The Punctuation of Footnotes, Bibliographies, and Letters, pages 145–147.)

Chapter 5

Quotation Marks

In American usage quotation marks normally are double quotes (""). Single quotes (') are used only for quotations within quotations. In British usage quotation marks are normally single quotes, with double quotes used for quotations within quotations.

Quotation marks have several uses, principally to indicate quoted speech and material quoted from another printed source. They are also used to indicate titles of certain works and to indicate that particular words are to be understood as words rather than as meanings conveyed by the words. This last use is explained on pages 71 and 72.

Two problems that face many writers are the use of quotation marks in combination with other marks of punctuation, and the abuse of quotation marks in what appears to be an attempt to imply that certain words mean more they normally mean.

Quoted Speech

Quotation marks are used to indicate directly quoted speech. There have already been many examples in this book of this use of quotation marks.

> Alfred said, "If I can build a greenhouse large enough to accommodate thousands of seedlings, I will be able to establish myself in the nursery business." (This is a direct quotation. *Alfred* said every word enclosed in quotation marks.)

An indirect quotation does not quote the exact words of a speaker and, therefore, is not enclosed in quotation marks.

> Alfred said that he will be able to get started in the nursery business if he can build a greenhouse large enough to accommodate thousands of seedlings. (Even though some of these words are *Alfred's*, others are not. Obviously *Alfred* would not refer to himself as *he* and *himself*. The quotation, therefore, is indirect and is not punctuated with quotation marks. Direct quotations are completely, not partially, direct.)

When speech is quoted directly, the speaker may be identified before the quotation, after the quotation, within the quotation, or not at all if the identity of the speaker is already clear to readers. This last situation occurs most frequently in dialogue. Notice that each time a new speaker is quoted, a new paragraph is needed.

> "Can you tell me where I can find the Director of Student Services?"
>
> "She's right down the hall. I'm going that way myself."
>
> "Thank you."

When quoted speech of a single speaker runs to more than a single paragraph, each paragraph is preceded by quotes, but only the final paragraph has final quotes. Indentation and spacing between lines are the same as for regular text.

> So Jesus spoke again:
> "In truth, in very truth I tell you, I am the door of the sheepfold. The sheep paid no heed to any who came before me, for these are all thieves and robbers. I am the door; anyone who comes into the fold through me shall be safe. He shall go in and out and shall find pasturage.
> "The thief comes only to steal, to kill, to destroy; I have come that men may have life, and may have it in all its fullness. I am the good shepherd; the good shepherd lays down his life for the sheep. The hireling, when he sees the wolf coming, abandons the sheep and runs away, because he is no shepherd and the sheep are not his. Then the wolf harries the flock

and scatters the sheep. The man runs away because he is a hireling and cares nothing for the sheep.

"I am the good shepherd; I know my own sheep and my sheep know me—as the Father knows me and I know the Father—and I lay down my life for the sheep. But there are other sheep of mine, not belonging to this fold, whom I must bring in; and they too will listen to my voice. There will then be one flock, one shepherd. The Father loves me because I lay down my life, to receive it back again. No one has robbed me of it; I am laying it down of my own free will. I have the right to lay it down, and I have the right to receive it back again; this charge I have received from my Father."

—John 9, 10

When a speaker must be identified, you must take care in deciding where to place the other required marks of punctuation.

He asked, "Are you going to stay at your desk all night?" (Comma before quotation. Question mark before final quote, because the quotation is a question. *He asked* is not enclosed in quotation marks because it is not part of the quotation.)

Did the teacher really say, "I am sick of this mess; we must all get out now or we will be in trouble"? (The entire sentence is a question, and so the question mark appears outside the final quote. The quotation needs no other final punctuation. The question mark serves to complete both the sentence and the quotation.)

"Can you remember what she asked you?" Richard said. (Question mark inside final quote, because the quotation is a question.)

"I hope you can find your way home easily," the police officer said. (Comma before final quote.)

"I must tell you," the principal said, "that you are just a fraction of a point above failing." (The quotation is a single sentence interrupted by *the principal said*. Comma before final quote in first part, period before final quote in second part.)

"There are many ways to solve this problem," Professor Morris said. "If you think through the directions already given, you will surely find the correct answer." (The quotation is in two sentences. Comma before final quote of the first sentence. Period before final quote of the second sentence.)

"You must recall that I told you I had found evidence of embezzlement," I insisted; "moreover, I advised you of your legal responsibility to take action." (Semicolon after *insisted*, because a semicolon would be required even if *I insisted* were not present.) (See pages 49–51.)

1. Insert quotation marks and other punctuation where appropriate in the following sentences. Extra space is provided for your convenience in writing.

> The child said, "I will not eat my dinner."
> The child said that she would not eat her dinner.

1. How will I ever get through graduate school now that tuition has been increased again   Grace asked

2. The police officers all demanded pay increases, claiming   that they could not pay their living expenses on what they were then earning

3. I ask you once more   Do you really intend to return the money I lent you

4. Rebecca prefers the Compact Oxford, although I don't know why   As Harry said yesterday   That damned compact majority dictionary has done more to ruin eyesight than all the movies in town

5. When are you going to mow the lawn   John   Mother asked

6. I cannot help recalling the ugly incident every time I see Mike   I said   He doesn't seem at all contrite

7. Of all the many types of trees in the woods near our house   he said   the copper beeches are the most spectacular

8. If you must disagree with me constantly   Hazel said   would you please just ignore me from now on

9. I told you   that I was surely not going to be with you last evening

10. Is there any point in continuing this conversation   she said   if we still are going to end up fighting

11. She insisted   that she was sorry about the trouble she had caused

12. If that teacher gives us one more assignment, I think I'll do something desperate to get out of it   Annette said

13. The headwaiter looked at us the way headwaiters always look at us and said   I'm sorry. I cannot seat anyone who is not dressed properly   He paused and then went on   You wouldn't want me to offend our other patrons, would you

14. Please stop that lawnmower for a while   I begged   The noise is killing me

15. Can you find your way by yourself   I asked   or should someone go with you for part of the way

16. Your mortgage payments have been at least one month late in each month of the past year   the bank president said   therefore, I shall have to ask you now to pay the rest of your mortgage in full

17. Does it hurt very much
    More than I can say. I've never felt worse pain
    Let me stop now and give you another injection before I complete the extraction

18. Were you in the room when the defendant said that   the attorney asked

19. Are you certain the child asked for another chance   the principal said

20. Are you willing to testify that the prisoner said   If I don't get my parole this time, I'll break out of this prison

Printed Sources

Quotation marks are used to indicate direct quotation from printed sources except when the material quoted is lengthy. With one exception, material quoted word-for-word from literature, newspapers, magazines, journals, or any other published source must be enclosed in quotation marks. The exception is quoted material running longer than five lines for prose and longer than two lines for poetry. These longer quotations are given special indentation and are single-spaced rather than double-spaced.

> The white man, turning his back upon the setting sun, looked along the empty and broad expanse of the sea-reach. For the last three miles of its course the wandering, hesitant river, as if enticed irresistibly by the freedom of an open horizon, flows straight to the east—to the east that harbours both light and darkness. Astern of the boat the repeated call of some bird, a cry discordant and feeble, skipped along the smooth water and lost itself, before it could reach the other shore, in the breathless silence of the world.

—Joseph Conrad, "Tropical River"

> Up! up! my friend, and quit your books,
> Or surely you'll grow double;
> Up! up! my friend, and clear your looks;
> Why all this toil and trouble?

—William Wordsworth, "The Tables Turned"

When material is quoted from printed sources, short quotations—like short quoted speech—are not set off in special indentation, but are run in with the text.

> The ringing phrase "Life, Liberty and the pursuit of Happiness" may not have been intended to assure all Americans of the right to work and support their families.   (The quotation marks enclose a phrase from the Declaration of Independence.)

> In light of recent exposures of corruption among attorneys, one can rightly wonder whether de Tocqueville would still stand with his characterization of the profession of law as "the only aristocratic element" in American life.   (The quotation is from *Democracy in America*.)

> Do you know the name of the vessel in Oliver Wendell Holmes' poem that begins: "Ay, tear her tattered ensign down! Long has it waved on high"?   (This quotation is two lines from "Old Ironsides." If the writer of the sentence wished to show that the first two lines were separate, the lines would appear this way: "Ay, tear her tattered ensign down!/Long has it waved on high," the slash mark indicating the break between the two lines.)

Notice that the opening words in these three quotations do not require capitalization unless they are already capitalized, as with *Life* in the first example and *Ay* in the two lines from Holmes. In addition, there is no need for a comma to introduce the quotations in the first two examples. The quoted material is run into the sentences containing the quotations. In the example quoting Holmes, the colon is used in accordance with the rule governing use of the colon to set off formal statements, quotations, and questions (see page 55).

As the following sentences show, commas or periods needed after quotations are placed inside the final quotes.

> Like Mrs. Malaprop you have "proof controvertible," and I shall now proceed to "extirpate you."   (In *The Rivals* Sheridan's famous Mrs. Malaprop massacres the language in most engaging fashion. Both *proof controvertible* and *extirpate you* are examples of her delightful way with the wrong words. Comma after *controvertible*, period after *you*.)

> Medicine can learn a great deal from Nietzsche, who said: "Contentment preserves one even from catching cold. Has a woman who knew that she was well dressed ever caught cold? No, not even when she had scarcely a rag to her back."   (Period inside final quotes.)

2. Insert quotation marks and other punctuation where appropriate in the following sentences. Extra space is provided for your convenience in writing.

> Do you believe, as Alexander Pope wrote, that "Hope springs eternal in the human breast" or, as Edmund Spenser wrote, that "hell it is . . . to feed on hope"?

> Yesterday was December 7, which many of us remember as a grim day in history. No one old enough to have heard President Franklin Roosevelt characterize December 7, 1941, as "a date that will live in infamy" can fail to greet December 7 without recalling where we were and what we were doing at the time of the announcement of the attack on Pearl Harbor.

1. In a poem written in 1892   William Butler Yeats commented on the brevity of human life   From our birthday until we die, Is but the winking of an eye

2. Mark Twain, in *Life on the Mississippi*, described the childhood ambition he shared with all his friends

> When I was a boy, there was but one permanent ambition among my comrades in our village on the west bank of the Mississippi River. That was, to be a steamboatman. We had transient ambitions of other sorts, but they were only transient. When a circus came and went, it left us all burning to become clowns; the first negro minstrel show that ever came to our section left us all suffering to try that kind of life; now and then we had a hope that, if we lived and were good, God would permit us to become pirates.

These ambitions faded out, each in its turn; but the ambition to be a steamboatman always remained.

3. What did Thoreau think of the way men and women spend their lives?   Our life   he wrote   is frittered away in detail

4. Why did Thoreau retreat to Walden?

I wanted to live deep and suck out all the marrow of life, to cut a broad swath and shave close, to drive life into a corner and reduce it to its lowest terms, and, if it proved to be mean, why then to get the whole and genuine meanness of it, and publish its meanness to the world; or if it were sublime, to know it by experience, and be able to give a true account of it in my next excursion

5. The old ballad goes on

John he made a steel-driving man,
   They took him to the tunnel to drive;
He drove so hard he broke his heart,
   He laid down his hammer and he died, my babe,
   He laid down his hammer and he died

6. Brutus continues   Not that I loved Caesar less, but that I loved Rome more

7. Milton referred to   Jonson's learned sock   meaning his ability to write drama

8. The Superintendent of the Census in 1890, commenting on the status of the American frontier, wrote   Up to and including 1880 the country had a frontier of settlement, but at present the unsettled area has been so broken into by isolated bodies of settlement that there can hardly be said to be a frontier line

9. Who can surpass Carl Sandburg's characterization of Chicago as   Hog-butcher for the world, Tool-maker, Stacker of Wheat   ?   Yes, this   Player with Railroads and the Nation's Freight-handler   even today is   Stormy, husky, brawling   indeed the   City of the Big Shoulders

10. In the fourth edition of *The American Language*, Mencken declared that   the pull of America has become so powerful that it has begun to drag English with it   and today many British scholars abhor the Americanisms that have become commonplace in British speech, just as the French inveigh against *franglais*

11. In his poem ''Locksley Hall Sixty Years After,'' Tennyson cautions writers and thinkers against careless expression: Authors—essayist, atheist, novelist, realist, rhymester, play your part,/ Paint the mortal shame of nature with the living hues of art

12. Franklin D. Roosevelt closed his first inaugural address with a call for the assistance of divinity: In this dedication of a Nation we humbly ask the blessing of God. May He protect each and every one of us. May He guide me in the days to come   He then proceeded to the reviewing stand to watch the inaugural parade

13. The record of Franklin D. Roosevelt's press conferences reveals the ability of the man to engage in give-and-take with members of the press, always with humor when appropriate. For example, a reporter once asked him whether a ban on highway use during a parade included   parking shoulders.   He replied:

Parking shoulders   ?
Yes, widening out on the edge, supposedly to let the civilians park as the military goes by
You don't mean necking places   ?

14. Herbert Hoover once said,   Corporations are not a thing apart from the people, for they are owned by somewhere between six and ten million families

15. And, what did businessmen think of American civilization? If you destroy the leisure class, J.P. Morgan once told a Senate committee, you destroy civilization,

Quotes within Quotes

Single quotes are used to enclose a quotation within a quotation. While not a common occurrence, quotations may themselves include quotations. When they do, single quotes are used for the enclosed quotation, and double quotes are used for the enclosing quotation.

> "Have you read the article in the *Los Angeles Times* that speaks of 'possible corruption in the legislature'? It goes on to say that only the leadership is under suspicion." (This entire example is conversation, and so it is enclosed in quotation marks. The words *possible corruption in the legislature* are an exact quotation from a newspaper. They must be enclosed in single quotes, since they are inside a quotation.)

> At that time a number of Pharisees came to him and said, "You should leave this place and go your way; Herod is out to kill you." He replied, "Go and tell that fox, 'Listen: today and tomorrow I shall be casting out devils and working cures; on the third day I reach my goal.' However, I must be on my way today and tomorrow and the next day, because it is unthinkable for a prophet to meet his death anywhere but in Jerusalem." (In the opening sentence of this excerpt from *Luke*, the warning of the Pharisees is reported word-for-word and enclosed in double quotes. In the second sentence Jesus replies, and the reply is enclosed in double quotes until the word *Listen*, which opens the exact words the Pharisees are instructed to use in responding to Herod. From *Listen* on, single quotes are needed. The final single quote follows *goal*, the end of the instructions to the Pharisees. The double quotes after *Jerusalem* end the direct quotation from Jesus.)

When a single quote is used just before a final double quote, any accompanying punctuation must appear either inside the single quote or outside the double quote. You already know that periods and commas are placed inside quotation marks, and the quotation mark rules on pages 77 and 78 govern the use of quotes with all the marks. The following examples illustrate the use of periods and commas with single and double quotes.

> I wrote Vera to invite her to attend the concert with us, saying, "You surely can steal time from your painting to spend an hour listening to Beethoven's Fifth, that 'most sublime noise that has ever penetrated into the ear of man.' " (The single quotes enclose a line from E.M. Forster's novel *Howard's End*.)

> "I must have your answer by tonight. You are not the only candidate for the position; in fact, I must tell you there are 'Multitudes in the valley of decision,' " the dean said in his letter. (The single quotes enclose a line from the Old Testament, which capitalizes *Multitudes*. Otherwise there would be no need to capitalize the word.)

Remember that other marks of punctuation are treated the same when a single quote appears just before a final double quote. The rules about the positioning of other marks with quotation marks apply directly to single quotes that appear just before final double quotes.

3. Supply single quotes, double quotes, and other marks of punctuation where appropriate in the following sentences. Extra space is provided for your convenience in writing.

> The lecturer said, "I cannot agree with Frost's 'Good fences make good neighbors.' "
> My father was fond of saying, " 'These are the times that try men's souls,' according to old Tom Paine, but he didn't know very much about times like ours."

1. The pompous man went on at great length: Have you considered, dear friends, whether you can, to quote the Old Testament, in the day of prosperity be joyful, but in the day of adversity consider or have you so wasted your inner resources that you no longer can be anything but joyful and in the day of adversity stop trying completely ?

2. The words I used in the examination were   Conrad manages to focus on moments of decision, moments when men must make difficult choices. This is why Conrad has been called   a historian of fine consciences

3. In conclusion   the speaker said   I want only to quote Kipling on the evils of tobacco: A woman is only a woman, but a good cigar is a smoke

4. In *The Autobiography of Benjamin Franklin*, we find the following: We have an English proverb that says   He that would thrive, must ask his wife   It was lucky for me that I had one as much disposed to industry and frugality as myself

5. Our biology teacher opened her lecture by saying,   I want to speak today of mosquitoes, described once as flying insects with a   damnably poisonous bite,   which everyone except hotel managers has seen, heard, or suffered from

Titles of Works of Art

Quotation marks are used when referring to titles of works included within other works—stories in a collection of stories, magazine articles, book chapters, individual poems in a collection of poems—and for paintings, sculptures, speeches, and song titles.

In typing a paper, quoted titles of books, magazines, newspapers, operas, symphonies, and long poems are underscored; in printing, these titles are italicized. Quotation marks are used for parts of books, magazines, and newspapers, and for speeches, parts of musical works, paintings, and single poems of less than volume length. Usage varies. Some editors prefer italics for paintings and sculpture. In any case no comma is used before a title unless there is some other valid requirement for one.

In Joyce's *Dubliners* "A Little Cloud" recounts the sad realization of a less than talented man that he will never write good poetry.   (The collection of stories is italicized, the single story enclosed in quotes.)

I came across a copy of *The Saturday Evening Post* of June 9, 1962, which contained an account of how Senator Joseph McCarthy was trapped by his own underhanded tactics. "The Final Irony of Joe McCarthy" is good reading for all of us.   (Magazine title italicized, article in quotes.)

"The Last Days of Peace" is a particularly gripping chapter of William L. Shirer's *The Rise and Fall of the Third Reich.*

Have you read Edwin Arlington Robinson's poem "Richard Cory"?

My favorite song in the musical *South Pacific* is "Some Enchanted Evening."

You ought to hear her sing "The Bell Song," from Delibes' *Lakmé.*

Notice that the rules governing use of punctuation marks with other marks apply equally when quotation marks are used to enclose titles. The last three examples above show quotation marks with a question mark, a period, and a comma. The question mark is outside the quote, because the entire sentence—not the quotation—is a question. The period and the comma are inside the quotes, as they always are.

When quotation marks are needed for a title that appears inside a sentence that is itself a quotation, single quotes are used for the title, since the quotation is enclosed in double quotes.

The critic wrote: "I find no fault with this production of *My Fair Lady* except for some sloppiness in enunciation. For example, in 'Get Me to the Church on Time,' I was not at all certain whether I really heard the singers or was merely singing to myself the words I know so well."

Titles of works such as plays and novels, which would normally be italicized, are enclosed in quotation marks when the works are cited as parts of larger volumes, for example, anthologies of plays or novels.

Yeats's play "The Countess Cathleen" can be read in *The Collected Plays of W.B. Yeats.* (*Because The Countess Cathleen is a play, it is normally italicized.*)

You can read "Nostromo, A Tale of the Seaboard" in *The Collected Works of Joseph Conrad*. (*Nostromo, A Tale of the Seaboard* is a novel and, therefore, normally italicized.)

4. Insert quotation marks and other punctuation where appropriate in the following sentences.

Nora Ephron's article "The Bennington Affair," *Esquire* (September, 1976) exposes the peculiar circumstances surrounding the departure of a former president of Vermont's Bennington College.

Ring Lardner's story "The Golden Honeymoon" was published in 1924 in a volume called *How to Write Short Stories*.

1. I was fortunate enough to be present at the Oberlin College commencement exercise in May 1938, when Robert Frost delivered an address entitled   What Became of New England   ?

2. Have you read Norman Mailer's   Nixon in Miami   which is included in his *Miami and the Siege of Chicago*

3. He specialized in such Gilbert and Sullivan songs as   I've Got a Little List   and   My Object So Sublime

4. He cited as one of his principal sources Chalmers Roberts' article on the decision not to intervene in Indochina in 1954   The Day We Didn't Go to War   *The Reporter*, September 14, 1956

5. They published a brief portion of the article   Telling the Employees   which appeared in *Time* in 1955.

6. When we saw *Madame Butterfly*, we were so late that we did not take our seats until the soprano was ready to sing   One Fine Day

7. *The New York Times* published the article   Which Way America?   during the year before the United States bicentennial

8. Frances Perkins, long a member of the cabinet in President Roosevelt's administrations, published   The Builder of Roosevelt's Presidency   in *The New Republic* in 1954

9. Matthew Arnold's poem   Dover Beach   is often quoted

10. Joseph Brodsky's poem   A Halt in the Desert   appears in his *Selected Poems*, published in the United States by HarperCollins.

Words as Words

Quotation marks are used to indicate words used as words rather than for their meaning. In this book, as in most books, italics (see page 101) are used to indicate words that are intended to be understood as words rather than as conveyors of meaning. Quotation marks are also used to indicate such words. What do we mean by "words as conveyors of meaning" and "words intended to be understood as words"? The sentence you have just read should indicate what is meant, but the following illustrations will make the distinction clear.

Words as Meanings

Children play happily with bicycles.   (All the words in this simple sentence convey meaning. If you had read them in an ordinary paragraph, you would have understood the thought intended.)

Words as Words

Children play happily with bicycles. In this sentence "bicycles" is the object of the preposition "with."   (The words *bicycles* and *with* in the second sentence are understood as words. Notice that *bicycles* in the second sentence is not plural. It is the subject of the verb *is*. When *bicycles* is used for its meaning, it is plural: *Bicycles are commonly used for transportation in many European countries*.)

Words as Words

Many people confuse "affect" and "effect" in their writing.   (These are the words *affect* and *effect*, not the meanings of *affect* and *effect*.)

Words as Words

> We wonder whether "at that point in time" means anything more than "then."   (If the quotation marks were removed, this sentence would be a hopeless jumble. Notice that *at that point in time* requires only one set of quotation marks, since the phrase is intended to be perceived as a unit.

Words as Words

> Are you always correct in your spelling of "to," "two," and "too"?   (Here, three sets of quotes are needed for three individual words used as words.)

Words as Words

> Audrey used ten "uh's" in a single sentence and five "and's."

5.   Insert quotation marks and other punctuation where appropriate in the following sentences.

> Intensifiers, such as "very" and "too," are words used to heighten meaning.
>
> In your first days at work on Wall Street, you will hear many new terms, for example, "margin," "bulls," "bears," "puts," and "calls."

1. Do you know that   normalcy   was coined by Warren G. Harding
2. We owe   ecdysiast   to the fertile mind of H.L. Mencken
3. The   ecdysiast   walked slowly across the stage, shedding articles of clothing as she went
4. If you are going to study rhetoric, you will have to learn such terms as   chiasmus   diacope   and   periphrasis
5. The old slang expression   twenty-three skiddoo   is rarely heard these days
6. Do you know anyone who uses   amanuensis   for   secretary
7. He was not above using such clichés as   stone-cold dead   gift of gab   and   rotten to the core
8. Few people today make a distinction between   disinterested   and   uninterested   in their speech or writing
9. Once she started her analysis, all we heard from Emma was Freudian jargon: libido   ego   superego   and the rest
10. High school teachers of English have prejudiced generations of students against starting sentences with   and   or   but

MISUSE OF QUOTATION MARKS

Quotes Cannot Apologize

Quotation marks are commonly used by writers to apologize for the words they enclose. This is poor practice, since punctuation marks cannot make up for improper or imprecise usage.

Speakers and writers attempt to choose words appropriate for the audience they are addressing and the degree of formality of the communication. For one audience a writer may use slang or even profanity; in another situation the same writer will deliberately avoid vocabulary that could give offense. (Candidates for public office know the importance of speaking carefully to potential supporters.) What applies to choice of words also applies to grammatical constructions. In one situation no care is given to such matters as agreement of subject and verb or to reference of pronouns; in another situation great pains are taken to ensure correctness of sentence structure, spelling, and punctuation.

These considerations relate to the levels of English usage, reflecting the educational background of the users of English and the situations in which they employ language. In *A Writer's Guide and Index to English*,

Porter G. Perrin calls attention to four levels, or varieties, of usage: *nonstandard, informal, general,* and *formal*. Since these levels overlap somewhat, all but the nonstandard may be used in various situations by people of the same educational background.

Nonstandard English is the language used by relatively uneducated people in the conversations they carry on in everyday life. Writing plays a small part in their lives.

> I ain't gonna do this nohow.
>
> He got no right to put me down like that.

Informal English is the language employed by better-educated people in relaxed conversation with friends and associates and in informal writing, such as personal letters. It may contain slang and the specialized jargon of occupational groups and social groups. Informal English is generally closer in correctness of grammar and structure to what is taught in most schools than is nonstandard English. In addition the user of informal English—unlike the user of nonstandard English—can move easily into general or formal English when the situation calls for it.

> Did you see those thirty-second spots the Republicans ran last night on TV?
>
> Maggie sure gave the kids whatfor yesterday when they told her the brakes froze while they were driving on Interstate 91.

General English is the language employed by better-educated people in business correspondence, newspaper articles, books, and magazines, and in conversation and public talks. General English is the language of people on their best behavior, cautious in selecting words and careful to observe as best they can all the rules they were taught in school.

> My subject today is a matter of great concern to all groups within our community.
>
> Whether we continue to operate successfully in the next five years depends on action we take now to build sales, improve the quality of our product, and develop the managerial skills necessary to compete successfully under present and future conditions.

Formal English is the language employed by better-educated people in a formal setting when speaking before audiences of similar background and when writing for such audiences. Technical, scientific, academic, and professional writing almost always employs formal English. Vocabulary may be specialized and beyond the grasp of people who lack special training, and all rules of grammar and syntax are scrupulously observed by writers and editors to the best of their ability. The difference between general English and formal English lies primarily in the writers' perceptions of their audiences.

> The dynamism of the construct impairs our perception of the essential interior organic whole.
>
> During the most recent quarter the company made important strides in overcoming market factors that heretofore precluded quantifiable economic gains, at the same time laying the groundwork for future capture of export markets in areas of burgeoning growth and capital accumulation accomplished primarily through more efficient use of natural resources exploited and exchanged with manufacturing economies at increasingly higher prices.

Better-educated people, then, employ informal, general, and formal English at various times, going from one level to another in response to the situation in which they find themselves. If they occasionally lapse into incomprehensible gobbledygook when employing formal English, their failure is human. Nonstandard English may also be incomprehensible at times to those who do not use it every day.

Even those who have never studied linguistics are aware that differences in usage mark the speech and writing of educated and uneducated users of English. This insight shows itself when writers employing a particular level of English become self-conscious over use of a word or phrase from another level. To indicate to their readers that, as writers, they know better, they will enclose the offending words in quotation marks. They want the strength that comes from the word or phrase they have chosen, but they do not want to be accused of ignorance. Not only do they do this in writing, but also in speech. How many times have you heard speakers say ''quote unquote'' to impart a special message to audiences about words they are using?

This practice is nonsensical and patronizing. There is no master list of language approved for any particular level of usage, even though some dictionaries supply their readers with discussions of good and bad usage. If, in the mind of a writer, slang or jargon or profanity is the most effective way to convey an idea, then that writer must take the chance. There is no point in apologizing for use of a word. If a word is inappropriate for an audience or a topic under discussion, it should not be used. Quotation marks do not make the unacceptable acceptable.

The message for you is clear: Select the best expression you can find for any thought you are discussing and use it without apology. Reserve quotation marks for their legitimate uses.

Wrong   Frank Lloyd Wright frequently designed "cantilevered" structures for his buildings.   (They were cantilevered, were they not? What purpose is served by quotation marks?)

Right   Frank Lloyd Wright frequently designed cantilevered structures for his buildings.

Wrong   The "perpetrator" was "apprehended" by the other officer and I.

Right   The perpetrator was apprehended by the other officer and me.

Right   Two of us arrested the accused person.

Wrong   Arlene was a member of the "fast" set in our high school, always smoking "grass" and "popping" pills.   (We know that *fast* in this sentence has nothing to do with acceleration or velocity. We also know that *Arlene* did not smoke lawn clippings and that *popping* means "swallowing." If these words are inappropriate for the audience, they should not be used. If they are appropriate, why apologize?)

Right   Arlene was a member of the fast set in our high school, given to smoking marijuana and taking psychic energizers and depressants.

Right   Arlene was a member of the fast set in our high school, smoking grass and popping pills almost every day.

Wrong   A really "hip chick" "knows her way around."   (Does the audience know what a *hip chick* is? What about *knows her way around*? If the audience does not know these terms, quotation marks will not help. Neither expression should be enclosed in quotation marks if the writer wants to write the sentence this way. If the audience does know these terms, what purpose is served by the quotation marks?)

Right   A really hip chick knows her way around.

Right   A sophisticated young woman needs no guidance.

6. In the following sentences, some quotation marks are used in accordance with the six rules previously laid down for your guidance, but other quotation marks are used mistakenly to apologize for a word or phrase. If a sentence is correctly punctuated, mark correct; if it is not correctly punctuated, eliminate the mistake.

My physician told me to stop playing "doctor." _____

Anne said she found "The Love Song of J. Alfred Prufrock" impossible to understand and added that many modern poems like that one were beyond her.   <u>*Correct*</u>

1. He habitually uses "ain't" and "dassn't" as a way of showing us that he knows better. _____

2. "Ain't you ever had any of these before?" the boy asked. _____

3. All we ever heard from her was "shouldn't" when we were dying to hear at least one "should" now and then. _____

4. The teachers all did their best to rid our speech of "I knows" and "you knows." _____

5. Paul was one of the "good" guys, but Sam was always a "bad" guy. _____

6. "Get off your 'duffs' and get out there and win," the coach said. _____

7. The slang word "dude" has recently acquired a new meaning in American slang.
   _____

8. Do you remember when boys wore "knickers" and girls wore "bloomers"?
   _____

9. He told me he was a "psychoanalyst," but I didn't believe him. _____

10. "Have you read 'In Memoriam' in your English class? Our class really 'dug' it even though we thought it was pretty 'heavy' stuff," George said. _____

11. Every third word the girl said was "hell," but I can't repeat the dirty words she "threw around." _____

12. A really "fine" person just does not try to "push you around" like that. _____

13. They were willing to pay for "first-class" seats, but only "tourist" accommodations were available. _____

14. The late Alexander Calder made his reputation by creating "mobiles" out of "sheet metal" and wire. _____

15. A book bound in "morocco" is more expensive than one bound in "cloth."
    _____

Words Mean What They Mean

Inexperienced writers and bumblers sometimes try to invest words with shades of meaning by enclosing them in quotation marks. These misguided writers send a coded message, telling readers that the words in quotation marks are entitled to special treatment. It is as though the writers are winking conspiratorially as they write, with the idea of letting their readers in on the conspiracy so they can share the secret message and understand the words precisely as the writers intend.

The problem is that quotation marks have no secret powers. They convey no more meaning than the word enclosed already conveys. They do not contribute to the humor of what is said. They do not convey irony. They do not add emphasis. They merely mark their users as inept.

If a word is intended to mean something other than what it means, another word should be used in its place. If the word conveys the meaning intended, the word may stay but the quotation marks must go. A "beauty" is no more than a beauty. A "bargain" is only a bargain. If something else is meant, other words must be found.

Find the words that express your meaning. Do not use words that mean less and then decorate them with quotation marks.

Wrong   My mother-in-law always thought she was the "district attorney" in our "conversations."
          (We know what a *district attorney* is, and we know that the *conversations* were less than pleasant. In short we understand the humor intended, heavy-handed as it is. We do not need quotation marks to get the point. Does the writer of this sentence think we would miss it without the quotation marks?)

Right   My mother-in-law always thought she was the district attorney in the grillings she conducted every time we met.

Right   My mother-in-law always thought she was the district attorney when we held our so-called conversations.

Wrong   Jack was acting "funny" when I saw him.   (If *Jack* was *funny*, no quotation marks are needed. If not, then *funny* is the wrong word.)

Right   Jack was acting funny when I saw him.

Right   Jack was acting strangely when I saw him.

Right   Jack was incoherent when I saw him, appearing to be under the influence of drugs or alcohol.

Wrong   You seem to consider yourself a member of the "intelligentsia."   (The dictionary provides an excellent definition of *intelligentsia*. What more do quotation marks add? If the writer means to convey irony, perhaps a better expression can be found.)

Right   You seem to consider yourself a member of the intelligentsia.

Right   You think you are more intellectual than you really are.

Wrong   I "really" hate you.   (What is stronger than *hate*? Even if we need *really*, it requires no quotation marks. Nothing can be more real than hate.)

Right   I hate you. I really do.

Wrong   He "bombarded" us with facts until we were ready to "scream."   (Of course there was no bombardment employing jet airplanes and napalm. In this sentence *bombarded* is used metaphorically and effectively. And what more is conveyed by *scream* enclosed in quotation marks than is conveyed without them?)

Right   He bombarded us with facts until we were ready to scream.

7. In the following sentences, some quotation marks are used in accordance with the rules, but other quotation marks are used mistakenly to add meaning, humor, irony, or emphasis. If a sentence is correctly punctuated, mark it correct; if it is not correctly punctuated, correct the sentence.

> Bert is a real "thinker."
>
> Our so-called "integrated" community has been labeled an "offense against decency by real estate operators," in the words of the Commission on Public Housing.

1. "So," he said, "you have written another 'masterpiece' that will go unnoticed by the world."

2. "Did he actually say, 'I'm going to conquer the world,' or is that another one of your 'embellishments?' "

3. In his poem "Il Penseroso" Milton described the pleasures of the "contemplative" life.

4. Her skin was as smooth as "velvet" and her eyes "deep pools" of mystery and promise.

5. He always promised more than he could "deliver" and never seemed at all embarrassed by his "failures."

6. "I want to caution you," she said, "against 'hasty' actions."

7. That cheese was "riper" than you can imagine.

8. You have been "booked" for the late train.

9. He always appeared "charming," as "charming" as a dead fish that has been sitting in the hot sun for six hours.

10. His "term paper" was as dull as most of them are.

11. Louise is a real "worker," isn't she?

12. His "democratic" attitude made me sick to my stomach.

13. When we had finished eating Bob's "gourmet meal," we went to the drug store to buy something for our stomachs.

14. They buy only the "finest" food and then "ruin" it.

15. I see you have been out "purchasing" a few "odds and ends."

Two Other Common Misuses of Quotation Marks

1. Quotation marks are not used with foreign language words or expressions unless they are quoted. Italics, or underscorings in writing or typing, call attention to foreign language words and expressions.

Wrong   She had a certain "je ne sais quoi."

Right   She had a certain *je ne sais quoi.*   (French for "indescribable something.")

Wrong   The "Weltschmerz" in the works of Goethe is not always apparent to young readers today.

Right   The *Weltschmerz* in the works of Goethe is not always apparent to young readers today.
      (*Weltschmerz* is a German noun meaning ''sentimental pessimism.'' It is capitalized because German nouns are capitalized.)

Wrong   The lecturer concluded her statement in a memorable sentence: "If you cannot see the significance of 'ego et meus rex' in the attitude of the Secretary of State, you will never understand the foreign policy we pursue today."

Right   The lecturer concluded her statement in a memorable sentence: "If you cannot see the significance of *ego et meus rex* in the attitude of the Secretary of State, you will never understand the foreign policy we pursue today."   (The Latin expression *ego et meus rex* translates as ''I and my king,'' the implication being that the speaker puts herself before the chief official served.)

   2.   Quotation marks are not used by students for titles of their own papers. They are not used by any writer in titling any article, story, song, or the like of which he or she is the author or composer. The rule governing use of quotation marks when referring to the work of others does not apply to titles written for one's own work and appearing on the title page or first page of that work.

Quotation Marks with Other Marks

No mark of punctuation is used immediately after opening quotes. Place periods and commas immediately before final quotes. Place colons and semicolons immediately after final quotes. Place exclamation points and question marks before final quotes if the quotation is an exclamation or question. Place exclamation points and question marks after final quotes at the end of a sentence if the sentence is an exclamation or question.

This is the longest rule in the book and one that gives many writers trouble. Read carefully through the examples and the discussions. This lengthy rule is really not difficult to learn.

Wrong   Jessie said ",There's nothing I can do for you."   (No discussion is needed. The comma must be placed before the opening quotes to set off the introductory element *Jessie said*. Nobody has trouble with this part of the rule.)

Right   Jessie said, "There's nothing I can do for you."

Right   The foreman of the jury announced the terrible verdict: "Guilty of murder in the first degree."

Wrong   The twelfth chapter of *The Russians,* by Hedrick Smith, is entitled "Patriotism: World War II Was Only Yesterday".   (Under no condition may a writer of American English place a period outside the final quotes and be correct. This restriction does not concern logic. It is standard practice.)

Right   The twelfth chapter of *The Russians,* by Hedrick Smith, is entitled "Patriotism: World War II Was Only Yesterday."

Wrong   In his chapter "Patriotism: World War II Was Only Yesterday", Hedrick Smith describes Russians as "perhaps the world's most passionate patriots."   Now the final period appears inside the final quotes, where it belongs, but the comma after the chapter title (see the comma rule on pages 19–21 governing use of the comma after introductory phrases and clauses) is mistakenly placed outside the final quotes. Under no conditions may a writer of American English place a comma outside final quotes and be correct. This practice is not a question of logic.

Right   In his chapter "Patriotism: World War II Was Only Yesterday," Hedrick Smith describes Russians as "perhaps the world's most passionate patriots."

Wrong   In our childhood Joe Louis was known as the "Brown Bomber:" this affectionate term reflected our respect for his ability to deliver a punch yet suggests we perceived him as a member of another race rather than as a man.   (Another violation of standard practice: the colon must never appear before final quotes.)

Right　　In our childhood Joe Louis was known as the "Brown Bomber": this affectionate term reflected our respect for his ability to deliver a punch yet suggests we perceived him as a member of another race rather than as a man.

Wrong　　He and I finally had a chance to study carefully Emily's new story, "A Wild Goose Chase;" we found it lacking in character development but strong in plot and details of locale, so we accepted it for immediate publication.　　(Again a violation of standard practice: semicolons must never appear before final quotes.)

Right　　He and I finally had a chance to study carefully Emily's new story, "A Wild Goose Chase"; we found it lacking in character development but strong in plot and details of locale, so we accepted it for immediate publication.

Although the rules for periods and commas (inside final quotes) and for colons and semicolons (outside) are strict and without exception, exclamation points and question marks require some thought.

Wrong　　Would that I could write something half as good as "The Fall of the House of Usher!"　　(The title of Poe's famous story does not contain an exclamation point. The sentence in which it is named is itself the exclamation, so the exclamation point must be moved.)

Right　　Would that I could write something half as good as "The Fall of the House of Usher"!

Wrong　　She was sufficiently angry to say, "To hell with your job"!　　(The exclamation in this construction is the quotation, not the sentence. The sentence would normally require only a period. It is a declarative statement. Since we do not use an exclamation point together with a period, the exclamation point serves in place of the period. But the exclamation point must be placed inside the final quotes.)

Right　　She was sufficiently angry to say, "To hell with your job!"

Wrong　　Has Joan completed her term paper on Picasso's "Guernica?"　　(This great painting is not a question. The sentence is a question. The question mark must be moved.)

Right　　Has Joan completed her term paper on Picasso's "Guernica"?

Wrong　　The new minister delivered a sensational sermon entitled "Is God Only Half Alive"?　　(This sentence is not a question. The title of the sermon is. The question mark must be moved.)

Right　　The new minister delivered a sensational sermon entitled "Is God Only Half Alive?"

Placement of an exclamation point or a question mark depends on whether the material within quotes is an exclamation or a question or whether the sentence including the quotation is an exclamation or a question.

Thus, the exclamation point goes *inside* quotes if the *quotation* is an exclamation and outside quotes if the *sentence* is an exclamation.

Likewise, the question mark is placed *inside* quotes if the *quotation* is a question and *outside* quotes if the *sentence* is a question.

8.　Insert quotation marks and other punctuation where appropriate in the following sentences. Extra space is provided for your convenience in writing.

> "If you really care about people," Margaret said, "you will not hesitate to volunteer for a few months of work among migrant workers."
>
> "Can you expect," I said, "to find happiness when you consider only your own needs?"

1.　Let the music and dancing begin　the pompous host said
2.　As we left the stadium, Jon said　What a baseball game that was　I replied　Bring on the Cincinnati Reds
3.　Can you remember Herman's tone when he said　I have changed my life completely
4.　How ridiculous　we found Alice's claim that her teaching was　unsurpassed in the department

5. I shall be going to St. Louis in a few weeks to see whether I can hire a new administrative assistant   she said   to replace my present assistant   Wish me luck

6. Why can't the English learn to speak   Rex Harrison sang

7. I have twice had the good fortune to see Da Vinci's   Mona Lisa   my cousin said as we walked in the garden   and don't care whether I never again have the chance to see another painting

8. Sylvia cares enough about her sisters, brother, and father   I suggested   I want to know why she does not care about herself

9. Kenyon quickly said   Unless the city plays a more active role, our neighborhood will sicken and die

10. When you have a chance to read   Sports of the Times   in this morning's *Times,* you will know why professional football no longer is a sport   he said

11. I replied   You have only to hear him read   To be or not to be   to understand why he is called the finest young Shakespearean actor now performing

12. A friend of mine who fought in Germany during World War II says there is considerable doubt over whether General McAuliffe was the one who replied   Nuts   when the Germans demanded surrender of the 101st Airborne Division   she said   What's more, there's even greater doubt that the actual reply was   Nuts

13. I quote Noel Coward on   mad dogs and Englishmen   whenever my friends ask me to spend a day on the beach   her letter said   Why turn your skin to leather by the time you reach forty, when it does not take much strength to resist a chance to loll about half-naked in front of a gallery of gawking young men eager to exhibit their rippling biceps and hair chests

14. The first question on the test really stumped me   If Moby Dick is the symbol of evil, what does Captain Ahab symbolize   What does Queequeg symbolize

15. All of us agreed that Selma gave the best reading of   Ode to the West Wind   she gave each line its full poetic impact, modulated her voice beautifully, and appeared to understand and experience all the lines, from   O wild West Wind, thou breath of Autumn's being   through   If Winter comes, can Spring be far behind   ?

Chapter 6

The Dash and the Hyphen

THE DASH

The dash may have many uses, but it is almost never used by some writers, seldom used by most writers, and overused by inexperienced writers. Only the amateur substitutes careless use of dashes for good diction and effective sentence structure. The fact is that modern writing does not often require use of the dash. Yet, when a dash is needed, there is nothing better. Notice that a dash is made on a typewriter by two hyphens, with no spacing either before or after.

Dashes indicate greater separation of elements of a sentence than can be accomplished with commas. In this sense the dash is a supercomma. Dashes can also play the same role as parentheses in setting off material not central to the thought of a sentence. Where parentheses tend to deemphasize enclosed material, dashes tend to emphasize it.

For Abrupt Breaks in Thought

A dash is used to indicate an abrupt break in thought within a sentence. For stylistic effect writers may use a dash to break off suddenly within a sentence and change subjects or end a sentence completely.

> During the campaign the underdog spoke constantly of the role of her opponent in recent Washington scandals, the waste and corruption in the legislature, the personal habits of leading officials—you know the whole story.   (By breaking off at the dash, the writer of this sentence implies there is much more to be told. The reader may fill in the rest. The reader becomes an assenting insider, privy to shameful secrets.)

> Imagine a situation like this, so degrading for the individuals involved, so damaging for their families—how can anyone but a novelist intent on revealing the sordid nature of humanity do justice to it?

> They said they could not find suitable jobs—had they really looked?—so we continued to support them.   (A dash can be used with a question mark. See pages 84–85.)

> "Jimmy, please don't lean out so far—." Too late. The boy had already begun to slide down the face of the sharp cliff.   (A dash can be followed by a period. See pages 84–85.)

> Now I shall tell you the entire story of how the affair started and died—but first have another cup of coffee.

As you can see, such sentences are not often needed, so the dash is not often needed to indicate an abrupt break in thought within a sentence.

1.   Insert dashes where appropriate in the following sentences, as shown in the examples.

> Now I would like to hear everything you know about the matter—or have you already told me more than you know?

> The girls were ecstatic—is that a strong enough word?—when they heard who their visitor was.

1. Everything was turning out just the way I wanted it: I was rich and famous and sought after but my alarm clock ruined everything.
2. Just when the crops were ready for harvesting, a storm flattened our fields how can one predict the weather?
3. Catherine had planned for every contingency she had foreseen how could she have done more?

4. The feeble voice of the electorate spoke once again slightly less than half of the eligible voters went to the polls.

5. I called to him again and again, ''Please, John, don't go. Please, John, don't go. Please, John '' but I could not get him back.

6. What she really meant was you know what she meant.

7. We were all concerned you know how much we cared that the brothers were getting in too deep.

8. I think we overfed the poor thing you know how pups look at you with those sad eyes.

9. These are not hard times if only you had lived during the Great Depression.

10. A new threat has arisen you may not understand it now.

With Appositives

Dashes are used to set off nonrestrictive appositives worthy of greater emphasis than is achieved with commas and to set off appositives that contain commas. Ordinarily commas are used with nonrestrictive appositives, as noun repeaters that point out or identify the nouns with which they are in apposition. You will recall that nonrestrictive appositives are appositives that can be omitted without damaging the meaning of a sentence. (See pages 29–31 for full discussion of commas with appositives.)

> I like romances, fictional accounts of heroic achievement, and often read myself to sleep with a paperback that takes me far away from today's troubled world.   (The commas enclose the nonrestrictive appositive *fictional accounts of heroic achievement.*)

> The problems—unemployment and inflation—perplex economists and mystify the public.
> (Use of dashes gives greater emphasis to the nonrestrictive appositive *unemployment and inflation* than would be achieved through use of commas. Notice that commas would not be incorrect, merely less emphatic.)

> The role of the Securities Investigating Commission proposed in the bill—seeking out corruption among investment bankers, recommending new legislation, and checking abuse of securities practices—was poorly understood by most investors.   (The commas used within the nonrestrictive appositive *seeking out corruption among investment bankers, recommending new legislation, and checking abuse of securities practices* make it mandatory to set off the appositive in dashes rather than commas. Use of commas to set off the appositive would confuse readers.)

Notice that when a nonrestrictive appositive occurs at the end of a sentence, a single dash is used.

> She asked me to buy three things at the supermarket, and I forgot all three of them—bread, hamburger, and tuna fish.

A comma would suffice if there were no internal commas.

> She asked me to buy two things at the supermarket, and I forgot both of them, bread and hamburger.

2. Insert dashes or commas where appropriate in the following sentences. Use your judgment to determine whether an appositive is worthy of the emphasis achieved through use of dashes rather than commas.

> My mother could always be counted on to come up with a meal on a moment's notice—a concoction that would disturb my sleep for an entire night.
>
> Ron hunts any animal the law says he can hunt—raccoon, muskrat, squirrel, moose, bear, deer—and stocks his freezer with the meat the animals provide.

1. The neighborhood insists on all its rights proper housing, hot lunches for schoolchildren, safe streets, fire protection and gets them too.

2. The young couple wanted so few things a small house, a faithful dog, and decent air to breathe and couldn't get any of them.

3. Alice is looking for a job in either of her fields editing or teaching.

4. The suit he was wearing a four-button yellow velvet achieved its purpose fully when he entered the theater lobby.

5. His old car a battered Studebaker is now up on blocks.

6. Their favorite drinks coffee and tea were becoming too expensive for their budget.

7. Three dogs an Irish setter, a Russian wolfhound, and a German shepherd were the scourge of the neighborhood.

8. His degree Master of Arts in Social Work will enable Robert to gain useful employment among the hill people of South Carolina.

9. Anne's achievement a Doctor of Medicine degree *cum laude* made her entire family happy.

10. The promised reforms improved city planning, provision for open space in the city center, and rent allowances for the indigent became important issues in that year's elections.

For Parenthetic Elements

Dashes are used to set off parenthetic elements when commas are insufficient and parentheses inappropriate.

Ordinarily commas are used to set off interrupters, parenthetic elements that break into the expected movement of a sentence.

> Bernice is, however, concerned with the administration of student affairs at her high school.

A parenthetic element that can stand logically and grammatically as a sentence or that is internally punctuated requires more than commas. When a parenthetic element is not part of the main thought, yet sufficiently pertinent to include in a sentence, parentheses are used (see pages 59–61).

> I frequently consult *The Reader Over Your Shoulder* (Macmillan, New York, 1943) to find out what Robert Graves and Alan Hodge have to say about sentence structure.   (Bibliographic information is a good example of parenthetic information that is usually enclosed in parentheses within a sentence.)

When a parenthetic element is too closely related to the main thought of a sentence to justify use of parentheses and can stand logically and grammatically as a sentence, dashes are used. As pointed out above, dashes give greater emphasis than parentheses give to the material they set off.

> Her final examinations—may I never have to take another one!—are legendary instruments of student torture.   (Notice that exclamation points can be used with dashes.)

> Corky's usual appearance—I'm not sure it's what you expect in one so talented—attracts a great deal of interest wherever he goes.

> Ned's earnings as a stockbroker—he made more than $200,000 last year—do not qualify him for welfare payments by our current standards.

3. Insert commas, parentheses, or dashes where appropriate in the following sentences. Extra space is provided for your convenience in writing.

> By the time I spoke with Frank, the oldest son, the entire family had decided to move out of Ohio.

> Many students find Mawson's *Dictionary of Foreign Terms* (first published in 1934, reprinted in paperback format in 1961) a handy reference work for library research.

1. Popular conceptions of political morality   one must use that word no matter how far-fetched it seems   do not speak well of our practicing politicians.

2. John Milton   1608–1674   is considered one of the three greatest English poets.

3. Zircon   a common mineral   is frequently used in inexpensive jewelry.

4. The Rocky Mountains   I last saw them in 1970   are one of the great tourist attractions in the United States.

5. Rockville   Maryland   is one of the finest suburbs of Washington, D.C.

6. By the time we had finished talking   Joseph later told me we had talked for three hours   both of us were so tired we fell asleep in our chairs.

7. I don't mind spending a good deal of money for a word processor   how would I pursue my writing if I did not have one?   yet $2,600 is a great deal more than I can justify for even the finest machine.

8. Once a furnace wears out   they all must wear out eventually   the homeowner can do nothing but buy a new one.

9. We overlook the tremendous variety of beautiful terrain one can see in just a few hours' drive from New York City   we overlook other advantages as well   and miss the chance for a relatively inexpensive camping vacation.

10. Cemeteries   would God we could do without them!   charge so much for their services that only the grief of bereaved families and the awkwardness of death without burial preclude a consumers' boycott.

With Summaries Following Series

A dash is used to set off a summary statement following a series of words, phrases, or clauses. Writers sometimes vary sentence structure to place a summary or assertion after a series of words, phrases, or clauses. This is an excellent way to achieve variety of sentence structure and to emphasize the elements of the series. A dash is used before the summary statement.

The three elements of the trivium leading to a bachelor's degree in medieval universities were grammar, logic, and rhetoric.

Grammar, logic, and rhetoric—these were the three elements of the trivium leading to a bachelor's degree in medieval universities.

Three attributes do more for an engineer's career than technical knowledge: clear writing, effective speech, and willingness to work hard.   (See page 53–55 for use of the colon before enumerations or lists.)

Clear writing, effective speech, and willingness to work hard—these attributes do more for an engineer's career than technical knowledge.

My English professor spends her summers enjoying hard work and good exercise: she works on her research; she swims, rides, and runs daily when the weather permits; and she perfects her knowledge of fine cooking and dining.

My English professor works during the summer on her research; she swims, rides, and runs daily when the weather permits; and she perfects her knowledge of fine cooking and dining—these are the ways she spends her time enjoying hard work and good exercise.

The use of the dash to set off summaries and assertions after a series is a rare one, since such constructions are rare. Used sparingly, these inversions of the usual structure of a sentence achieve variety and emphasize the elements of the series.

4. Insert commas, semicolons, and dashes where appropriate in the following sentences. Extra space is provided for your convenience in writing.

Potable water, fresh air, and good food—all these are essential for a healthy life.

"That great but unequal poet," "the gloomy master of Newstead," "the meteoric darling of society"—these were just some of the sobriquets applied to Byron.

1. A dictionary   thesaurus   word processor   and paper   these tools of the trade are the main-stays of a modern writer's life.

2. Police officers   fire fighters   and sanitation workers   no municipality can do without these men and women.

3. Beagles   coon hounds   and spaniels   these breeds often serve the hunter well.

4. *Finnegans Wake   Alice's Adventures in Wonderland   Looking Backward*   and *Pilgrim's Progress*   all are concerned with dreams.

5. Sloops   schooners   yawls   such ships are commonly seen in coastal waters.

6. Joseph Conrad   Herman Melville   and William Faulkner   these and other fine novelists are studied in her English class.

7. The young boys frequently set fires in vacant buildings   they robbed vagrants   old women and helpless children   they burglarized neighborhood shops   there was nothing they wouldn't do.

8. Lithographs   prints   and   etchings   you will find them all for sale in most art galleries.

9. A walk in the park   a Sunday stroll on Fifth Avenue   a trip to the Cloisters   these were the things we missed when we left New York.

10. Theater   concerts   libraries   and museums   these are the attractions of a great city.

With Other Marks

Dashes are used when necessary to set off sentence elements punctuated as questions or exclamations. When a question is set off by dashes within a sentence, the question mark precedes the second dash.

> My sister-in-law—why was I home when she called?—asked me again about the money we owe her.

When the question is set off at the end of a sentence, only a single dash is needed in addition to the question mark.

> I have always had trouble with mathematics—do you know anyone who hasn't?

When an exclamation is set off by dashes within a sentence, the exclamation point precedes the second dash.

> The Dodgers won the pennant in the last game of the season—what a season it was!—leaving their fans emotionally drained but happy.

When the exclamation is set off at the end of a sentence, only a single dash is needed in addition to the exclamation point.

> Despite all our initial difficulties, our marriage has turned out to be the happiest I can imagine—how few of my friends still are married!

Notice that the exclamation point in this example serves as punctuation for the entire sentence as well as for the exclamation.

A dash can also be followed by a period.

> I asked her where she would find the book if she could not—. Again she interrupted me.
>
> They were about to go to the old woman's rescue, but when they saw the gun in the assailant's hand—.

5. Insert dashes, exclamation points, question marks, and periods where appropriate in the following sentences. Extra space is provided for your convenience in writing. (You may wish to review the uses of some of these marks before attempting this exercise.)

First be sure you have enough lumber, nails, tools, and experience in carpentry and then—are you sure you want to try to build your own cabin?

I have told you this again and again—what a bore I must be!—and still you have not changed your ways.

1. How I wish   can you understand why   I were closer to death
2. Eloise insisted on remaining behind when the group left base camp   what a mistake that was
3. The entire play   what a fiasco   took four and a half hours to run through during dress rehearsal
4. The basic problem   how can we pay for the new car   will not be solved by sitting here and worrying
5. Everyone in the family   what a crowd   squeezed into the camper for the trip to the lake
6. Once you have determined what the roofing repairs will cost   I hope you are still listening
7. The mountains are so beautiful in autumn   how I wish we were still there
8. Some politicians can never manage to maintain a discreet silence on sensitive matters when questioned by the press   they refer to reporters as interrogators   and do themselves more harm by speaking than they would by respectfully declining to answer
9. The tired old champion   what a runner she was in her prime   sat in the dressing room for almost an hour without looking up
10. Norman Mailer   will anyone ever write a better first novel   is a marvelous stylist and an engaging public personality

The Double Dash

A double dash is used to indicate deleted expressions and to suggest hesitant speech. We live in times of relaxed rules of decorum, so writers tend to use so-called explicit language in their work. Yet family newspapers and some magazines still use dashes from time to time to replace offensive expressions.

The candidate then used the word   ——, leaving his partisan audience unwilling to believe their ears but certain that the outcome of the election was in greater jeopardy than ever. (Some newspapers hypocritically show such omissions by a series of hyphens, carefully counting out each letter of the omission so that the reader will know exactly what has been omitted, for example, --- -- - -----. They may as well spell out the offending item.) A double dash (——) is sufficient, no matter how the offender is spelled. In print a double dash appears as a solid bar twice the length of a dash. Notice that the double dash in this use is spaced as a word; a dash normally does not have a space before it or after it.

Dashes are also used to indicate that part of a name has been omitted from an account. We see this usage most often in works of fiction, such as spy novels. Some writers of serious fiction also use the dash this way to heighten the effect of their work.

Colonel L—— drew his pistol from its holster and carefully pointed it at his right temple. (This is a double dash no matter how long the full name is. Notice that there is no space after the first letter of the name, but there is a space after the dash.)

In the novel she is referred to only as Mlle. P—l.   (Writers usually use a single dash when supplying the last letter of the name. Notice the spacing of the dash.)

The Half Dash

A half dash is used to indicate inclusive dates, times, and page references.

The convention was scheduled for Philadelphia, Pennsylvania, November 23–25, 1993.

The meeting will be held in our dormitory, 6:30–8:30 p.m.

I refer you to *Time* of April 19, 1969, pp. 52–54, for a fuller discussion.

THE HYPHEN

Book publishers, editors of current magazines and newspapers, and teachers of composition disagree with one another on use of the troublesome hyphen mark more than they agree. Although certain rules can be offered for your guidance, you will have to become accustomed to relying—as most writers do—on an up-to-date standard dictionary for whatever comfort it can give. It is ironic that a mark intended to prevent confusion causes so much dispute.

In Numbers and Fractions

Hyphens are used with spelled-out numbers from twenty-one through ninety-nine and with spelled-out fractions. Numbers from zero through twenty are single words, so they are not hyphenated: *two*, *eight*, *nineteen*.

Numbers above one hundred are usually written as numerals, except for two hundred, three hundred, etc.: *104, 675, 892, 1166; six hundred, twelve hundred, one thousand, two million*. We never hyphenate numerals, and we never hyphenate multipliers; in the number five hundred, for example, *five* is the multiplier of *hundred*.

Numbers between twenty-one and ninety-nine that consist of two words can be thought of as having the word *and* understood between them: *thirty-four* can be thought of as *thirty and four* (the hyphen replaces the *and*); *sixty-seven* is *sixty and seven*. Contrast this with *seven hundred*, in which we really have *seven times one hundred*.

In fractions written as words the sign of the fraction, which means *divided by*, is usually replaced by a hyphen: *1/6* is written as *one-sixth*; *3/4* is written as three-fourths. A hyphen is not used for the division sign when the numerator or denominator requires a hyphen: *3/32 is written as three thirty-seconds*; *31/64* is written as *thirty-one sixty-fourths*. Needless to say, few writers find a need for writing such fractions.

6. Write the following numerals and fractions as words.

    200   two hundred

      49   forty-nine

1. 100 _____
2. 600 _____
3. 5/9 _____
4. 7/16 _____
5. 26 _____
6. 11 _____
7. 24 _____
8. 2,000,000 _____
9. 5/8 _____
10. 88 _____

Compounds with Self-

Hyphens are used in compounds employing the word *self-*. One unabridged dictionary includes more than nine hundred words employing *self-*. Most are hyphenated. There are other prefixes, such as *all-*, *ex-*, *auto-*, *non-*, and *anti-*, that are occasionally hyphenated. The dictionary is your best source when you are not certain of whether to hyphenate.

7. Use your dictionary to do the following exercise. Part of the sentence is italicized. Rewrite the italicized portion, making single words and inserting hyphens where appropriate.

Her hypnosis was *self induced*.   <u>self-induced</u>

She accused him of *self ishness*.   <u>selfishness</u>

1. Albie Booth was a famous *all American* football player. _____
2. My *ex wife* lives in Kansas City. _____
3. Like many other people, she sought *self fulfillment* through work.

   _____
4. How dare he speak *ex cathedra* on something he knows nothing about?

   _____
5. She suffered from *ex ophthalmic* goiter. _____
6. Many people who do not take the time to understand current trends in religion condemn certain movements as *self worshipping* indulgence. _____
7. They decided to buy Cathy a *self winding* watch for her birthday.

   _____
8. What can you expect *self less* individuals to do in such a business situation?

   _____
9. The Miranda decision sought to protect accused persons against giving *self incriminating* evidence when they were not aware of their right to remain silent.

   _____
10. How often do you find *self starters* among people who can never hope to earn more than a minimal wage? _____

Family Relationships

Hyphens are used in terms that express family relationships, such as *in-laws*. Some family members are designated in two-word expressions: *half sister, half brother, kissing cousin*. Others are designated in single words: *sister, brother, grandmother*. Family relationships employing *in-law* are hyphenated: *sister-in-law, brother-in-law*. Some expressions preceded by *great* are also hyphenated: *great-aunt, great-grandmother*.

8. Rewrite the following terms as single words, two words, or hyphenated expressions. Use your dictionary for meanings of unfamiliar terms.

mother in law   <u>mother-in-law</u>

step sister   <u>stepsister</u>

1. first cousin   _____
2. father in law   _____
3. step son   _____
4. step father   _____
5. daughter in law   _____
6. son in law   _____
7. grand father   _____
8. great grand father _____
9. great grand son   _____
10. grand daughter   _____

Awkward Combinations

Hyphens are used between syllables of words to prevent harsh or misleading combinations of letters. Words made of two words—*red-hot, secretary-general*—or of a prefix and root word—*anti-imperialistic*, *semi-abstract*—sometimes can be difficult to pronounce without a hyphen. When no problem of pronunciation exists, the words are spelled without a hyphen: *redhead, antihuman, semifinal*. But how would you like to read *red-hot* as *redhot, secretary-general* as *secretarygeneral, anti-imperialistic* as *antiimperialistic*, or *semi-abstract* as *semiabstract*?

Would you know what a *halllike* lavatory looks like? You know what a *fireman* is, but can you tell what a *fireeater* is? The hyphen makes hall-like and *fire-eater* easy to understand.

Don't trust your judgment in this use of the hyphen. If you are not certain, check your dictionary.

9.   Rewrite the following terms as single words where appropriate with or without hyphens or as two words where appropriate. Use your dictionary to check words you do not know.

lieutenant colonel	<u>lieutenant colonel</u>
anti immigration	<u>anti-immigration</u>

1. semi industrialized   _____
2. semi finalist   _____
3. anti logarithm   _____
4. anti gravity   _____
5. anti intellectual   _____
6. full length portraits   _____
7. still life   _____
8. fire resistant   _____
9. ice free winters   _____
10. trash can   _____

With Compound Modifiers before Nouns

Hyphens are used in compound modifiers that appear directly before the nouns they modify. Many modifiers are made of two or more words acting as a single word: *clear-minded, first-rate, up-to-date*. These modifiers are hyphenated when they appear before a noun they modify.

A *clear-minded* individual with a good grasp of the language will have no trouble making a good grade on the Law School Aptitude Test.

Christine is a *first-rate* tennis player.

Up-to-date dress is imperative for salespersons in Madison Avenue shops.

When a modifier is made of an adverb that ends in *-ly* plus another modifier, the term is not hyphenated, even when it appears before the noun it modifies.

A *clearly addressed* envelope is essential.

Have you enclosed a *well-addressed* envelope?

Be sure to include a *self-addressed* envelope.

Notice that most of these compound modifiers are not hyphenated when they follow the nouns they modify or when they function as predicate complements (sentence elements that complete copulative verbs, such as *be* and, in certain senses, *feel*).

The envelope was *well addressed.*

Are you certain you are *clear minded* today?

Jane feels *first rate* for her match.

In that frock you look *up to date* and chic.

10. Insert hyphens where appropriate in the following sentences.

> The union was demanding a one-dollar wage increase for its members.
>
> Are you ready for the question-and-answer period?

1. That man's rule can surely be termed iron fisted government.
2. The long term outlook for the economy is sound.
3. Our medical school faculty includes two Nobel laureates.
4. A five foot three shortstop is as unusual as a left handed catcher.
5. Early blooming roses can be damaged by late frosts.
6. Dave and Dina are a poorly matched pair.
7. The 1976 New York Yankees and Cincinnati Reds were unevenly matched.
8. A well suited couple can expect a happy life together.
9. Fast moving films always attract large audiences even if their casts are poorly chosen.
10. He felt bright eyed and bushy tailed that morning, ready for the rapid fire discussion his advisers predicted.
11. Down at the heels salesmen cannot expect to achieve sure fire results.
12. The so called teacher addressed his students in a quavering, pity me voice that revealed his insecurity.
13. Open minded students can learn a great deal from such a teacher.
14. She was open minded, but her associates could not bring themselves to treat her as anything but a stereotype.
15. Third rate scholars produce third rate scholarship.

With Prefixes and Capitalized Root Words

Hyphens are used in terms consisting of prefixes and capitalized root words. Many terms in English are made of prefixes and capitalized root words, or proper nouns. The capital letter is often retained in the new word. When it is, a hyphen is required: *trans-Siberian*, *pro-Liberian*. When the capital letter is not retained, no hyphen is required: *transatlantic*, *prepaleolithic*.

11. Rewrite the italicized terms in the following sentences, inserting a hyphen where appropriate or closing up the terms where a hyphen is not used.

> The *pro-Lebanese* forces could not develop the teamwork they surely needed to end the senseless struggle.
>
> The statement showed the group's neofascist orientation.

1. The *trans continental* railroad was completed late in the last decade.
2. A *trans Canadian* pipeline will carry oil inexpensively.
3. They must not fish in *extra territorial* waters.
4. The idea of a *Pan American* Union is not new.
5. *Pan Germanism* was one of the reasons for Hitler's rise.
6. Do you understand the difficulties facing anyone who attempts to lay a *trans pacific* cable?
7. *Trans Adriatic* travel is subject to petty interference by two governments.
8. We expect to be in our new house by *mid July*.
9. The *pre Roosevelt* years were not as grim as many would have us believe.
10. If you persist in taking an *anti Islamic* position, what can you expect in return?

Suspension Hyphen

Hyphens are used with incomplete modifiers whose meanings are in suspense. When two or more modifiers employing hyphens precede a noun, writers will often leave incomplete all but the final modifier. When they do, they must retain the hyphens within the modifiers.

> We would like to buy tourist-class or second-class tickets.
>
> We would like to buy tourist- or second-class tickets.

Notice that a space is left after the hyphen following *tourist*.

This practice of retaining the hyphen ensures that readers see that incomplete modifiers are completed by the same term as the final modifier.

12. Copy the following sentences, inserting hyphens where appropriate.

> Museums often display reconstructed third and fourth century pottery without informing visitors that the pottery was not found intact.
>
> Museums often display reconstructed third- and fourth-century pottery without informing visitors that the pottery was not found intact.
>
> This is your third and final chance to pass the entrance examination.   *Correct*

1. My fourth and fifth grade teachers were especially valuable in teaching me essential study techniques.

_____

2. They stood second and third in their classes.

_____

3. Much of the great literature of the eighteenth and nineteenth centuries goes unread today.

_____

4. We were fortunate to win red and blue ribbons at the dog show.

_____

5. A cat we had for many years was neither a blue nor a red ribbon winner yet managed to bear almost twenty prize winning kittens.

_____

6. Next year, according to our landlord, all second, third, and fourth floor rooms will be completely redecorated.

_____

7. First, second, and third ranked pupils will be eligible for the final competition.

_____

8. Did you know that the Titan missile had first and second stage rockets?

_____

9. Entering students will be assigned by time of receipt of applications to pre, mid, and post July classes.

_____

10. First and second semester students register last in our school.

_____

Linked Numerals and Letters

Hyphens are used with numerals that are part of a modifier, and letters that are linked to nouns. Numerals often appear as part of a modifier: *10-inch planks*, *50-cent candy bars*. The hyphen attaches the numeral firmly to the rest of the modifier (*inch*, *cent*).

Letters used as part of a noun also are attached to the rest of the noun by hyphens: *X-rays*, *D-day*.

13. Copy the following sentences, inserting hyphens where appropriate.

The machine lacked two O rings.	The machine lacked two O-rings.
He owned two .22 calibre rifles.	He owned two .22-calibre rifles.

1. Under the city statutes then in existence, he was entitled to two 6 month delays.

2. The judge gave her a suspended 30 day sentence.

3. A champion weight lifter cannot be bothered with 50 pound weights unless they are added to barbells already loaded with a few hundred pounds.

4. H hour instructions were as precise as the company commander could write; the G 2 had made sure of that.

5. We have lived through development and deployment of the A bomb and the H bomb, but we have yet to see the latter used in anger.

6. The F 15 aircraft has not been without its failures.

7. The battalion S 3 developed plans for the attack.

8. We will have to buy seven 6 inch boards in order to make that bookcase.

9. The designer decided to use three 5 inch rules on each page of the magazine.

10. We bought a dozen 14 ounce beer mugs to prepare for the party.

Word Division at the End of a Line

Hyphenate between syllables to divide words at the end of a line. This rule is simple to state but hard to follow, since logic sometimes appears to fall apart in deciding where syllables begin and end. Consider *de moc ra cy* and *dem o crat ic*, *bar ba rism* and *bar bar i ty*. If any of these words appears at the end of a line and cannot be completed on that line, you may divide them and use a hyphen to show the division. You can see that your dictionary will be well thumbed if you practice word division according to the rule.

But there is more to the problem than has yet been presented. The following practices must also be observed:

- Never divide a word to leave a single letter at the end of a line or the beginning of a new line.
- Never divide a hyphenated word except at the hyphen, so that you will not have more than one hyphen in the word.
- Never divide a hyphenated expression except at one of the hyphens.

- Never divide a one-syllable word. This would seem to be obvious if you follow the hyphen rule stated above, but you may forget that adding the suffix *-ed*, for example, to single-syllable words does not always change the word from one syllable to two. *Watch* and *watched* are both one-syllable words, as are *patch* and *patched*. But how about *dis-in-ter-est-ed* and *un-re-quit-ed*?
- You may always divide words between double consonants: *com-mit*, *pat-tern*, *suf-fer*.

Chapter 7

The Apostrophe

The apostrophe—considered a mark of punctuation by some and a mark of spelling by others—has three principal uses: to show possession, to form contractions, and to form plurals of letters or numbers. The first two uses come into conflict in *its* and *it's*, the possessive of *it* and the contraction of *it is*. While English usage is clear on what *its* and *it's* mean, beginning writers are bedeviled by this apparent inconsistency.

Possession

An apostrophe is used to show possession.

Singular Nouns

The rule is applied directly to most singular nouns, but with an added twist: In forming the possessive of singular nouns, add an apostrophe plus an *s*:

John	John's	boy	boy's
Norma	Norma's	lady	lady's

When a singular noun ends in *s* or an *s* sound, add an apostrophe and an *s* unless the additional *s* produces an unpleasant sound or results in the awkwardness of *s's* followed by a word beginning with an *s*:

James	James's	goose	goose's
Hortense	Hortense's	horse	horse's

If addition of an *s* after an apostrophe is undesirable because of sound or appearance, add only an apostrophe:

Hippocrates	Hippocrates' contributions
goodness	goodness' sake
Socrates	Socrates' sayings
Pleiades	Pleiades' six visible stars

(The awkwardness of *Hippocrates's*, *goodness's sake*, *Socrates's*, and *Pleiades's* is obvious, not to mention *Pleiades's six*.)

Notice that not all writers and editors agree on certain aspects of this rule. For example, many writers and editors refer to Henry *James's* novels as Henry *James'* novels. Again, many writers prefer *Keats'* poetry to *Keats's* poetry. You will always be correct in following the rule stated here. Unless the sound or appearance offends the ear or eye, use the apostrophe plus *s*.

1. Form the possessive of the italicized singular nouns in the following sentences.

   I went to *Henry* party. ___Henry's___

   Enos tail was caught in the door. ___Enos's___

   1. The entire group was satisfied with *Alice* performance as president of the club.

      _____

   2. Our *city* record in public housing is far from outstanding. _____

   3. One *hour* delay is about all we can take at this point. _____

   4. Are you studying *Aristophanes* plays this semester? _____

5. *Luis* new hat is the envy of all the men in the neighborhood.　＿＿＿＿＿＿

6. *Lois* approach to management solved most of our *company* problems.　＿＿＿＿＿＿
＿＿＿＿＿＿＿＿＿＿

7. A *moment* hesitation may be fatal in such situations.　＿＿＿＿＿＿

8. Mr. *Harris* old car will not survive the winter.　＿＿＿＿＿＿

9. Have you ever read any of Gene *Hawes* books?　＿＿＿＿＿＿

10. Please attend our meeting on Old *Timer* Day.　＿＿＿＿＿＿

Plural Nouns

When a plural noun does not end in *s*, add an apostrophe plus an *s* to show possession.

women	women's	alumni	alumni's
firemen	firemen's	bacteria	bacteria's

When a plural ends in *s*, only an apostrophe is added.

actors	actors' lines	the Fords	the Fords' old house
artists	artists' easels	two minutes	two minutes' silence

2. Form the possessive of the italicized plural nouns in the following sentences.

　　Men clothing is becoming more colorful than *women*.　<u>Men's, women's</u>

　　All the algae vanished into the *geese* stomachs.　　<u>geese's</u>

1. Have you noticed the color of the *Thomases* house?　＿＿＿＿＿＿

2. I always enjoy a good reading of *children* stories.　＿＿＿＿＿＿

3. The *mothers* conversation always turned to their *children* behavior at home and their progress in school.　＿＿＿＿＿＿

4. Three *hours* interruption of electrical service is not enough to thaw food in a good home freezer.　＿＿＿＿＿＿

5. The *alumnae* annual reunion is seldom lively.　＿＿＿＿＿＿

6. Urban *workers* problems have been growing worse with the passing of the years.
＿＿＿＿＿＿

7. I look forward each year to three *weeks* stay in the country.　＿＿＿＿＿＿

8. His six months in the penitentiary will have the same effect as ten *years* absence from home.
＿＿＿＿＿＿

9. *Physicians* malpractice insurance adds considerably to their operating costs and their *patients* bills.　＿＿＿＿＿＿

10. The *guards* uniforms are more dismal than they have to be.　＿＿＿＿＿＿

Indefinite Pronouns

Certain indefinite pronouns can show possession. This is done by adding an apostrophe and an *s*:

anyone	anyone's	each one	each one's
somebody	somebody's	someone	someone's

3. Form the possessive of the italicized indefinite pronouns in the following sentences.

　　Everybody paper was returned ungraded.　<u>Everybody's</u>

　　She finds *nobody* work satisfactory.　<u>nobody's</u>

1. She would rather eat *anybody* cooking than her own.　＿＿＿＿＿＿

2. They were surprised when *no one* painting won first prize.　＿＿＿＿＿＿

3. *Somebody* coat has been stolen. _____
4. *Everybody* desks must be cleared by quitting time. _____
5. *Each one* turn will come soon. _____

Compound Constructions

In compound constructions, such as *mother-in-law* and *someone else*, the possessive is formed by adding an apostrophe and an *s*, where appropriate, to the last word in the compound: *mother-in-law's room*, *mothers-in-law's rights*, *someone else's happiness*.

4. Form the possessive of the italicized compounds in the following sentences.

Everyone else privileges are observed.   Everyone else's

He hopes to find a copy of the *Surgeon General* report.   Surgeon General's

1. They were always doing *one another* work. _____
2. They found *each other* papers just before the deadline for submittal at the end of the term. _____
3. My *brother-in-law* art gallery will soon close. _____
4. The *sergeant-at-arms* request for silence was ignored. _____
5. The *Chief Justice* opinion was beautifully phrased. _____

Joint Possession

To indicate joint possession by two or more nouns, the apostrophe and an *s* are added, where appropriate, only to the last noun.

Have you a copy of Strunk and White's *Elements of Style*?   (The book was written by both men.)

Stay out of the mare and goat's stall if you want to stay healthy.   (The *mare* and *goat* share a common *stall*.)

Mary and John's party was the best I have ever attended.   (One *party* given by two people.)

5. Form the possessive of the italicized nouns in the following sentences to show joint possession.

They decided to look for *Burton and Taylor* old house.   Burton and Taylor's

Anne and Paul marriage did not last long.   Anne and Paul's

1. Have you ever been a client of *Wodehouse, Clark,* and *Peal* law firm?
_____

2. *Puerto Rico and Haiti* fishing agreement was violated.
_____

3. *Colgate and Skidmore* joint program will be terminated if registration does not improve.
_____

4. *Wentworth and Flexner* book on slang is almost a classic.
_____

5. *Maria and José* relationship has lasted a long time.
_____

Individual Possession

To indicate individual possession by two or more nouns, the apostrophe and an *s* are added, where appropriate, to each noun.

May's and June's receipts were higher than expected.   (Each of the months had individual *receipts*.)

The advanced course deals with Maurois' and Proust's literary works.   (Each author had his own *literary works*.)

Every minute's, hour's, and day's output was carefully measured.   The *output* was *measured* individually by the minute, hour, and day.)

6. Form the possessive of the italicized nouns in the following sentences to show individual possession.

Sophie and Elaine engagements did not last long.   <u>Sophie's and Elaine's</u>

Pittsburgh and Kansas City baseball teams have become stronger in recent years.   <u>Pittsburgh's and Kansas City's</u>

1. *Janet and John* tennis rackets need restringing.   _____
2. *Frank and Anne* intellectual interests are similar.   _____
3. One of my chores was to prepare *Pooch, Willy, and Louie* dinners before sitting down to my own.   _____
4. Who can tell where *Plato and Socrates* ideas diverged?   _____
5. *April, July, and October* gross profits were the lowest by far in that year. _____

Contractions

An apostrophe is used to indicate the omission of letters and numbers in a contraction. A contraction is a shortened form of a word or group of words: *won't* for *will not*, *she's* for *she is*, *'76* for *1776* or any other year for which this contraction would be understood. The apostrophe substitutes for the missing letters or numbers.

Will-o'-the-wisp is the common name for *ignis fatuus*, the light sometimes seen over marshy ground and now taken to represent anything deluding that we chase in vain.   (*Will-o'-the-wisp* is the contraction of *will-of-the-wisp*.)

The word *ain't* is a variant form of amn't, a contraction of *am not*.   (Here we have two contractions of the same original expression.)

"She goin' back no more."   (In writing dialogue some fiction writers attempt to reproduce the sounds of the dialect characteristic of their characters. The apostrophe in contracted forms assists readers in understanding the speech represented.)

7. Change the italicized expressions in the following sentences to contractions.

Do you recall the desperate situation of many Wall Street speculators in *1929*?   <u>'29</u>

Carolyn *could not* understand the laziness shown by some of her friends in the office.   <u>couldn't</u>

1. They *have not* been home in nine months.   _____
2. We *would have* given you what you wanted if you had been more polite in asking.   _____
3. They *cannot* do any more than *they have* already done.   _____
4. The class of *1992* will find itself more readily employable than the class of *1991*.   _____
5. I *shall not* be home when you call.   _____

Its and It's

Unfortunate individuals—numbering in the millions in the United States alone—confuse the rules governing use of the apostrophe when dealing with *it* in the contraction *it's* and in the possessive *its*.

It may help to remember that possessive adjectives and pronouns ending in *s* do not take an apostrophe: *his home*; *this is hers*; *its broken leg*; *the mistake is ours*; *those are yours*; *we lost theirs*. Other possessives, such as *my* and *our*, do not take an apostrophe.

> The cat lost *its* way.   (Possessive form of *it*.)
>
> Rain damaged *its* binding.   (Possessive form of *it*.)
>
> The party interpreted *its* victory as a mandate to plunder the treasury.   (Possessive form of *it*.)

It may also help to remember that the contraction of *it is* is *it's*.

> *It's* much earlier than you think.   (Contraction of *it is*.)
>
> I think *it's* improper to demand so much of the young.   (Contraction of *it is*.)
>
> She thinks *it's* an acceptable way to proceed.   (Contraction of *it is*.)

8.   Supply either *its* or *it's* where indicated in the following sentences.

> I find   <u>it's</u>   too much for me to do in one day.
>
> I found   <u>its</u>   solution far too difficult for me.

1.   Three of _____ puppies went on to win major prizes at the show.
2.   _____ more than a day's journey, I think.
3.   The agent advised us to clean up the house in order to ensure _____ prompt sale.
4.   I could tell that yesterday was going to be a long day from _____ beginning.
5.   The cat spent an hour chasing _____ tail.
6.   You can tell a book from _____ cover.
7.   If we only had known of _____ tendency to break down in hot weather, we would have bought another automobile.
8.   Do you think _____ too late to look for a solution?
9.   He hopes _____ going to turn out all right.
10.   Most of those who still say _____ a mistake to go ahead with the project are probably thinking only of their own needs.

Plurals of Letters and Numerals

An apostrophe and an *s* are used to form the plurals of letters and numbers. Businesspeople, bureaucrats, and others have been influenced by military writing style, which omits the apostrophe. The rule for abbreviating letters and numerals still holds for formal prose, particularly scholarly writing, but you can anticipate that at some future time the apostrophe will no longer be required for this purpose. Both forms are shown in two of the following examples, but you are cautioned that the omission of the apostrophe may not be acceptable in school and college writing.

> That child seems unable to learn his ABC's (ABCs).
>
> If you learn that *accommodate* has two c's and two m's, you will have no trouble with it.   (The apostrophes in this sentence will never disappear. Without them the sentence would be impossible to decipher: *two cs and two ms*? Both *cs* and *ms* happen to be standard abbreviations for special terms.)
>
> There were three 7's (7s) in the winning lottery number.

Here is a good example of a rule that is undergoing change but must not be abandoned yet. It is better to be safe than misunderstood.

9. Form the plurals of the italicized numerals and letters in the following sentences. Follow the apostrophe rule as you work.

> The *1980* hold promise of being a decade of world peace if we do not ignore the lessons of the past.   1980's
>
> "Mind your *p* and *q*" is a cliché.   p's, q's

1. I do not know of a single formula that does not have more *x* and *y* than I can manage. _____

2. She made straight A in her first semester at school.   _____

3. Do you have any 33 *rpm* around that you would care to swap for some of my compact disks? _____

4. That furnace is rated at better than 1200 BTU an hour   _____

5. Will we still be around after the '90?   _____

Chapter 8

Italics and Ellipsis

ITALICS

Underscored typewritten and handwritten words are the equivalent of italicized words in printed matter. Italics can be considered a form of punctuation in the sense that italics, like punctuation marks, clarify meaning. Italics perform certain well-defined functions performed by no other mark. They share other functions with quotation marks. Italics can also add emphasis to particular words in a sentence, but writers who use italics often for this purpose risk being perceived as screaming at their readers.

Reference to Books, Other Published Works, and Ships and Aircraft

Italics are used when referring to titles of books, newspapers, magazines, films, plays, operas and other full-length musical works, paintings, sculpture, book-length poetry, ships, and aircraft.

Italics are used when referring to a title that appears on the title page of a published work. Quotation marks are used when referring to any part of the work. For example, a chapter or section title is enclosed in quotation marks, as stated on page 70.

The names of newspapers and magazines appear on the first, or title, page. The titles of books, plays, published operas, and the like appear on the title page. The titles of films appear on the screen credits. When a poem is long enough to be published as a single volume, its title appears on the title page. All these titles are italicized.

When referring to paintings, sculpture, and other works of art, the usual practice is to employ quotation marks, but many publishers regularly employ italics for this purpose.

The names of ships and aircraft are italicized when they appear in print.

Newspaper

> Do you read the St. Louis *Post-Dispatch*?   (Only the name that appears on the masthead of the newspaper is italicized.)

Magazine

> I once had an article in the *Journal of the National Association of Deans of Women.*
> Do you find *Time* as interesting as *Newsweek*?

Film

> I hear Hollywood has made a sequel to *Gone With the Wind.*
> Do you remember Clark Gable and Claudette Colbert in *It Happened One Night*?

Play

> Many critics believe Eugene O'Neill reached his peak in *Long Day's Journey into Night.*
> Oscar Wilde's *Lady Windermere's Fan* is played only on college campuses these days.

Full-Length Musical Works

> I never miss a chance to see Gilbert and Sullivan's *Pirates of Penzance.*
> Beethoven's *Fifth Symphony* is probably the most frequently performed symphonic work.

Painting

> Rembrandt's *Aristotle Contemplating the Bust of Homer* brought a record price at auction some years ago.

Sculpture

> Rodin's *Balzac* looks out at tourists in stern rebuke for the follies of humankind.

Book-Length Poem

> When you have read the *Odyssey, Aeneid*, and *Paradise Lost*, you have read the best that humanity has produced.

Ships

> We will never see the likes of the *Normandie* for beauty and comfort in ocean travel.

Aircraft

> The most famous B-29 of World War II was the *Enola Gay*.

1. Underscore and insert quotation marks where necessary in the following sentences. An underscore indicates that a term is to be italicized.

> His favorite book is <u>Huckleberry Finn</u>.
>
> I wonder if I will have a chance to travel on <u>Queen Elizabeth</u> II before the ship is decommissioned.

1. Wallace Stegner's most successful novel was Remembering Laughter, which appeared in 1937.
2. They were fortunate enough to find a copy of the Nation that carried the article they wanted to read.
3. The Return of a Private is one of Hamlin Garland's best stories in his volume Main-Traveled Roads.
4. Hemingway's story The Three-Day Blow appeared in his In Our Time, which was published in 1925.
5. Charles Lindbergh's name is inseparable from his companion on the long journey to Le Bourget, The Spirit of St. Louis.
6. If you know only The Great God Brown and Ah Wilderness!, you know only half of Eugene O'Neill's greatness.
7. Many statues of Aphrodite have been attributed to Praxiteles (fourth century B.C.), but none more lovely than the Aphrodite from Arles.
8. The Archaeological Museum in Salonika has a mosaic signed Gnosis that is entitled Stag Hunt.
9. Have you ever seen La Traviata or The Barber of Seville? If you have not, you have not seen Italian opera at its best.
10. Have you read Annabel Lee, Ulalume, or Lenore—three of Poe's most frequently quoted poems?

Foreign Expressions

Italics are used for foreign words and phrases that appear in English sentences. English owes much of its strength to its practice of making foreign words its own. This process of adoption goes on all the time, and dictionary makers watch carefully to determine when a foreign word is used frequently enough to consider it part of the English language.

When a writer uses a foreign word that has not been recognized by the lexicographers, that word must be italicized to show its alien status. The best practice is to check a recent standard dictionary to determine the status of any foreign word or expression you wish to use in your writing. If the word or expression appears in italics in the dictionary, it must be italicized in your writing. If it does not appear at all, it is surely not an English word and, of course, must be italicized. Above all do not enclose foreign words or foreign expressions in quotation marks.

Wrong   Anyone that young who can be said to have "savoir-faire" is indeed remarkable.   (The *Random House Dictionary of the English Language* lists this expression as English.)

Right   Anyone that young who can be said to have savoir-faire is indeed remarkable.

Wrong   A good story begins "in medias res."   (The same dictionary identifies this phrase as Latin, meaning "in the middle of things.")

Right   A good story begins *in medias res.*

2. In the following sentences certain expressions are enclosed in quotation marks. Remove the quotation marks and underscore foreign expressions; remove the quotation marks and do nothing else if the expressions are English. Check your dictionary as you consider each sentence.

The lovely young Japanese woman wore a yellow "kimono" tied at the waist with a scarlet "obi."

He was a dedicated collector of "objets d'art."

1. The sculptor lived "circa" 360 A.D.

2. Many students in my classes have "chutzpa" to a degree seldom approached in people my own age.

3. Greek tragedy relates the failure of heroes to ignore warnings from the gods; the "hubris" of these tragic figures leads inevitably to catastrophe.

4. We had a dozen "escargots" before going on to "escalope de veau" with plenty of "vin ordinaire."

5. He never failed to complete his poems with a brief "envoi" that restated the principal theme.

6. The cadets of Company A showed sufficient "esprit de corps" to win the prize month after month.

7. As far as I am concerned, Saul Bellow's novels are "ne plus ultra."

8. Who can forget the "Schrecklichkeit" of Nazi concentration camps?

9. Their summers were perfect examples of "dolce far niente" that more than made up for winters of intense activity.

10. As far as I can tell, the voters were more interested in "via trita, via tuta" (the beaten path, the safe path) than in taking a chance on an unknown candidate who promised much but never explained how he would carry out his ambitious programs.

Words as Words

Italics are used to indicate words used as words rather than for their meaning. This rule is the alternative technique for identifying words that are intended to be understood as words rather than as conveyors of meaning. Quotation marks are generally used for this purpose, but most books use italics. (For full discussion and practice in using quotation marks for this purpose, see pages 71–72.) Understand that italics can be used wherever quotation marks are used for this purpose. The important thing to remember is that one cannot mix the two marks in a single piece of writing. If you begin using quotation marks to identify words used as words, stay with them throughout. If you begin using italics for this purpose, stay with them throughout.

Emphasis

It is hard to resist the occasional urge to underscore a word that deserves special emphasis. Italics used in this manner are almost equivalent to telling your readers to raise their voices for that word.

Many writers do use italics for emphasis occasionally, so we would be wrong if we said italics are not to be used for emphasis. When writers fall into the habit of italicizing frequently to increase emphasis, they appear to be saying to their readers: The only important words in my writing are italicized, so you can skip the rest.

Although the use of italics for emphasis is tempting, it might be wise to avoid this use altogether. If you make the necessary effort to write emphatically, the words you choose will not need artificial support.

ELLIPSIS

Ellipsis is a mark consisting usually of three spaced periods (. . .) or four spaced periods (. . . .). It is used most often to indicate an incomplete quotation or an incomplete presentation of information. Question marks and exclamation points sometimes are combined with ellipsis (? . . . and ! . . .).

Fiction writers may use ellipsis artistically to indicate pauses in dialogue or hesitation in speech, and advertising copywriters may use ellipsis to dramatize their commercial messages. These uses are highly individual and will not be treated here.

Above all, good writers never use ellipsis to endow a message with mysterious or arcane meanings. This mistaken use of ellipsis is futile and childish, a doomed attempt to establish a private communication channel through which the reader is presumed to be able to read the writer's mind.

Ellipsis is given four spaced periods when the ellipsis occurs at the end of a sentence punctuated ordinarily by a period. You may think of the additional spaced period, therefore, as the period of a sentence from which a quotation is taken or as the period of a sentence that is written incompletely. Except for quotations in which lines of poetry or paragraphs of prose are omitted, ellipsis never contains more than four spaced periods.

Omissions in Quotation

Ellipsis is used to indicate omission of words in quoted matter. Writers frequently must quote published material to support or illustrate an argument they are making. The quotation need not include every word of the original, but must retain the meaning of the original. Read the following excerpt from *The Gospel of St. Matthew*. It will be used in the discussion that follows.

> Jesus then got into the boat, and His disciples followed. All at once a great storm arose on the lake, till the waves were breaking right over the boat; but He went on sleeping. So they came and woke him up, crying: "Save us, Lord; we are sinking!" "Why are you such cowards?" He said, "How little faith you have!" Then He stood up and rebuked the wind and the sea, and there was a dead calm. The men were astonished at what had happened and exclaimed, "What sort of man is this, that even the wind and the sea obey Him?"

In quoting from this paragraph, ellipsis is used to indicate any omissions.

> "Jesus then got into the boat. . . . All at once a great storm arose on the lake. . . ."   (Four spaced periods used twice. The two omissions include the ends of sentences.)

> "Then He stood up and rebuked the wind and the sea, and there was a dead calm. The men . . . exclaimed, 'What sort of man is this, that even the wind and the sea obey Him?' "   (Three spaced periods. The omission comes in the middle of a sentence.)

When ellipsis is used to indicate omission at the end of a sentence that is punctuated by a question mark or exclamation point, three spaced periods are used along with the question mark or exclamation point if either mark is needed to preserve the original sense.

> "The men were astonished at what had happened and exclaimed, 'What sort of man is this? . . .' "   (If the question mark were omitted, the meaning of the quotation would be obscured.)

"So they came and woke Him up, crying: 'Save us, Lord! ...' " (The exclamation point is retained to preserve the meaning of the quotation.)

Notice that ellipsis is not used to indicate omissions of words from the beginning of a quoted sentence.

Jesus "stood up and rebuked the wind and the sea, and there was a dead calm."

Commas, colons, and semicolons in the original material are omitted in quoting unless those marks are essential for understanding.

"All at once a great storm arose on the lake ... but He went on sleeping."

"So they ... woke Him up, crying ... 'we are sinking!' "

Ellipsis can save space in quotation but must not damage the essential meaning of the original material.

3.   Use ellipsis to replace the italicized words in quoting from the following sentences.

His way of answering such questions was always to pull out his face; *it was his only means of putting any expression into it.*

"His way of answering such questions was always to pull out his face. ..."

Imagine my satisfaction *at being allowed to carry them to my room!*

"Imagine my satisfaction! ..."

1.   But the Airedale, *as I have said*, was the worst of all my dogs.

2.   When you sit by a pond or winding stream, *the city's hurry drains away, and* from the corners of the mind thoughts come out and sun themselves.

3.   People who owned closed models *rebuilt along different lines: they* bought ball grip handles for opening doors, windows, anti-rattlers, and deluxe flower vases of the cut-glass anti-splash type.

4.   He fell into the habit of stealing out at night and engaging in long drinking bouts *at the village tavern.*

5.   Whether Thurber's drawing requires psychiatry or not, a great many people, *including Harold Ross*, cannot get enough of it.

Incomplete Presentation

Ellipsis is used to indicate that information presented is incomplete. Ellipsis is not used merely in quoting material from sources other than the writer's own mind. When you do not wish to include all elements of a series you are presenting or when you wish to suggest that more information is available than you are presenting, ellipsis can indicate the incompleteness. In this use ellipsis is a welcome substitute for *etc.*, *and so forth*, and *and the like*.

Televised sports programs (football, baseball, hockey ...) have become the controlling force in professional and intercollegiate athletics.   (Three spaced periods to indicate that the list of sports goes on.)

Recall the many conjunctive adverbs available for your use: *however*, *moreover*, *thus*. . . .   (Four spaced periods because the omission occurs at the end of a sentence.)

Remember: three spaced periods or four. No more.

Lengthy Omissions

A line of spaced periods is used to indicate omission of a line or more from poetry, a paragraph or more from prose.

Poetry

> And I made a rural pen,
> And I stained the water clear,
> And I wrote my happy songs
> Every child may joy to hear.
>   —William Blake

> And I made a rural pen,
> . . . .
> And I wrote my happy songs
> Every child may joy to hear.

Prose

When quoting prose material longer than a paragraph, the purpose of the writer may be served through omitting one or more paragraphs. This omission is also shown by a line of spaced periods.

> I think that in no country in the civilized world is less attention paid to philosophy than in the United States. The Americans have no philosophical school of their own, and they care but little for all the schools into which Europe is divided, the very names of which are scarcely known to them.
> Yet it is easy to perceive that almost all the inhabitants of the United States use their minds in the same manner, and direct them according to the same rules; that is to say, without ever having taken the trouble to define the rules, they have a philosophic method common to the whole people.
> To evade the bondage of system and habit, of family maxims, class opinions, and, in some degree, of national prejudices; to accept tradition only as a means of information, and existing facts only as a lesson to be used in doing otherwise and doing better; to seek the reason of things for oneself, and in oneself alone; to tend to results without being bound to means, and to strike through the form to the substance—such are the principal characteristics of what I shall call the philosophical method of the Americans.
>   —Alexis de Toqueville

> I think that in no country in the civilized world is less attention paid to philosophy than in the United States. The Americans have no philosophical school of their own, and they care but little for all the schools into which Europe is divided, the very names of which are scarcely known to them.
> . . . .
> To evade the bondage of system and habit, of family maxims, class opinions, and, in some degree, of national prejudices; to accept tradition only as a means of information, and existing facts only as a lesson to be used in doing otherwise and doing better; to seek the reason of things for oneself, and in oneself alone; to tend to results without being bound to means, and to strike through the form to the substance—such are the principal characteristics of what I shall call the philosophical method of the Americans.

Chapter 9

Capitalization

There are many uses of capitalization, some clearly understood by most writers and some not so clearly understood. The review that follows begins with the easiest rule of all and then develops all the other individual requirements for capital letters.

Despite the many rules that are presented, modern English uses far fewer capitals than German, for example, and English of earlier centuries.

Sentences

The first word of every grammatical unit punctuated as a sentence is capitalized. What starts out as a simple rule includes the problem words *every grammatical unit punctuated as a sentence*. Why? Everyone who has had even a few years of formal schooling knows that the first word of a sentence is capitalized.

> Now is the time for all good men to come to the aid of their party.
> Let there be light!
> Is there any doubt about their position on this troubling matter?

A sentence is normally defined as a group of words expressing a complete thought and containing a subject and predicate. In the paragraph you are now reading, the third sentence consists of a single word: *Why?* Where is the subject? Where is the predicate? Yet *Why?* is punctuated as a sentence and is a sentence. Certain grammatical units, sometimes referred to as *incomplete sentences* or as *fragments,* are used as sentences and punctuated as sentences by professional writers as well as by the rest of us. For this reason, the rule governs capitalization of the first word of any grammatical unit punctuated as a sentence.

Consider the following sentences, none of which is a complete sentence:

> At last!
> Now!
> Now?
> No.

Now consider this dialogue:

> "Which do you prefer?"
> "Neither."
> "Which will you buy?"
> "The cheaper one."
> "Now?"
> "Yes."

Only the first and third sentences of this dialogue are complete sentences in the traditional sense, yet all are treated as sentences, complete with capitalization of the first word.

1. Capitalize the first word of each of the following sentences.

> are you certain?   <u>Are</u>
> you will soon tire of her.   <u>You</u>

1. nothing bothers me more than talkative strangers.   _____
2. can you deliver the goods when we need them?   _____
3. haying time is near.   _____
4. the neighborhood is quiet tonight.   _____
5. everyone will be there.   _____

Poetry

The first word of every line of conventional poetry is capitalized. Some poets, notably e.e. cummings, choose not to capitalize conventionally. In cummings' case, unconventionality of capitalization extends to the way he chose to write his own name. The great majority of poets start each line with a capitalized word. When quoting a line or more of conventional poetry, then, you must capitalize conventionally. When quoting cummings or any other unconventional poet, follow the lead of the poet. In your own poetry you may choose whatever style suits you.

> One impulse from a vernal wood
> May teach you more of man,
> Of moral evil and of good,
> Than all the sages can.
> —William Wordsworth

2. Capitalize the first word of every line of the following stanza taken from a poem by William Wordsworth.

for oft, when on my couch I lie   1. _____

in vacant or in pensive mood,   2. _____

they flash upon that inward eye   3. _____

which is the bliss of solitude;   4. _____

and then my heart with pleasure fills,   5. _____

and dances with the daffodils.   6. _____

Quotations

The first word of a quotation is capitalized, unless the quotation is less than a sentence long. Quotations sometimes do not consist of complete sentences. When they do not, the opening word of the quotation is not capitalized unless there is some other reason for capitalization. When the quotation is a complete sentence, the first word is capitalized.

> Dave's father said, "You must learn to fend for yourself."

> "We will do exactly as you wish," the children said.

> Hobbes's famous phrase "a kind of sudden glory" describes the feeling of the onlooker when he sees misfortune befall another.

Sometimes a quotation of a complete sentence is broken into two parts in the sentence quoting it. The second part is not capitalized if it is not treated as a sentence.

> "You will," he went on, "do exactly as I say."

> "You will do exactly as I say," he went on; "you will leave tonight and be with your sister by morning."

> "You will do exactly as I say," he went on. "You will leave tonight and be with your sister by morning."

3. Capitalize where necessary in the following sentences.

The thief said quietly, "if you do not cry out, you will be safe."   <u>If</u>

"if you do not cry out," the thief said, "you will be safe."   <u>If</u>

1. "be patient," my father said. _____

2. "there is no point in worrying," the physician said. "you will be up and about in a few weeks." _____

3. As Shakespeare said, "something is rotten in the state of Denmark." _____

4. I grew tired of "at this point in time" as I listened to the hearings of the Senate committee. _____

5. Will we ever hear the word *expletive* again without recalling "expletive deleted"? _____

6. Wordsworth's "impulse from a vernal wood" does not have a chance of doing slum children much good. _____

7. "stop what you are doing," the teacher said, "and pass in your examination papers." _____

8. "go quietly through life if you want the world to be ignorant of who and what you are," the old woman said. _____

9. "gather ye rose-buds while ye may," Herrick advised, and who is to say he was wrong? _____

10. "the committee will meet one more time," the dean said; "moreover, it will sit until a decision is reached." _____

The Words *I* and *O*

The pronoun *I* and the interjection *O* are capitalized. Except for *I*, pronouns are not capitalized unless they are the first word of a sentence or a line of poetry. Do not confuse the pronoun *I* with the letter *i*.

He and I are going into business together.   (*He* is capitalized because it is the first word of a sentence, *I* because it is *I*.)

Please see that she and I are seated together.

There are three i's in *invidious*.

The interjection *O*, which is seen mainly in literature and prayer but is rarely used today, is always capitalized, even though the interjection *oh* is not. Do not confuse the interjection *O* with the letter *o*.

Ben Jonson is responsible for the famous line: "O me no O's."

Hear me, O Israel!

The word *cooperate* has two o's and is spelled three different ways: *cooperate, co-operate,* and *coöperate*.

4. Capitalize the i's and o's in the following sentences wherever appropriate.

o Lord, what did i do to deserve this?   O, I

She then said, "invite me to the ball game, and i will go."   Invite, I

1. Have you ever heard anyone say "o God, just give me another year of life"? _____

2. Life was so cruel to her that she prayed nightly: "o God, please spare me any further torture and i will be grateful through eternity." _____

3. This i cannot say no matter how often i am asked. _____

4. How many i's are there in the word *implication*? _____

5. Can you count the o's in Thurber's famous story? _____

Names

Proper Nouns and Adjectives

Proper nouns and adjectives are capitalized. A proper noun is the name of a particular person, place, or thing. A proper adjective is an adjective derived from a proper noun.

Frank met Lucy for dinner.   (*Frank* and *Lucy* are proper nouns.)

France attracted artists and writers from all over the world during the 1920's.   (*France* is a proper noun.)

The White House is the center of political activity in the United States.   (*White House* and *United States* are proper nouns.)

After many years of absence from the finest tables, German wines are commanding a great deal of attention.   (*German* is a proper adjective. In the sentence *He is a German, German* is a proper noun.)

The baby was delivered by Cesarean section.   (*Cesarean* is a proper adjective derived from Julius *Caesar*.)

Eleanor Holm was expert in the Australian crawl.   (*Australian* is a proper adjective.)

Be certain when you deal with words such as *china* (a ceramic material commonly used for dishes) and *China* (the country) that you do not confuse proper nouns with common nouns. The rule for capitalization affects only proper nouns and proper adjectives.

She decided to join the Republican Party   (*Republican Party* is the name of a political party.)

As a Republican she decided there was no reason to have a party to celebrate the 1992 presidential election.   (The only proper noun in this sentence is *Republican*. The *party* mentioned has nothing to do with *Republican Party*.)

5.   Capitalize all proper nouns and proper adjectives in the following sentences.

Do you recall that norman thomas was a member of the socialist party?   <u>Norman Thomas   Socialist Party</u>

We studied euclidean geometry when I went to school.   <u>Euclidean</u>

1. Is she a member of the freudian group?   _____

2. What damage has been done to native americans of our southwest that can still be undone?
_____

3. They traveled abroad during their last year in college to see ireland, england, and wales.
_____

4. Historians are taking a new look at the truman years.   _____

5. Young students now seem at home in newtonian physics.   _____

6. The british are dismayed at the number of americanisms that are used daily in their newspapers and magazines.   _____

7. Frederick law olmsted designed new york's central park.   _____

8. I hope that I do not have to undergo an appendectomy.   _____

9. She is a member of the anglican church.   _____

10. Wealthy men often buy aberdeen angus cattle as investments.   _____

11. We admire winston churchill for his eloquence as well as for his leadership of a nation deep in crisis.   _____

12. The roosevelt family has contributed many leaders to american life.
_____

13. The shakespearean sonnet and the petrarchan sonnet are identical in length and metric pattern, but not in rhyme scheme.   _____

14. He was never known as a francophile even though he admired french painting and poetry, particularly the work of gauguin and mallarmé.   _____
_____

15. Auctioneers love to offer chippendale furniture to sophisticated new york and london bidders.
_____

Particles

American family names beginning with the particles *Van, Von, De, Du, Di,* or *Da* are capitalized. Do not capitalize foreign family names beginning with the particles *van* or *von*. Do not capitalize foreign family names beginning with the particles *de, du, di,* or *da* unless they appear without first names or titles.

Many family names of foreign origin include particles. *Van* is of Dutch origin. *Von* is of German origin. *De* and *du* are of French origin. *De* is also of Spanish origin. *Di* and *da* are of Italian origin. All have the same meaning: *from* or *place of origin*. Thus, someone named *Simon de Versailles* would literally be *Simon of Versailles*.

As names employing the various particles become Americanized, the particles often are treated as separate and capitalized parts of the names rather than as particles with the meaning of *of*: the *Van Cortlandt* family, Agnes and Cecil *De Mille*. Names of foreign families are given special treatment following European custom: Ferdinand *de* Lesseps, builder of the Suez Canal; Paul *von* Hindenburg, President of Germany from 1925 to 1934. In the European custom, these two names would be given as *Lesseps* and *Hindenburg* if first names and titles were omitted. In the American custom they would be given as *De Lesseps* and *Von Hindenburg*.

> One of the best engineers I know in Connecticut is Paul Von Hardenburgh.   (An American name.)
>
> The Van Doren family boasts two distinguished members: Carl and Mark.   (An American name.)
>
> Most of the Du Pont family still resides in Delaware.   (An American name.)
>
> Do you know the works of Pietro di Donato?   (An Italian name.)
>
> Have you read Donato's works?   (An Italian name appearing without a first name.)
>
> Wernher von Braun started his career as a rocketeer at Dortmund, Germany.   (A German name.)
>
> We know that Braun lived and died in Alabama.   (A German name appearing without a first name.)

6.   Capitalize italicized particles wherever appropriate in the following sentences.

> Joe *di* Maggio set the record for hits in consecutive ball games when he was a Yankee star.   Di
>
> Lee *de* Forest was an American inventor who did much to advance the development of the radio.   De

1.   Can you remember when Norm *van* Brocklin was a football star?   _____
2.   John *von* Neumann was an American mathematician.   _____
3.   W. E. B. *du* Bois was a distinguished American writer and educator and founder of Pan-Africanism.   _____
4.   The American actor Erich *von* Stroheim was born in Austria.   _____
5.   Although he was born in the Netherlands, author Pierre *van* Paasen considered himself American.   _____
6.   The nickname given to American General Stephen *van* Rensselaer was "the Patroon."   _____
7.   Lucas *van* Leyden, the Dutch painter and engraver, is mistakenly thought by some to have been the inventor of the Leyden jar.   _____
8.   Do you know the works of *van* Gogh and *van* Dyck?   _____
9.   The full name of Lope *de* Vega, the Spanish dramatist and poet, was Lope Felix *de* Vega Carpio.   _____
10.   The great Italian ocean liner was named after Conte *di* Savoia.   _____

Geographical Names

Since geographical names are proper nouns, they are capitalized. There are several conventions that are followed with geographical names, however, that make special discussion worthwhile.

Before beginning, be certain you understand that words such as *river, ocean, mountain,* and *gorge* are geographical terms that are used both alone and as part of the names of geographical features: *Mississippi River, Atlantic Ocean, Doe Mountain, Quechee Gorge.* When *river* and the others occur as part of a geographical name, they are capitalized. When they do not occur with a geographical name, they are not capitalized.

In all the examples given thus far, the geographical term has been singular. Other terms are often plural, for example, *Harbor Hills, Thousand Islands, Rocky Mountains,* and *Verrazano Narrows.* Again, since these terms are part of a proper geographic name, they are capitalized. When they are not, they are not capitalized: *hills, islands, mountains,* and *narrows.*

The final group of geographical terms to be considered consists of singular words that are used both before and after place names: *Bay of Fundy, Cape of Good Hope, Lake Louise,* and *Mount Rainier; Baffin Bay, Howe Cape, Churchill Lake,* and *Rocky Mount.* These terms follow the same practice. When they are part of a geographical name, they are capitalized. When they are not, they are not capitalized.

> I have seen mountains in my time, but none to rival the Rocky Mountains.
>
> Of all the rivers in the United States, there is none to rival the Mississippi River.
>
> I would like to own just one of the islands of the Thousand Islands or just one of the lakes of the Finger Lakes.

7. Capitalize all geographical names in the following sentences.

> We are going to sail the gulf of mexico next year.   Gulf of Mexico
>
> Have you ever seen indian head or indian point?   Indian Head, Indian Point

1. The caspian sea is a favorite resort area for many people in europe.

2. We hope to travel to pike's peak next year.   _____

3. A desert area is home to more life than you realize.   _____

4. I spent a summer near little egg harbor, new jersey.   _____

5. Of all the lakes I have seen, salt lake is the most interesting.

6. My parents come from county cork and now live in cuyahoga county.

7. A narrows frequently is subject to dangerous currents.   _____

8. I once was aboard a ship that went through the strait of macassar.

9. Mount lebanon, pennsylvania, is an attractive suburb of pittsburgh.

10. During World War II, lingayen gulf saw the arrival of the invasion fleet that helped retake luzon.

Compass Directions

Compass directions are capitalized when they are part of the names of specific regions. We do not capitalize *east, west, north,* and so on when they merely indicate directions: *Travel east on this road.* We do capitalize directions when they serve as part of the name of a place or region.

An old song referred to the region just a little bit south of South Carolina.

Voters in Southern California behave quite differently from their fellow Californians to the north.

8. Capitalize all geographical names in the following sentences.

The northern part of vermont is known as the northeast kingdom.   Vermont, Northeast Kingdom

Texas is part of the southwest.   Southwest

1. We were told to go west when we were young. _____
2. The west was considered the land in which opportunity abounded.
   _____

3. F. Scott Fitzgerald was the chronicler of the east.   _____
4. Chicago is considered the heart of the midwest.   _____
5. Can you believe that west new york is in new jersey?
   _____

6. War seems to have left southeast asia for a while.   _____
7. He loved to hunt near the lakes in western michigan.
   _____

8. The most beautiful part of the united states is the far west.
   _____

9. Do you think we will ever regard the south as an equal member of the united states?
   _____

10. Do you know the foothills of south carolina?   _____

Regional Names and Nicknames

The names and nicknames of geographic regions and political units are capitalized. As in compass directions used in regional names, all terms commonly used to name geographic regions and political units are capitalized. Not only are the proper names of countries and regions capitalized, but so are the nicknames used by the press, historians, and political commentators to designate such units.

Columbus set forth from the Old World to find what turned out to be the New World.

Mystery writers often use the Orient as a locale.

9. Capitalize the geographic names and nicknames used in the following sentences.

All football fans know that iowa is called the hawkeye state.   Iowa, Hawkeye State

Steinbeck's famous novel dealt with the people who fled the dust bowl in the 1930's.   Dust Bowl

1. New jersey is one of the middle atlantic states.   _____
2. Massachusetts is known as the bay state.   _____
3. Political commentators are fond of differentiating between the old south and the new south.   _____
4. The black forest is a mountainous region of germany.   _____
5. How often do we hear ireland referred to as the emerald isle today?
   _____

6. The semiarid region east of the rocky mountains is known as the great plains.
   _____

7. The salton sea was once known as the salton sink.
   _____

8. The nickname of california is the golden state.   _____

9. Do you know the proper name of the nutmeg state?   _____

10. Many cities claim the title of athens of the midwest.   _____

Streets, Buildings, Parks, and Companies

The names of all formally designated streets, buildings, parks, public places, companies, and other organizations are capitalized.

All the world has heard of New York City's Fifth Avenue.

The Flatiron Building was once considered a New York landmark.

Have you ever visited Yellowstone Park?

Lenin's tomb is on Moscow's Red Square.

The General Electric Company manufactures a wide variety of equipment for nuclear power plants.

The United Nations accomplishes a great deal through the work of its many committees.

10. Capitalize the proper names in the following sentences.

Have you ever had the pleasure of walking along boston's massachusetts avenue?
Boston's Massachusetts Avenue

My sister worked for many years in the main office of pratt & whitney aircraft company.
Pratt & Whitney Aircraft Company

1. Although the empire state building is no longer the largest building in new york, it is still a feature of the midtown skyline.

_____

2. One of the most famous addresses in the world is 1600 pennsylvania avenue, washington, d.c.

_____

3. You will receive valuable assistance from the bureau of media services, florida department of commerce, 107 w. gaines street, tallahassee, florida.

_____

_____

4. Many of arizona's public offices are located on north central street in phoenix.

_____

5. The john hancock tower, in chicago, is one of the tallest buildings in the united states.

_____

6. Many tourists overlook the archaeologic interest of italy's paestum.

_____

7. St. marks cathedral is not immune from the effects of the air pollution that has attacked venice for so many years.

_____

8. The royal dutch petroleum company is one of the major companies controlling the international oil industry.

_____

9. Have you ever visited the world trade center, two buildings so large that they have their own ZIP code?

_____

10. The pennsylvania academy of the fine arts houses an outstanding collection of american art.

_____

Organizations and Other Groups

The proper names of all organizations, religions, races, nationalities, and so on are capitalized. This rule is another specific expansion of the rule governing the capitalization of proper names: *Columbia University, Seventh-Day Adventists, Asians, Poles, Department of Commerce, Los Angeles Police Department, The Salvation Army.* The list is almost endless.

When anything but the proper name of such a group is used, no capitals are required: *college departments, fundamentalists, bureaucrats, government officials, charities.*

When a phrase is used that could serve as the name of an organization but does not, the phrase is not capitalized. Only official names are capitalized.

> We ought to organize a cheerleaders' club.
>
> The Tenafly Cheerleaders' Club is a popular group.
>
> In the 1930's our political leaders recognized that the government had a responsibility to organize a commission that would keep watch over securities transactions.
>
> The Securities and Exchange Commission, consisting of five members, oversees the public offer and sale of securities.

11. Capitalize all the proper names in the following sentences.

> The hollywood chamber of commerce promotes tourism and business.   <u>Hollywood Chamber of Commerce</u>
>
> We ought to develop an organization that would bring tourists and business to our community.   <u>*Correct*</u>

1. The united states senate has a membership of one hundred men and women, who are elected by their states for six-year terms.

———————————————————

2. The commonwealth of massachusetts legislature consists of a senate and a house of representatives.

———————————————————

3. Mary Baker Eddy founded the church of christ, scientist in 1879 to reinstate the healing power of original christianity.

———————————————————

4. Baseball played by professionals in the United States is regulated by the national league and the american league.

———————————————————

5. Canada is a self-governing member of the commonwealth of nations, with executive powers nominally in the hands of the governor-general, who represents the queen and is appointed by her on the recommendation of the canadian government.

———————————————————

———————————————————

6. He served for many years as an officer of the toastmaster's club in his company, representing the club at many international meetings.

———————————————————

7. Many universities are organized by department rather than by colleges, with administrative responsibility resting in the hands of department heads rather than deans.

———————————————————

8. The chairman of the english department at the university of pennsylvania served also as provost of the university and dean of the graduate school of fine arts.

———————————————————

9. Six deacons of the local church were named corecipients of the annual brotherhood award of the rotary club.

_____

10. His company was known as the bridgeport gas and electric works until it was merged into the connecticut utilities companies, a holding company for firms in the energy field.

_____

Deity and Sacred Writings

Nouns and pronouns referring to God and writings held to be sacred are capitalized. American usage requires that all references to God, members of the Trinity, religious observances, and the books sacred in religious traditions be capitalized.

God, the Father, the Son, and the Holy Ghost were celebrated in a special Mass.

The reading of the Haggadah during the Passover Seder is a symbolic reminder of the deliverance of the Israelites from Egypt.

12. Capitalize all proper names, nouns, and pronouns in the following sentences.

The koran is the holy book of the nation of islam.   Koran, Nation of Islam

The anglican church is one of many protestant denominations that interpret the bible in various ways.   Anglican Church, Protestant, Bible

1. Are you familiar with deuteronomy and numbers?   _____
2. Then jesus spoke and reminded his disciples of his obligation to god.

    _____

3. The veda is the body of hindu sacred writings.   _____
4. The hebrew word *adonai* is but one of the terms used by orthodox jews to refer to god.

    _____

5. Bach's *missa solemnis* is heard many times during the christmas season.

    _____

6. Do you believe in the coming of the messiah?   _____
7. Moses delivered the ten commandments to the children of israel.

    _____

8. He prayed to the almighty for relief from pain.   _____
9. The young woman addressed the virgin mary in prayer, seeking her intervention.

    _____

10. During ramadan all believers in islam fast from dawn until dusk.

    _____

Events, Eras, Prizes, Documents

The proper names of all wars, battles, historic events, treaties, documents, prizes, and important historical periods are capitalized. This rule is still another extension of the general rule governing capitalization of proper names. Proper names of wars, battles, and so on merit capitalization just as much as the names of people or companies.

The end of the Spanish Civil War saw the death of democracy in that country.

A civil war is the saddest of wars.

The Nobel Prize for Literature was won by Saul Bellow in 1976.

Those who lived through the Great Depression will never recover from its effects.

13. Capitalize all proper names in the following sentences.

> Rollin Kirby won the first of his several pulitzer prizes in 1922.   <u>Pulitzer Prizes</u>
>
> *Gone With the Wind* is one of the top movie money earners of all time.   <u>*Correct*</u>

1. Paul A. Samuelson, of the united states, won the nobel prize for economics in 1970 for his efforts to improve the level of scientific analysis in economic theory.

2. The north atlantic treaty, enacted on july 21, 1949, resulted in the establishment of the potent north atlantic treaty organization military forces.

3. The mason-dixon line is the boundary between pennsylvania and maryland.

4. A copy of the magna carta was presented to the american people on the occasion of the bicentennial year of the founding of the united states.

5. Pope John XXIII convoked two great meetings of the catholic church, the first vatican council and the second vatican council.

6. In 1936 the leaders of germany and italy organized the rome-berlin axis, later to be joined by japan.

7. The versailles treaty is said by some historians to have been an indirect cause of world war II.

8. In the casablanca conference prime minister churchill and president roosevelt agreed that they would seek an unconditional surrender of enemy forces.

9. The american civil war ended with surrender at appomattox by general lee.

10. Normans led by william the conqueror invaded england to fight the battle of hastings in 1066.

11. The middle ages extended from the late fifth century to about 1350, the period in european history between classical antiquity and the italian renaissance.

12. The statement of beliefs and doctrines of the lutherans, the augsburg confession, was drawn up by melanchthon and endorsed by the lutheran princes for presentation at the diet of augsburg in 1530.

13. An interregnum is the period between the end of a ruler's reign and the formal accession of a successor.

14. After an unbroken string of victories in state primary elections, gerald ford met his waterloo in 1976.

15. A truce signed on july 27, 1953, formally ended the korean war, which was fought by north korea and south korea with the assistance of other countries.

Titles

Civil and Military Titles

Military and civil titles are capitalized when they precede a name, indicate high rank, or are used as substitutes for the names of individuals.

Did you know that *Consul* Burton was in danger of losing his position at that point in his career? (Title preceding a name.)

The *Secretary of State* is generally the most important person in the administration of the country's foreign affairs. (Title of high rank. Notice that unimportant words that are part of a title are not capitalized. Unimportant words are generally considered to be articles and prepositions and conjunctions of fewer than five letters.)

After André was apprehended, the *Major* was kept captive until his trial. (Title used as substitute for the name of an individual: *Major John André.*)

The mortality rate for lieutenants in World War I was shockingly high. (No capital letter for *lieutenants*. The word does not precede a name, does not indicate high rank, is not used as a substitute for the name of an individual.)

14. Capitalize wherever appropriate in the following sentences.

A yeoman in the United States Navy generally performs clerical work.   *Correct*

The president entered the room precisely at noon to meet the prime minister.   President, Prime Minister

1. He was referred to as sir Winston Churchill in certain documents, as prime minister Churchill in others. _____

2. In later years the old civil servant wondered why he had not received recognition from the Queen. _____

3. Hollywood turned the story of sergeant York into a vehicle for Gary Cooper. _____

4. I have heard that professor Barnard is preparing a paper on the national objectives of our country. _____

5. Professors earn less than police sergeants in many sections of our state. _____

6. We wonder how president Bush will be able to fulfill promises he made as a candidate. _____

7. Two instructors and two assistant professors will be named by chancellor Emilio to study student complaints. _____

8. Can you imagine a person less qualified for appointment as the next ambassador to the court of st. james? _____

9. Most ambassadors are unqualified for the positions they hold. _____

10. The principal speaker at our next commencement will be university professor Morris L. Chaffee. _____

Academic Degrees

Capitalize all academic degrees and their abbreviations.

Many lawyers who hold the degree of Bachelor of Laws (LL.B.) would prefer to receive the degree Doctor of Law (J.D.), which is now common in most American law schools as the initial law degree.

She is one of the few people I know of who may write R.N. and M.D. after her name.

15. Capitalize where appropriate in the following sentences.

The j.d. degree is an abbreviation of the latin *juris doctor.*   J.D., Latin, *Juris Doctor*

Do you know that many universities will award honorary degrees in return for substantial financial contributions?   *Correct*

1. She received the degrees litt.b. and litt.d. within three years.

　　　　_____

2. The ph.d. degree is no longer a guarantee of employment.

　　　　_____

3. James Mellhorn, ph.d., will be appointed to the french department of middleford college next year.　　_____

4. After earning a d.d.s. degree, Tom spent the next forty years of his life probing jaws and cavities.　　_____

5. Few chemical engineers hold the d.ch.e. degree.　　_____

Books, Plays, and Periodicals

　　　Capitalize the first word and all important words in the title of a book, play, story, article, poem, musical work, journal, magazine, and newspaper. The only problem in this rule is definition of *all important words.* Important words are anything but short articles, prepositions, and conjunctions. Prepositions and conjunctions of five letters or more are considered important.

　　　The House of Seven Gables　　(*The* is the first word; *of* has fewer than five letters.)

　　　Much Ado About Nothing　　(*About* has five letters.)

　　　The Way of All Flesh, All's Well That Ends Well, For Whom the Bell Tolls, Long Day's Journey into Night, The Importance of Being Earnest, "*Recent Additions to the Morgan Library,*" "*Dover Beach,*" *How to Succeed in Business,* "*When the Red Red Robin Goes Bob Bob Bobbin' Along,*" *Statistical Abstracts, Journal of the National Association of Deans of Women, Playboy, Harper's,* Greenwich *Time,* St. Louis *Post-Dispatch.*

16.　　Capitalize wherever appropriate in the following sentences.

　　　Thomas Hardy's *desperate remedies* appeared in 1871.　　Desperate Remedies
　　　Few people today read George Meredith's first great novel, *the ordeal of richard feverel.*
　　　　The Ordeal of Richard Feverel

1. Many important stories by Hemingway first appeared in *collier's* and *the saturday evening post.*　　_____

2. *The saturday review of literature* had a long life under various names.

　　　_____

3. I love the vignettes of farm life that appear in *vermont life.*

　　　_____

4. Edgar Allan Poe's "the fall of the house of usher" has been reprinted in many anthologies.

5. Students chuckle over Chaucer's "the wife of bath's tale."

　　　_____

6. He tried unsuccessfully to place his article "women in the literature of the middle ages" in the *proceedings of the modern language association.*

　　　_____

7. Bob Dylan's songs were again praised highly in a recent issue of *rolling stone.*

　　　_____

8. High school students are introduced to the art of Thomas Hardy in *the mayor of caster-bridge.*　　_____

9. I have never seen a production of *two gentlemen of verona.*

　　　_____

10. A recent article in the *wall street journal,* entitled "prices of commodities and their effect on food prices," attracted little attention.

　　　_____

Chapter 10

Spelling

Despite many inconsistencies, English spelling to a large extent follows a pattern that enables most of us to spell most words in the same recognizable ways.

This chapter presents guidelines—spelling has no rules—and exercises to help you improve your spelling. If you work carefully through the chapter and sustain your interest in spelling, you will find considerable improvement in your grasp of this skill.

Double Letters

Doubling Consonants when Adding Suffixes

When adding a suffix beginning with a vowel to a word of one syllable that ends in a single consonant, double the final consonant if that consonant is preceded by a single vowel.

sit	sitting	
bat	batting	batted
pet	petting	petted

These words—*sit, bat, pet*—have only one syllable and end in a single consonant, *t*. The suffixes being added—*ing, ed*—begin with a vowel. *Sit, bat,* and *pet* have single vowels: *i, a,* and *e*. Because all the necessary conditions are present, we double the final consonant, *t*.

seat	seating	seated
beat	beating	beater
read	reading	reader

All these words—*seat, beat, read*—have double vowels. The final consonant is not doubled.

When adding a suffix beginning with a vowel to a word of more than one syllable in which the accent is on the final syllable, double a single final consonant that is preceded by a single vowel if the accent does not shift to another syllable.

prefer	preferred	preference
infer	inferred	inference

Both words—*prefer, infer*—have two syllables. They end in single consonants preceded by single vowels. The suffixes being added begin with a vowel: *ed* and *ence*. The final syllables are accented: **pre fér, in fér.** Adding *ed* does not cause the accent to shift: **pre férred, in férred.** All conditions have been met. The final consonant, the letter *r* in both words, is doubled.

Adding *ence*, however, causes the accents to shift: **pré fer ence, ín fer ence.** All conditions but one have been met. The final consonants are not doubled.

Now consider two other words, *repeat* and *unseat*.

repeat	repeating	repeated
unseat	unseating	unseated

No doubling, because the final syllables of *repeat* and *unseat* have double vowels.

Now consider *develop* and *deliver*.

develop   developing   developed
deliver   delivering   delivered

No doubling, because the accents in *develop* and *deliver* are not on the final syllables.
Finally, consider *entrap*.

entrap   entrapping   entrapped   entrapment

Do you see why *entrapping* and *entrapped* have double *p*'s? Right, they meet all requirements. But why does *entrapment* not have a double *p*? Right, the suffix added does not begin with a vowel.

1. Supply the missing forms in the following sentences.

They decided to go (trap + ing) this week.   <u>trapping</u>
They are fond of (tramp + ing) in the woods.   <u>tramping</u>

1. The boy (stab + ed) himself in the finger when carving the turkey. _____
2. If you are not careful, you will find yourself (slip + ing) on the icy sidewalk. _____
3. The local theater group will not be (appear + ing) in *Ghosts* this season. _____
4. They went (tear + ing) through the hallways, creating so much noise that classes were disturbed. _____
5. It is one thing to show (defer + ence); it is another to be servile. _____
6. The little boy and girl (pester + ed) their parents until they were given their allowances. _____
7. After many attempts to design a new bomber, the company (scrap + ed) its plans and turned to other projects. _____
8. Money was so tight last year that the young couple were constantly (scrap + ing). _____
9. The crime the man had (commit + ed) was so bloody that many in the courtroom expressed outrage. _____
10. To succeed in any major project, you must have a sense of (commit + ment) as well as the required talent. _____
11. After the two of us have (confer + ed), the entire committee will meet in a formal (confer + ence) and dispose of the matter. _____
12. I agree that we have made a good (begin + ing), but we must not stop now. _____
13. The river was (widen + ing) and (deepen + ing) slowly through the months of winter. _____
14. If you manage to get a (run + ing) start, you may be able to clear the obstacle. _____
15. (Bar + ing) circumstances beyond our control, we ought to be in town this Saturday for the (unveil + ing) of the statue. _____
16. They spent most of the day (sun + ing) themselves. _____
17. The bridge (span + ed) the river just outside town. _____
18. They have (control + ed) the unruly crowd for almost an hour and are rapidly becoming fatigued. _____

19.   With your (concur + ence) we will proceed to have the money (allot + ed) among the heirs.
_____

20.   Do you accuse me of giving him (prefer + ential) treatment? _____

Doubling Consonants when Adding Other Elements

When a word is formed by adding a prefix that ends in a consonant to a stem that begins with the same consonant, keep the double consonant.

com + mode = commode   dis + sent = dissent
con + note = connote   mis + spell = misspell

When a word is formed by joining a word that ends in a consonant with another word that begins with the same consonant, keep the double consonant.

book + keeper = bookkeeper   over + reach = overreach
can + not = cannot   over + ride = override

When a word is formed by adding a suffix that begins with a consonant to a stem that ends in the same consonant, keep the double consonant.

accidental + ly = accidentally   immoral + ly = immorally
cool + ly = coolly   judicial + ly = judicially

If you do not have a good grasp of prefixes, stems, and suffixes, these guidelines may not help you. Pronunciation is helpful if you have a good ear, but you will see from the next discussion that pronunciation is not an infallible guide.

Doubling Vowels

When a word is formed by adding a word that ends in silent *e* to a word that begins with *e*, drop the silent *e*.

where + ever = wherever   whose + ever = whosever

You can see that pronunciation is not a help. You may take consolation in the fact that few words are made in this way.

When a word is formed by adding a prefix that ends in a vowel to a stem that begins with the same vowel, keep the double vowel.

anti + inductive = anti-inductive   de + emphasize = de-emphasize
co + operate = cooperate   re + entry = reentry

Pronunciation helps in these words and in the many other words formed in this manner. You can easily hear the double vowel. Notice that the initial vowel is long, the second vowel short.

2.   Form words in the following list.

ac + com + modate =   _accommodate_
ag + gravate =   _aggravate_

1.   dis + sect =   _____
2.   bi + sect =   _____
3.   glow + worm = _____
4.   out + talk =   _____

5. pen + name = _____

6. who + so + ever = _____

7. drunken + ness = _____

8. bath + towel = _____

9. bath + house = _____

10. mean + ness = _____

11. mean + est = _____

12. former + ly = _____

13. formal + ly = _____

14. un + com + mon + ness = _____

15. com + mon + al + ity = _____

16. dis + appear + ance = _____

17. sum + mons = _____

18. beach + house = _____

19. il + literate = _____

20. over + rule = _____

21. over + react = _____

22. un + necessary = _____

23. re + gard + less = _____

24. ir + refutable = _____

25. mis + shaped = _____

26. cut + throat = _____

27. re + emphasize = _____

28. con + nect = _____

29. con + nubial = _____

30. co + in + cidental + ly = _____

Final Silent *e*

For most words ending in a silent *e*, drop the *e* when a suffix is added that begins with a vowel, and retain the *e* when a suffix is added that begins with a consonant.

slope	sloping	sloped
elope	eloping	eloped

Notice that the *e* has disappeared from *sloping* and *eloping*. When we added *ed* to make the past tense of these two verbs, the final *e* also disappeared. The guideline works for most words ending in silent *e*.

elope	elopement
amuse	amusement

Notice that the *e* remains in these words, because the suffix *ment* begins with a consonant. This guideline always works for words ending in silent *e*.

Now consider what happens with words such as *courage* and *salvage* when adding suffixes that begin with a vowel.

courage	courageous
salvage	salvageable

Notice that the *e* remains in these words even though the suffixes *ous* and *able* begin with vowels. This is one of the exceptions to the guideline for words ending in silent *e*. Read on.

For words ending in silent *e* preceded by a *g* or *c*, retain the *e* if the *g* or *c* remains soft when adding a suffix beginning with *a* or *o*.

service	serviceable
change	changeable
practice	practicable

The silent *e* at the end of *service* and *change* is preceded by a *c* in one case and a *g* in the other. The *c* and *g* in *serviceable* and *changeable* remain soft—they do not sound like the *c* in *cash* or the *g* in *gift*. The suffixes that we added begin with *a*. The silent *e* is retained. Why is the *e* in *practice* dropped from *practicable*? Because the *c* in *practicable* is hard.

advise	advisable
revise	revision

The silent *e* is dropped. In both *advise* and *revise* the *e* is preceded* by an *s*. Also, since the suffix added to *revise* begins with an *i*, the silent *e* must be deleted.

Lest you think the matter of the silent *e* is finished, examine the following exceptions to this guideline.

argue	argument	hoe	hoeing	singe	singeing
awe	awful	judge	judgment	true	truly
dye	dyeing	nine	ninth	whole	wholly

3.   Choose the correctly spelled words in the following sentences.

His (spitefulness, spitfulness) was too much for me to swallow.   ___spitefulness___

She considered her wedding ring (irreplacable, irreplaceable).   ___irreplaceable___

1.   They managed to make a (tracing, traceing) of the key and duplicate it in soap.
   _____

2.   By the time the final quarter opened, all our hopes were (hingeing, hinging) on the performance of a third-string quarterback.   _____

3.   The critics left the theater (singeing, singing) the score of the brilliant musical comedy.
   _____

4.   The vice president's behavior since leaving office was considered (outragous, outrageous) by his enemies.   _____

5.   We are (bracing, braceing) for a hard winter.   _____

6.   Does anyone remember the song "(Embracable, Embraceable) You"?
   _____

7.   That (likable, likeable) child is able to charm every teacher in the school.
   _____

8.   The weather is (changable, changeable) in spring.   _____

9.   My dishwasher is no longer (serviceable, servicable).   _____

10.   I will take the matter under (advisement, advisment).   _____

11.   Once the family money was dissipated, Emma found her entire world (collapsing, collapseing).   _____

12.   Disregarding the churning water of the river, they went (charging, chargeing) into the rapids.
   _____

13. We still admire the work of the English (Suffrageettes, Suffragettes) in pioneering women's rights. _____

14. To the dismay of the health authorities, the dryers were slowly (dying, dyeing) as a result of the lethal gas seeping into the factory. _____

15. Slow (dyeing, dying) produces faster colors than rapid (dyeing, dying). _____

16. Your rights are (impinging, impingeing) on mine. _____

17. The hair (singeing, singing) was badly done. _____

18. I particularly dislike the (vengeance, vengance) she showed in her dealings with the defeated candidate. _____

19. We think it is not too early to begin making final (arrangements, arrangments) for the burial. _____

20. When the farmer had finished his (hoing, hoeing), he went into the barn to feed the cattle. _____

i **Before** *e* **Except After** *c*

Who has not heard this jingle in one form or another?

> Use *i* before *e*
> Except after *c*
> Or when sounded as *a*
> As in *neighbor* or *sleigh*.

As with most spelling guidelines, there are exceptions to this old standard. In general, however, the guideline is a good one.

i Before e

achieve	fierce	priest	siege
belief	grief	relief	sieve
believe	grieve	relieve	thief
brief	mien	reprieve	tier
chief	niece	retrieve	wield
fief	piece	shield	yield
field	pierce	shriek	

Except after c

ceiling	conceive	deceive	receipt
conceit	deceit	perceive	receive

Or When Sounded as a

deign	freight	reign	weight
eight	heinous	rein	weighty
eighth	neigh	sleigh	
eighty	neighbor	vein	

Exceptions

In addition to comparatives such as *fancier* and *saucier,* and superlatives such as *fanciest* and *sauciest,* there are at least seven known exceptions to the *i* before *e* guideline.

financier	leisure	seize	weird
either	neither	sheik	

Notice that some of this last group of seven are pronounced in various ways. We are all familiar with the *eethur/Ithur*, *neethur/nIthur*, and *leezhur/lehzhur* disagreements. All three words are pronounced *ee* in American dictionaries as a first choice. The word *sheik* is pronounced *sheek* by speakers of English even though speakers of Arabic pronounce it *shake*.

If you want help in trying to overcome the obstacle of seven exceptions to the *i* before *e* guideline, you can learn a silly mnemonic;

Neither financier-sheik seized either weird leisure.

Derivative forms like *seizure* are also exceptions.

4. Choose the correctly spelled words in the following sentences.

The movie star (diegned, deigned) to grant the young reporter a personal interview.
____deigned____

Upon (receipt, reciept) of the telegram, she withdrew to her room and began to cry. ____receipt____

1. The eighth (freight, frieght) car that went by was loaded in an (unwieldy, unweildy) manner.
   _____

2. Each time we encounter that type of error in our computer, we become more and more convinced that (wierd, weird) forces are at work. _____

3. Imagine the (conciet, conceit) of the man who signed that (receipt, reciept).
   _____

4. A (brief, breif) (seige, siege) will have no effect on those (thieves, theives).
   _____

5. (Pierced, Peirced) ears are slowly going out of style again, to the (releif, relief) of millions of parents. _____

6. A (shriek, shreik) in the night brought fright to the (preists, priests).
   _____

7. Do you (believe, beleive) what they told you? _____

8. I am (relieved, releived) that the (cheif, chief) complaint of your (nieghbors, neighbors) has been satisfied. _____

9. Some (thieves, theives) look upon a strong bank vault as nothing more than a (seive, sieve).
   _____

10. A (riegn, reign) of fifty years is exceptional. _____

11. The physician tried in vain to find a healthy (vein, vien) in his patient's arm.
    _____

12. When you have finished planting that (field, feild), I am sure I can find another task for you.
    _____

13. A crime so (hienous, heinous) can frighten the entire (nieghborhood, neighborhood).
    _____

14. I do not wish to (decieve, deceive) you. _____

15. She was at her (fiercest, feircest) in her karate class. _____

16. We will have to (yeild, yield) on some points or give up everything to your (neice, niece).
    _____

17. I (beleive, believe) that a (breif, brief) conference will serve to convince most of us.
    _____

18.   How much can one person (achieve, acheive) in a single life?

_____

19.   I feel as though I am walking across the (ceiling, cieling).

_____

20.   (Seize, Sieze) your opportunity or (grieve, greive) forever.

_____

Words Ending in _y_

Nouns

To form the plural of a noun ending in _y_, add an _s_ if the _y_ is preceded by a vowel.
To form the plural of a noun ending in _y_, drop the _y_ and add _ies_ if the _y_ is preceded by a consonant.

This guideline is straightforward, and the exceptions are all proper names. To form the plural of a proper name ending in _y_, add an _s_ no matter how the rest of the name is spelled.

y _Preceded by Vowel_

| valley | valleys | birthday | birthdays |
| boy | boys | way | ways |

y _Preceded by Consonant_

| wallaby | wallabies | walky-talky | walky-talkies |
| army | armies | antibody | antibodies |

Names Ending in **y**

| Gary | Garys | May | Mays |
| Peabody | Peabodys | Joy | Joys |

5.   Choose the correctly spelled words in the following sentences.

She kept the child's (toys, toies) in the attic.   ___toys___

Do you really have two (libraries, librarys) in your town?   ___libraries___

1.   The (Goodbodys, Goodbodies) are the new family on our street.

_____

2.   Both her sons are (attorneys, attornies).   _____

3.   The legislature proposed the abolition of (countys, counties) throughout the state.

_____

4.   When they were in Paris, they loved to walk along the (quays, quaies).

_____

5.   I love to talk with the (barflies, barflys) at our local tavern.   _____

6.   As long as your country employs (spys, spies), it will also employ (counterspys, counter-spies).   _____

7.   Destroyers often served as (convoys, convoies) during World War II.

_____

8.   The (Terries, Terrys) invited us to dinner the night we moved into our apartment.

_____

9. Two (sulkys, sulkies) touched during the race and spilled their drivers.
_____

10. That Christmas was noteworthy for the number and quality of the (partys, parties) we attended.
_____

Verbs

To form the third person singular of a verb ending in *y*, add an *s* if the *y* is preceded by a vowel.

To form the third person singular of a verb ending in *y*, drop the *y* and add *ies* if the *y* is preceded by a consonant.

say	says	worry	worries
pay	pays	tarry	tarries
annoy	annoys	bury	buries
convey	conveys	glory	glories

Adjectives

To form the comparative of an adjective ending in *y* and preceded by a vowel, add *er*. To form the superlative of an adjective ending in *y* and preceded by a vowel, add *est*.

To form the comparative of an adjective ending in *y* and preceded by a consonant, drop the *y* and add *ier*. To form the superlative of an adjective ending in *y* and preceded by a consonant, drop the *y* and add *iest*.

Comparatives and Superlatives

gay	gayer	gayest	happy	happier	happiest
coy	coyer	coyest	angry	angrier	angriest

Notice that a final *y* often changes to *i* when adding suffixes.

gay	gaiety	(an adjective becomes a noun)
bounty	bountiful	(a noun becomes an adjective)
tarry	tarrier	(a verb becomes a noun)
witty	wittily	(an adjective becomes an adverb)

6. Choose the correctly spelled words in the following sentences.

His conversation usually (annoys, annoies) his wife.   annoys

I enjoy watching a mouse as it (scurrys, scurries) along looking for food.
scurries

1. Who is (sorryer, sorrier) than the person who has missed an opportunity because he was unprepared to take advantage of it? _____

2. The (wispiness, wispyness) of the little creature made it the object of concern.
_____

3. She is paid well to comment (dayly, daily) on the news of the world.
_____

4. During an examination by Dr. Olsen, you quickly find that her calm manner (allays, allaies) your fears. _____

5. Your furniture is even (tawdrier, tawdryer) than mine. _____

6. My eyes are much (drier, dryer) than yours. _____

7. Your (happyness, happiness) means a great deal to me. _____

8. (Cattyness, Cattiness) is a trait that you should discourage.

    _____

9. I never have met a (slyer, slier) person. _____

10. World War I soldiers were even (grimyer, grimier) than G.I. Joe of World War II.

    _____

Words Ending in *o*

Words ending in *o* form their plurals sometimes by adding *s*, sometimes *es*, and sometimes either *s* or *es*.

Making plurals of uncommon words ending in *o* usually involves consulting a dictionary. Words in common use become second nature. Practice with less common words eventually will fix them in your memory.

Plurals in **os**

You can be almost certain that musical terms ending in *o* require only addition of *s* to form the plural, but an ever-increasing number of other *o* words also take *s* to form their plurals.

alto, altos	Eskimo, Eskimos	pronunciamento, pronunciamentos
avocado, avocados	Filipino, Filipinos	radio, radios
banjo, banjos	folio, folios	ratio, ratios
barrio, barrios	impetigo, impetigos	silo, silos
basso, bassos	lanugo, lanugos	soprano, sopranos
canto, cantos	neutrino, neutrinos	studio, studios
cameo, cameos	patio, patios	tremolo, tremolos
dynamo, dynamos	piano, pianos	

Plurals in **oes**

echo, echoes	nonhero, nonheroes	tornado, tornadoes
hero, heroes	potato, potatoes	torpedo, torpedoes
mosquito, mosquitoes	tomato, tomatoes	veto, vetoes
mulatto, mulattoes		

Plurals in **os** and **oes**

Some words have both plural forms. In the following list the more common plural form is given first.

buffalo, buffaloes, buffalos	hobo, hoboes, hobos
cargo, cargoes, cargos	motto, mottoes, mottos
desperado, desperadoes, desperados	no, noes, nos
flamingo, flamingos, flamingoes	virago, viragoes, viragos
ghetto, ghettos, ghettoes	volcano, volcanoes, volcanos
halo, halos, haloes	zero, zeros, zeroes

7. Supply the plural forms of the italicized words in the following sentences.

There were two *soprano* in our singing group.   sopranos

I do not want a salad with so few *tomato*.   tomatoes

1. Do you know how many *tornado* we experienced that year?

    _____

2. Susan asked for *avocado* in her salad. _____

3. He and his father specialized in building *patio*. _____

4. More *radio* are sold each year than ever before. _____

5. Prosperous farmers build several *silo*. _____

6. Damn the *torpedo*! _____

7. The *echo* in that canyon attract many visitors. _____

8. At one time they operated several *studio*. _____

9. The *barrio* in our city are fun to visit. _____

10. How many *potato* shall I peel for dinner? _____

Foreign Plurals

Many foreign words that have been taken into English retain their spelling in the plural as well as in the singular. The dictionary is your best guide when dealing with foreign words, but the following list will give you some of the more common words and their plurals. Wherever anglicized plurals are also in use, these are given too. As particular words of foreign derivation are used more and more, they tend to be given English plurals, for example, *memorandums* instead of *memoranda*. Certain foreign plural forms are so commonly seen that English plurals will never replace them, for example, *crises* and *axes*. Another factor preventing adoption of English plural forms for these words and others like them is the awkwardness of some sounds. Consider *crisises* and *axises*.

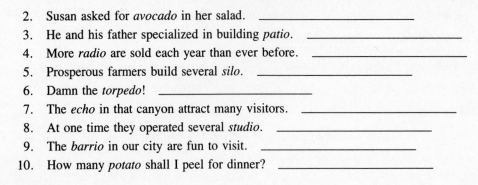

addendum, addenda, addendums   larva, larvae
alumna, alumnae   libretto, librettos, libretti
alumnus, alumni   locus, loci
ameba, amebas, amebae   matrix, matrixes, matrices
analysis, analyses   medium, media, mediums
antenna, antennas, antennae   memorandum, memorandums, memoranda
apparatus, apparatus, apparatuses moratorium, moratoriums, moratoria
appendix, appendixes, appendices neurosis, neuroses
automaton, automatons, automata   nucleus, nuclei, nucleuses
axis, axes   oasis, oases
bacillus, bacilli   opus, opuses, opera
basis, bases   ovum, ova
beau, beaus, beaux   parenthesis, parentheses
cactus, cactuses, cacti   phenomenon, phenomena, phenomenons
chateau, chateaus, chateaux   psychosis, psychoses
cherub, cherubs, cherubim   radius, radii, radiuses
crisis, crises   sanatorium, sanatoriums, sanatoria
criterion, criteria   species, species
curriculum, curricula, curriculums stadium, stadiums, stadia
datum, data   stimulus, stimuli
diagnosis, diagnoses   stratum, strata, stratums
erratum, errata   syllabus, syllabi, syllabuses
focus, focuses, foci   symposium, symposiums, symposia
formula, formulas, formulae   synopsis, synopses
fungus, fungi, funguses   synthesis, syntheses
gladiolus, gladioluses, gladioli thesis, theses
hypothesis, hypotheses   vertebra, vertebrae, vertebras
index, indexes, indices   vortex, vortices, vortexes

8. Supply the singular form for the following plural words.

analyses   <u>analysis</u>

memoranda   <u>memorandum</u>

1. media _____	6. curricula _____
2. alumni _____	7. syntheses _____
3. indices _____	8. errata _____
4. criteria _____	9. parentheses _____
5. automatons _____	10. ova _____

Silent Letters

Just because a letter is not heard in pronouncing a word is no reason to omit it. The following are examples of words that are difficult to spell because one or more letters are not pronounced. Pay particular attention to them.

acknowledge	February*	knife	psychology
aisle	ghetto	knight	psychotherapy
answer	ghost	knot	raspberry
balm	ghoul	know	salmon
condemn	gnat	knowledge	scene
could	gneiss	laboratory	schism
courtesy	gnome	listen	solemn
debt	gnomic	mnemonic	subtle
disciple	gnostic	mortgage	temperament
doubt	handsome	muscle	temperature
doubtful	hymn	often	undoubtedly
doubtless	indict	pneumatic	Wednesday
fascinate	island	pneumonia	yacht

* Sometimes pronounced Feb-yoo-eh-ree

9. Select the correctly spelled words in the following list.

yachting/yahting   <u>yachting</u>

gostly/ghostly   <u>ghostly</u>

1. costly/cohstly _____
2. ghoulish/goulish _____
3. goalie/ghoalie _____
4. bahmy/balmy _____
5. condemnation/condemation _____
6. dissiplinary/disciplinary _____
7. goulash/ghoulash _____
8. subtelty/subtlety _____
9. doutless/doubtless _____
10. gout/ghout _____
11. detridden/debt-ridden _____
12. nowledge/knowledge _____
13. solennity/solemnity _____
14. temperment/temperament _____
15. February/Febuary _____
16. neumonia/pneumonia _____

17. labratory/laboratory _____

18. mussle/muscle _____

19. mussle/mussel _____

20. pyschological/psychological _____

Commonly Confused Words

Certain spelling errors are due as much to carelessness as to ignorance. Be alert to the following sound-alikes and look-alikes. They are all correctly spelled. Learn their meanings so you call tell them apart.

accept, except	cast, caste	extant, extent
access, excess	cell, sell	faint, feint
adapt, adopt	censor, censer, censure	fair, fare
advice, advise	cent, scent, sent	fate, fete
affect, effect	cereal, serial	flautist, flouter
air, heir	choose, chose, chosen	flea, flee
aisle, isle	chord, cord	flew, flue
aloud, allowed	cite, sight, site	flour, flower
allude, elude	click, clique	for, fore, four
allusion, illusion	cloths, clothes	formally, formerly
already, all ready	coarse, course	forth, fourth
altar, alter	colonel, kernel	foul, fowl
altogether, all together	complement, compliment	gait, gate
always, all ways	counsel, council, consul	gamble, gambol
anecdote, antidote	creak, creek	garret, garrot
angel, angle	cue, queue	gild, guild
arc, arch	currant, current	gorilla, guerilla
ascend, ascent, assent	cymbal, symbol	grate, great
assistance, assistants	dairy, diary	gray, grey
bail, bale	days, daze	grisly, grizzly
ball, bawl	dear, deer	groan, grown
band, banned	decent, descent, dissent	hail, hale
bare, bear	desert, dessert	hair, hare
base, bass	desperate, disparate	hall, haul
beach, beech	device, devise	hart, heart
beat, beet	dew, do, due	heal, heel
beau, bow	die, dye	hear, here
bell, belle	discreet, discrete	heard, herd
berry, bury	done, dun	heir, air
berth, birth	doughy, doughty	him, hymn
beside, besides	dual, duel	hoar, whore
blew, blue	dudgeon, dungeon	hole, whole
boar, bore	dyeing, dying	holy, wholly
board, bored	earn, urn	hoping, hopping
boarder, border	earnest, Ernest	human, humane
born, borne	eerie, eyrie	idle, idol
bough, bow	elicit, illicit	illicit, elicit
brake, break	elude, allude	illusion, allusion
bread, bred	emanate, eminent, imminent	imminent, eminent, emanate
breath, breathe	envelop, envelope	in, inn
bridal, bridle	ever, every	its, it's
but, butt	excess, access	Jews, juice
buy, by	except, accept	kernel, colonel

knead, need
knight, night
knot, not
know, no
known, none, nun
lain, lane
later, latter, ladder
lead, led
lessen, lesson
lie, lye
load, lode
loan, lone
local, locale
loose, lose
made, maid
mail, male
main, mane
manner, manor
marital, martial
maybe, may be
meant, ment (a suffix)
meat, meet
medal, meddle, metal
moral, morale
muscle, mussel
naval, navel
nay, neigh
need, knead
night, knight
nil, null
not, knot
none, nun
ordinance, ordnance
pail, pale
pain, pane
pair, pare, pear
passed, past
patience, patients
pause, paws
peace, piece
peak, pique
peal, peel
pear, peer, pier
pearl, purl
pedal, peddle
peer, pier, pear
personal, personnel

physics, psychics
plain, plane
porpoise, purpose
pray, prey
pride, pried
principal, principle
prophecy, prophesy
propose, purpose, porpoise
queue, cue
quiet, quite
rain, reign, rein
raise, rays, raze
rap, wrap
read, red
real, reel
right, rite, wright, write
road, rode, rowed
role, roll
root, route
rote, wrote
rye, wry
sail, sale
scene, seen
scent, sent, cent
sea, see
seam, seem
sell, cell
sense, since
serial, cereal
serf, surf
serge, surge
sew, so, sow
shear, sheer
shone, shown
sight, site, cite
sign, sine
slay, sleigh
sleight, slight
soar, sore
soared, sword
sole, soul
some, sum
son, sun
staid, stayed
stair, stare
stake, steak
stationary, stationery

statue, stature, statute
steal, steel
step, steppe
stile, style
straight, strait
symbol, cymbal
tail, tale
taught, taut
team, teem
tear, tier
than, then
their, there, they're
tied, tide
thorough, through
though, thought
threw, through
throne, thrown
tide, tied
toe, tow
to, too, two
trail, trial
urn, earn
vain, vane, vein
vale, veil
wail, whale
waist, waste
wait, weight
waive, wave
ware, wear, where
way, weigh
weak, week
weather, whether
were, where, whir
wet, whet
which, witch
while, wile
whine, wine
whole, hole
wholly, holy
whore, hoar
who's, whose
wrap, rap
wright, write, right, rite
wrote, rote
wry, rye
yoke, yolk
your, you're

10. Choose the correctly spelled words in the following sentences.

I tried to find out (where, ware) I could buy Delft (where, ware) inexpensively.
<u>where, ware</u>

The horse was (tide, tied) to a post and left for (days, daze).   <u>tied, days</u>

1. Are (there, they're) (to, too) many people (here, hear)? _____

2. My (personnel, personal) preference should not be considered in your deliberations.
    _____

3. The new stadium grandstand has three (tiers, tears). _____

4. The (stationery, stationary) store will open next week with a full supply of office equipment.
    _____

5. The physician's (weighting, waiting) room was filled with (overwait, overweight) people.
    _____

6. Who can be bold enough to (prophecy, prophesy) the future?
    _____

7. We (pride, pried) the old (boards, boreds) (loose, lose) with our fingers and then went (upstairs,
    upstares) to find a supply of nails.
    _____

8. He made a (rye, wry) face when we asked him what his (principal, principle) complaint was.
    _____

9. I feel a sense of loss whenever I realize once again that the (local, locale) of O. Henry's best
    stories is forever gone. _____

10. (Their, They're) (morale, moral) was never lower. _____

11. (Mussel, Muscle) fishermen must have good (mussels, muscles) to lift the heavy bags of
    shellfish. _____

12. How many times must you (need, knead) the dough when you bake (rye, wry) bread?
    _____

13. (Maybe, May be) you ought to hurry more if you think you (maybe, may be) late.
    _____

14. We were unable to secure a (loan, lone) at the (local, locale) bank.
    _____

15. That is (holy, wholly) your affair. _____

16. Do you believe (its, it's) time for a change?_____

17. You spend (to, too, two) much time (hoping, hopping) about from one unfinished task to the
    next. _____

18. She was recognized as an (imminent, eminent) researcher in her field of specialization.
    _____

19. After a meal like that one, who (kneaded, needed) (dessert, desert)?
    _____

20. A (descent, decent) night's sleep was all they wanted. _____

21. (There, Their) is no room for (descent, dissent) in that organization.
    _____

22. Their (disparate, desperate) points of view meant that they were forever irreconcilable.
    _____

23. Psychologists are now suggesting that (dual, duel) custody of children after divorce may not be
    the worst possible decision. _____

24. An (excess, access) of money is never a problem in most marriages.
    _____

25. They were unable to gain (excess, access) to jobs during Reagan's tenure in the White House.
    _____

26. The boxer (feinted, fainted) several times in succession and then (threw, through) a knockout
    punch. _____

27. They kept their prisoners in a (dudgeon, dungeon) far below the castle, where (their, there) cries were never heard. _____

28. He was fond of (allusions, illusions) so literary that most of his audience understood little of what he said. _____

29. (Accept, Except) for his own vote, Jules was the unanimous choice of the members. _____

30. Nothing you can say will (affect, effect) the outcome of the election. _____

31. They were (already, all ready) so far behind the others that they could not catch up. _____

32. She was (altogether, all together) indifferent to the (way, weigh) we felt about her husband.

33. What we need is someone courageous to come to the (four, fore) and help us find a means of climbing out of our depression. _____

34. I particularly like the way she prepares (foul, fowl). _____

35. What was (formerly, formally) a grand and colorful garden now is a disorderly patch of weeds. _____

36. The (flue, flew) at our house is in (desperate, disparate) need of repair. _____

37. Few original marble (statutes, statues) of that period are (extant, extent). _____

38. (Accept, Except) our thanks for the marvelous dinner you made. _____

39. The community does not have the power to pass (its, it's) own (ordnances, ordinances). _____

40. Some experts feel that (naval, navel) forces are no longer of value in today's world. _____

41. The old man will soon (breath, breathe) his last, I fear. _____

42. She was a real (bore, boar) as a lecturer as far as her students were concerned. _____

43. I enjoy (beats, beets) when they are prepared without vinegar. _____

44. Local libraries (band, banned) Vonnegut's books for a time. _____

45. My mother was inordinately fond of telling the same old (anecdotes, antidotes) again and again. _____

46. You will have to learn to do his (biding, bidding) if you expect to move ahead in that department. _____

47. The (bridle, bridal) we bought for Nell was far too small. _____

48. The foal we (bred, bread) last winter will be a great champion. _____

49. I am tired of being the (but, butt) of all your jokes. _____

50. Do they still (garret, garrot) people on the streets of your city? _____

51. I would gladly make a journey of many miles for succulent (fare, fair) of that kind. _____

52. He was known everywhere for his rambling (gate, gait) and drawling speech.
    _____

53. A (gorilla, guerrilla) war is difficult to win with conventional forces.
    _____

54. The orchestra was not responding to (queues, cues) from the conductor.
    _____

55. I like fresh (currants, currents) after turkey, don't you?
    _____

56. He owned nothing but the (clothes, cloths) he wore. _____

57. Do you remember the (serials, cereals) we saw each Saturday at the motion picture houses?
    _____

58. I need a tie that will (complement, compliment) my new suit.
    _____

59. I find him (course, coarse) of speech and unacceptable. _____

60. If you (cite, site) articles in your paper, you must include them in your bibliography.
    _____

61. They usually maintain a (discreet, discrete) silence.
    _____

62. We (sighted, sited) many (dear, deer) during the hunting season but chose not to fire our guns. _____

63. The gambler picked up a single (die, dye) and (threw, through) it to the floor.
    _____

64. If you can (devise, device) a new method, be certain to tell us at once.
    _____

65. They stood (for, fore) good government above all. _____

66. The fox managed to (allude, elude) the hunters' dogs. _____

67. She wrote daily in her (diary, dairy), taking care to hide the volume from her family.
    _____

68. Our (current, currant) sales record is better than last year's.
    _____

69. The musicians had every percussion instrument (accept, except) (symbols, cymbals).
    _____

70. The mugger had a bottle of (lye, lie) in his pocket when he was arrested.
    _____

71. Can you (elicit, illicit) any response from the drowning swimmer?
    _____

72. She was (hale, hail) into her ninetieth year. _____

73. The House of Representatives seldom (censures, censors) its own members, no matter how grievous the proven misconduct. _____

74. The glider (sword, soared) far above the hills, taking full advantage of thermal updrafts.
    _____

75. I (propose, purpose) that no one run for office until the duties and responsibilities of the office are explained. _____

76. She (piered, peered) into the darkness. _____

77. Robin Hood (preyed, prayed) on the rich to give to the poor.
    _____

78. The (quiet, quite) was (quite, quiet) a bit (to, too) much for them (to, too) take.
    _____

79. Her (role, roll) in the crime was never clearly understood.
   _____

80. The clerk (rapped, wrapped) the parcel and (maled, mailed) it for his customer.
   _____

81. He learned to spell by (wrote, rote). _____

82. The cube (root, route) is often a small number. _____

83. They decided to take the shortest (root, route) home from the game so that they would not be late for dinner. _____

84. Thieves made a big (hall, haul) last night at the airport.
   _____

85. The cat sat licking (its, it's) (paws, pause). _____

86. In a fit of (peak, pique) the young boy (through, threw) away the chance he had been waiting for. _____

87. Many towns pass (statues, statutes) that do less for them (than, then) they anticipate.
   _____

88. We enjoy a (sleight, slight) advantage over our opponents.
   _____

89. There was much at (steak, stake) in the election. _____

90. That house is no longer for (sail, sale). _____

91. Nerves of (steal, steel) are needed. _____

92. He (peddled, pedaled) home on his bicycle as quickly as he could.
   _____

93. My grandmother spent much of her last years (sewing, sowing) in her bedroom.
   _____

94. The (scene, seen) was unforgettable. _____

95. We consider that (site, sight) perfect for the home we want to build.
   _____

96. The excavation (sight, site) was so rocky that we had to call in experts in blasting.
   _____

97. He thought that the sun (shone, shown) exceptionally brightly that day.
   _____

98. A (staid, stayed) person will not enjoy working in our office.
   _____

99. His (whiles, wiles) proved to be more than we could take.
   _____

100. Calculus and (plain, plane) geometry were my most difficult (coarses, courses) in high school.

Miscellaneous Guidelines

Some words are so peculiar that the dictionary is your best bet until you lean them by rote.

Verbs Ending in c

A few English verbs end in *c*. When adding a suffix that begins with *e*, *i*, or *y*, a *k* is needed after the *c*. Addition of the *k* ensures that the *c* will be hard (pronounced *k* rather than *s*).

frolic, frolicked, frolicking, frolicker

mimic, mimicked, mimicking

panic, panicked, panicking, panicky

picnic, picnicked, picnicking, picknicker

traffic, trafficked, trafficking, trafficker

Verbs Ending in **sede, ceed,** *and* **cede**

English has only one word that ends in *sede*, a few in *ceed*, many in *cede*.

supersede

exceed, proceed, succeed

accede, antecede, cede, concede, intercede, precede, recede, secede

able *Versus* **ible**

The suffixes *able* and *ible* are found in many words that must be learned one by one.

attainable, unattainable	manageable, unmanageable
blamable, unblamable	marriageable, unmarriageable
changeable, unchangeable	measurable, immeasurable
chargeable, unchargeable	movable, immovable
comparable, incomparable	mutable, immutable
consolable, inconsolable	navigable, unnavigable
curable, uncurable	peaceable
damageable, undamageable	placeable, unplaceable
dispensable, indispensable	practicable, impracticable
enforceable, unenforceable	provable, unprovable
formidable, unformidable	replaceable, irreplaceable
imaginable, unimaginable	serviceable, unserviceable
lovable, unlovable	traceable, untraceable

There are fewer *ible* words even though the following list is longer than the previous list.

accessible, inaccessible	indelible
admissible, inadmissible	intelligible, unintelligible
audible, inaudible	invincible
compatible, incompatible	legible, illegible
contemptible	perceptible, imperceptible
controvertible, incontrovertible	permissible, impermissible
convertible, unconvertible	plausible, implausible
credible, incredible	possible, impossible
defensible, indefensible	reprehensible, unreprehensible
discernible, indiscernible	responsible, irresponsible
eligible, ineligible	sensible, unsensible, insensible
feasible, infeasible	susceptible, unsusceptible
flexible, inflexible	tangible, intangible
forcible	terrible
horrible	visible, invisible

11. Choose the correctly spelled words in the following sentences.

He was the most notorious drug (trafficker, trafficer) in our neighborhood.   <u>trafficker</u>

Sophomores (precede, preceed) freshmen in academic processions and (succeed, succede) juniors.   <u>precede, succeed</u>

1. We resented her (mimicing, mimicking) the motions of the physically handicapped teacher.

   _____

2. You will soon (exceed, excede) your authority, and I find that (inadmissable, inadmissible).

   _____

3. She was a (formidible, formidable) opponent in debate and an (incomparable, incomparible) public speaker. _____

4. I find his behavior (contemptible, contemptable) and want him dismissed as soon as (practicible, practicable). _____

5. We hope that she will come (peacibly, peaceably). _____

6. They were glad they had not (panicked, paniced) during the emergency. _____

7. The new orders are intended to (supercede, supersede) the old ones. _____

8. Her hair is (unchangeable, unchangible, unchangable) for two days after she has it set. _____

9. I cannot (accede, acceed) to your demands. _____

10. I find her story (incredable, incredible). _____

11. By keeping her voice almost (inaudible, inaudable), she is able to say almost anything she wants to her husband without being overheard. _____

12. I thought you told me the goods were (undamagable, undamageable, undamagible). _____

13. I believe her progress will prove (measurable, measurible). _____

14. She is not a (lovable, loveable, lovible) person. _____

15. Charles would be an (incomparably, incomparibly) better supervisor than the person you now have in the position. _____

PRACTICE LIST

The following list contains the most commonly misspelled words in English.

absence	accuser	administer	aggressive
absent	accustom	administration	agitation
absolutely	achievement	administrative	airplane
abundant	acknowledge	admission	aisle
abutting	acknowledgment	admittance	allay
academic	acquaint	adolescent	alleviate
academically	acquaintance	advantage	alley
academy	acquire	advantageous	alleys
accept	acquisition	advertisement	allies
acceptability	acre	advertising	all right
acceptable	across	advice	all together
acceptance	activity	advise	allude
accepting	actual	adviser	allusion
accommodate	actuality	aeroplane	ally
accommodating	actually	affect	already
accompanied	additional	affectionately	altar
accompaniment	additionally	affirmative	alter
accompany	address	afraid	altogether
accomplish	adequately	against	amateur
accuracy	adjournment	aggravate	ambulance
accurate	adjustment	aggregate	ambulatory

amendment	assistants	beneficial	carry
among	assured	benefit	carrying
amount	atheist	benefited	castle
analysis	athlete	berth	catastrophe
analyze	athletic	bicycle	category
ancient	attack	bidding	caucus
announce	attempt	bigger	cavalry
announcement	attendance	birth	ceases
announcing	attendants	biscuit	ceiling
annually	attorney	boring	cellar
another	audience	born	cemetery
anticipate	author	borne	censer
antique	authoritative	boundary	censor
anxious	authority	breadth	censure
apologetically	authorize	breakfast	censurious
apologies	auxiliary	breath	century
apologize	availability	breathe	certainly
apology	available	bridal	challenge
apostrophe	avalanche	bridle	chancel
apparatus	average	brief	chancellor
apparently	aviator	brilliant	change
appeal	awfully	Britain	changeable
appearance		Briton	changing
appetite	bachelor	bruise	chapel
applies	baggage	budget	characteristic
apply	banana	buoy	characterize
appointment	bankruptcy	buoyant	charity
appreciate	banquet	bureau	chauffeur
approaches	bar	burglar	chief
appropriate	barbarous	burglaries	chieftain
approximate	bare	burglarize	children
architecture	bargain	business	chimney
arctic	baring	busy	choice
areas	barrel		cholera
argue	barring	cabbage	choose
argument	basement	Caesar	choosing
arise	basic	cafeteria	chose
arising	basically	calendar	Christian
arouse	basis	campaign	cigarette
arousing	beautifully	candidacy	Cincinnati
arrangement	beautify	candidate	circle
arrival	becoming	canvas	circular
arrive	before	canvass	cite
article	began	capability	civil
artistic	beggar	capable	client
artistically	begin	capital	climate
artistry	beginning	capitalism	clothes
ascend	behavior	capitol	cloths
ascendant	belief	captain	coarse
ascent	believe	career	coherence
assassin	believing	carefully	collar
assent	beneficence	carelessness	colonel
assistance	beneficent	carried	color

column
comfortable
comfortably
coming
comma
commence
commencement
commerce
commercial
commission
commit
commitment
committed
committee
committing
communal
communist
community
companies
comparative
compare
comparison
compatible
compel
compelled
compete
competitive
competitor
complement
complete
complexion
compliment
compulsion
concede
conceivable
conceive
concentrate
conception
condemn
condemnation
condescend
confer
conference
conferred
conferring
confidence
confident
confidential
confidently
congressional
Connecticut
connotation
connote

conquer
conqueror
conscience
conscientious
conscious
consequence
consequently
considerable
considerably
consist
consistency
consistent
conspicuous
contemporary
contempt
contemptible
contemptuous
continual
continuous
contribution
control
controlling
controversial
controversy
convenience
cool
coolie
coolly
cooly
cooperate
corollary
coronary
corps
corpse
correlate
counterfeit
country
county
course
courteous
courtesy
cousin
crazy
create
credible
creditable
creditor
credulous
criminal
crisis
criticism
criticize
cruel

cruelly
cruelty
cubic
cupola
curiosity
curious
currant
current
curriculum
curtain
curtsy
custard
customary
customer
cylinder
cylindrical
cynosure

dairy
damage
dangerous
deal
dealer
dealt
debauch
debouch
debris
debt
deceit
deceive
decent
decentralize
deception
decide
decision
default
defendant
defense
defer
deference
deferral
deferred
define
definitely
definition
deity
delegate
deliberately
deliver
dependant
dependent
depth
deputy

descend
descendant
descent
describe
description
desert
desirability
desirable
desire
desirous
despair
despatch
desperation
despicable
despite
dessert
destruction
detriment
devaluate
devastate
develop
developed
development
device
devise
diary
die
different
difficult
dilemma
diligent
dining
dinning
dirigible
disagreeable
disappear
disappearance
disappoint
disapprove
disaster
disastrous
disciple
disciplinary
discipline
discriminate
discriminatory
disease
disgust
disillusion
dispatch
disposal
dissatisfied
dissent

dissimilar	emphatic	experience	gaiety
dissipate	empirical	experiment	gallant
divinity	employee	explanation	garage
division	encouragement	extraordinarily	gasoline
doesn't	endeavor	extraordinary	general
dominant	enjoyment	extravagant	generally
dominate	enlightenment	extremely	generate
dormitory	enough		generation
dough	enterprise	facility	genius
dropped	entertain	fallacious	gilt
due	entirely	fallacy	goddess
dully	entrance	familiar	government
duly	envelop	familiarity	governor
duped	envelope	fantasy	gradually
during	environment	fascinate	grammar
dye	equal	fashion	grammatically
dyeing	equality	favorable	grieve
dying	equally	favorite	grievous
	equip	February	grocery
eager	equipment	federal	group
earnest	equipped	federated	guarantee
easily	escapade	feminine	guardian
economical	especially	fictitious	guidance
economically	everything	filial	guilt
economics	evidently	Filipino	gymnasium
ecstasy	exactly	finally	
edge	exactness	financial	handkerchief
edgy	exaggerate	financier	handled
editor	exaggeration	finial	handsome
editorial	excavation	folios	happened
effect	exceed	forehead	happiness
efficiency	excellence	foreign	headache
efficient	excellent	forewarn	health
egress	except	foreword	hear
eight	exceptionally	forgive	heard
eighth	excessive	formally	heavily
eighty	excitable	formerly	height
electoral	excitement	forth	herald
electrical	exclusively	fortunate	herd
elicit	excursion	forty	here
eligible	executive	forward	heroes
eliminate	exercise	fourth	heroic
elude	exhaust	franchise	heroin
emanate	exhaustive	fraternally	heroine
embarrass	exhibit	fraternity	hinder
embassies	exhibition	frequently	hindrance
embassy	existence	friendliness	holly
emigrant	existent	friendship	holy
emigrate	exorcise	frontage	honorable
eminent	exorcism	fulfill	hop
emperor	expedite	fulfillment	hope
emphasis	expedition	fundamental	hopeful
emphasize	expense	further	hopeless

hoping	influence	justify	lose
hopping	influential		losing
horizon	ingenious	kindergarten	loss
hose	ingenuity	knight	lovable
hosiery	ingenuous	knowledge	luncheon
hospital	ingredient	kowtow	lynch
hospitalization	inhabitant		
humor	initiative	laboratory	machination
humorist	injunction	laborer	machinery
humorous	innocence	laborious	magazine
hundred	innocent	laid	magnificence
hundredth	inquire	language	magnificent
hunger	inquiry	larynx	maintain
hungrily	insistent	later	maintenance
hypnotism	installment	latter	manage
hypnotize	instance	launch	management
hypocrisy	insurance	lawyer	maneuver
hypocrite	intellect	leather	manufacture
	intellectual	led	marine
icicle	intelligence	legacy	marriage
idea	intelligent	legend	marriageable
ideally	intentionally	legible	Massachusetts
ignorance	interest	legitimate	mater
illegal	interference	leisure	material
illicit	interior	lengthen	mathematics
illusion	interlocutor	level	matter
illusory	interpretation	leveled	may be
illustrate	interruption	liberally	maybe
image	intimate	library	meanness
imaginary	introducing	license	meant
imagine	inveigle	lighten	mean time
immediately	investigation	lightened	meantime
immense	involve	lightening	mechanical
immigrant	ironic	lightning	medal
immigrate	irony	likelihood	medallion
importance	irrelevant	likely	medical
incidentally	irresistible	lily	medicinal
increasing	irritable	limb	medicine
incredible	island	linen	medieval
indebted	isle	listening	melancholy
indefinite	its	literary	memorable
independence	it's	literature	mere
independent		livelier	metal
indicate	janitor	liveliest	metallurgy
indispensable	janitorial	livelihood	methodical
individually	jealously	liveliness	mettle
industrial	jealousy	lively	military
industries	jewelry	loath	militia
industry	journey	loathe	miner
inevitable	judge	location	miniature
inevitably	judgment	loneliness	minimum
infinite	justifiable	lonely	mining
infinitesimal	justification	loose	minor

minority
minute
misappropriate
mischief
mischievous
misdemeanor
missionary
Mississippi
misspell
monoplane
moral
morale
morally
mortgage
mosquitoes
movable
muscle
muscular
museum
mutilate
mysterious
mystery

narrative
nationality
native
naturally
necessarily
necessary
negative
Negroes
nevertheless
nickel
niece
ninetieth
ninety
notice
noticeably
notoriety
notorious
novel
nuclear
nucleus

oblige
obliged
obliging
obstacle
obtainable
occasion
occasionally
occur
occurred

occurrence
occurring
officer
official
officially
omission
omit
omitted
operate
opinion
opportunity
oppose
opposite
optimism
optimist
orchard
ordinarily
ordinary
organism
organization
organize
original
originally
outrage
outrageously
owing

package
pageant
paid
pamphlet
pamphleteer
papal
parachute
paradox
paradoxical
paradoxically
paragraph
parallel
parallelogram
paralysis
paralytic
paralyze
parentheses
parenthesis
parliament
parliamentarian
parliamentary
partial
partially
particle
particular
particularity

particularly
particulate
passage
passed
past
patient
patriot
patriotic
patriotically
peaceable
peaceful
peasant
peculiar
peculiarity
peculiarly
Pennsylvania
perceive
percentage
perception
performance
permanence
permanent
permissible
permission
permitted
persistence
persistent
personal
personality
personally
personnel
perspiration
persuade
persuasion
Philippines
philosopher
philosophy
physical
physically
physician
physiological
physiology
pianos
picnic
picknicker
picknicking
piece
pillar
pillow
planed
planned
plausible
playwright

pleasant
pledge
poem
poetic
poetry
polar
polarity
polish
Polish
political
politician
politics
pollen
pollinate
portion
possess
possession
possessive
possibility
possible
possibly
potatoes
poultry
practicable
practical
practicality
practice
prairie
prayer
precede
precedence
precedent
precedents
preciosity
precious
predominant
prefer
preference
preferential
preferred
preferring
prejudice
prejudicial
premium
preparation
preparatory
prepare
presence
presidency
president
pressure
prestige
prevalence

prevalent	radical	reunion	sergeant
priest	reality	reunite	series
primitive	realization	reveal	several
principal	realize	reveille	sew
principle	really	revelation	shepherd
prisoner	reasonable	rewrite	shining
privilege	reasonably	rewritten	shoulder
probability	rebellious	rhetoric	siege
probable	recede	rhetorical	sieve
probably	receipt	rheumatism	significance
procedural	receive	rhyme	significant
procedure	receiving	rhythm	similar
proceed	recession	ridicule	similarity
professional	recognition	ridiculous	simile
professor	recognize	roommate	simplicity
prohibitive	recollect	routine	simultaneous
prohibitory	recommend		sincerely
promenade	recommendation	sacrifice	skillful
prominent	recruit	sacrificial	skillfully
pronounce	reduction	sacrilege	socialism
pronouncement	refer	sacrilegious	socialistic
pronunciation	reference	safety	society
prophecy	referred	salary	sociology
prophesy	referring	sanitary	solemn
proprietary	regularly	satire	soliloquy
proprietor	reign	satisfaction	sophomore
psychoanalysis	rein	satisfactory	source
psychoanalytic	relative	satisfy	sow
psychology	reliability	saving	specimen
psychopath	reliable	scarcely	spiritual
psychosomatic	relief	scenery	sponsor
punctuation	relieve	scenic	stability
punish	religion	schedule	stabilize
pupil	religious	schism	stable
purchase	remember	scholar	standard
purchased	remembrance	science	stationary
purchasing	reminisce	scientific	stationery
pursue	repeat	scissors	statistical
pursuing	repetition	scrutinize	statistics
	representation	seamstress	statuary
qualification	representative	seance	statue
qualified	require	secede	stature
qualify	requisition	secretary	statute
qualitative	residence	sectional	stenographer
quality	resistance	security	stepped
quiescence	resource	seize	stories
quiet	resourceful	semicolon	straight
quite	respectful	senator	stratagem
	respectfully	sense	strategy
rabid	response	sentence	strength
rabies	responsive	sententious	strenuous
racing	restaurant	separate	stricture
racy	restaurateur	separation	structure

studying	telephone	troop	variety
subjunctive	telephonic	trough	various
substance	temperament	troupe	varying
substantial	temperature	truly	vegetable
subtle	temporary	Tuesday	vegetation
subtlety	tempt	turkey	vegetative
succeed	tendency	turnkey	vengeance
succession	than	twelfth	vengeful
successor	theater	twelve	vicinity
suddenness	their	two	village
suffice	then	typical	villain
sufficient	theory	typically	villainous
suicidal	there	tyrannical	
suicide	therefore	tyranny	warrant
summarily	they're	tyrant	weather
summary	thorough		Wednesday
summons	thought	unanimity	weird
superintendent	through	unanimous	welcome
suppose	to	unconscious	whether
suppress	tomorrow	undoubted	whiskey
surgeon	too	undoubtedly	whisky
surprise	topic	unmanageable	wholly
surprising	topical	unnecessary	wired
surround	topically	unprecedented	woman
susceptible	toured	unprecedentedly	women
suspicious	tournament	until	woolen
syllable	traffic	unusual	woolly
symbol	trafficked	unusually	worse
sympathize	trafficking	urgent	worst
sympathy	tragedy	useful	wound
synonym	tragic	usefully	write
synonymous	transfer	usual	writing
	transference	usually	written
tableau	transferral		
tailor	transferred	vacuous	yacht
tariff	transitive	vacuum	yield
taxation	traveler	valley	your
technical	tried	valleys	you're
technique	tries	valuable	

Appendix

Punctuation of Footnotes, Bibliographies, and Letters

PUNCTUATION OF FOOTNOTES AND BIBLIOGRAPHIES

Footnotes provide documentation, explanation, or comments related to material in the text of a student paper, published article, or book. Footnotes usually appear at the bottom of a page in a student paper or at the bottom of a page in published writing. Publishers of journals and books may choose to present footnotes at the end of an article, chapter, or entire book.

Regardless of where footnotes appear, they must follow a consistent form within a paper or publication. The most widely used guide for footnote form is the *MLA Style Sheet,* which is published by the Modern Language Association.

A bibliography is a list of readings on a subject. The list may be complete or selective. An example of a complete bibliography is a list of all of Ernest Hemingway's stories and novels. An example of a selective bibliography is a list of critical articles consulted by a student while preparing a research paper on Hemingway's novels. The *MLA Style Sheet* is the most widely used guide for bibliographic form.

Footnote form and bibliographic form are far from standard, and many different forms are used successfully. Experienced students know that the first requirement is that all necessary information be supplied to enable readers to locate a book or article to which reference is made. The second requirement is consistency of style within a single paper, article, or book. This consistency includes the items of information supplied and the punctuation of each entry. Students and scholars know that compilation of footnotes and bibliographies consumes a great deal of time and requires careful attention to detail.

Footnotes that provide documentation are discussed below to show one acceptable approach to the punctuation needed and the differences between footnote form and bibliographic form. A few examples are given to illustrate uses of punctuation in footnotes, and some bibliographic entries are provided to illustrate the types that are most frequently encountered in student papers.

Footnotes for an Article

[14] Gay Wilson Allen, "Biblical Echoes in Whitman's Works," *American Literature,* VI, 302–315 (November 1934).

Notice that the footnote number (14) is not spaced or followed by a period. The author's name appears in normal order: first name, middle name, last name. The full name is followed by a comma. The article title is enclosed in quotation marks. A comma appears after the title and, in accordance with the quotation mark guidelines, inside the final quotes. The journal title is italicized, in accordance with the italics guidelines, and is followed by a comma. The volume number (VI) is followed by a comma. The page numbers (302–315) are the first and last pages of the article. The date of publication is enclosed in parentheses. The entire footnote is followed by a period.

Footnotes for a Book

[31] Gay Wilson Allen, *Walt Whitman Handbook* (Chicago, 1946), 459–462.

Notice that the footnote number is not spaced or followed by a period. The author's name is given in normal order and followed by a comma. The book title is italicized. The place and date of publication are set off as a unit by parentheses and separated by a comma. A comma follows the final parenthesis. The page numbers are the first and last pages of the book to which the writer makes reference. The entire footnote is followed by a period.

Bibliographic Entries for an Article

> Golden, Arthur. "New Light on *Leaves of Grass*: Whitman's Annotated Copy of the 1860 (Third) Edition," *Bulletin of the New York Public Library,* 69 (May 1965), 283–306.

Entries in a bibliography are not ordinarily numbered. The author's last name is presented first and followed by a comma. The rest of the name of the author is given next and followed by a period. The article title is enclosed in quotation marks, with the comma following the article title placed inside the final quotes. *Leaves of Grass* is italicized because it is a long poem that was published as a book. The colon after *Leaves of Grass* and the parentheses enclosing *Third* are part of the article title. The title of the journal in which the article appeared is italicized and followed by a comma. The volume number (69) is not punctuated because it is followed by the date of publication. The date of publication (May 1965) is enclosed in parentheses and followed by a comma. The page numbers are the first and last pages of the article. The entire bibliographic entry is followed by a period.

Bibliographic Entries for a Book

> Allen, Gay Wilson. *Walt Whitman Handbook* (Chicago: Packard and Co., 1946).

The author's last name is given first and is followed by a comma. The first and middle names are then given, followed by a period. The book title is italicized. The place of publication, publisher, and date of publication are enclosed in a pair of parentheses. The place of publication is followed by a colon. In this case the publisher's name includes the abbreviation *Co.,* so a period is needed before the comma following the publisher's name. The entire bibliographic entry is followed by a period.

PUNCTUATION OF LETTERS

Personal letters and business letters follow certain conventions of punctuation. Two sample letters are presented here to illustrate the uses of punctuation in addresses, salutations, and the complimentary close.

Personal Letters

July 11, 1992

Dear Mrs. Turner,

    I am writing to thank you for the wonderful day in the country you provided for a tired student. A day off from summer school is just what the doctor ordered.

    Please tell Kathy I still think her blueberry pie is better than her sister's.

Sincerely yours,

Alfred

Notice that no inside addresses are needed in the personal letter. When a return address is needed, it may be placed in the upper right-hand corner of the letter, above the date. It may also be placed in the lower left-hand corner, below the body of the letter and the signature. Punctuation of the address would be the same as in a business letter.

Business Letters

532 North Hyatt Street
Washington, D.C. 20402
June 30, 1992

Dr. William L. Turner
72 Memorial Plaza
Pleasantville, New York 10570

Dear Dr. Turner:

I am writing to request your assistance in gaining admission to the Georgetown College of Medicine.

The application form I must submit requires recommendations by two physicians who know me well, can attest to my interest in medicine, and can evaluate my character and general ability.

Since I have been a patient of yours for many years and have worked in your office as a laboratory assistant for the past three summers, your name is first on my list. I particularly value your recommendation, since you are a distinguished Georgetown graduate.

If you can send me a note signifying your willingness to recommend me, I will include your name in my application. I am certain you will soon thereafter receive the recommendation form from the Admissions Office.

I look forward to an early reply and enclose a self-addressed stamped envelope for your convenience.

Sincerely,

Alfred Loew

Alfred Loew

Answers

Chapter 1

1.
1. We were amazed to find the judge so willing to hear our explanation.
2. Do four laps before you stop.
3. Only six of them may stay.
4. The theater will be dark this season if we do not convince the unions to work for the same money they earn now.
5. No answer.
6. Common sense dictates that caution is needed in that part of town.
7. Read your novel aloud.
8. You will find happiness in your work if you apply yourself to the full extent of your ability.
9. Hugh's project will keep him busy for many years.
10. Please take your seats now.

2.
1. Mrs. Lewis will soon receive a B.S. degree and then go on to work toward an R.N.
2. Cicero is believed to have been born in 106 B.C. and died in 43 B.C.
3. She was a WAC during World War II and later became an instructor at UCLA.
4. Has Dr. Wells arrived yet?
5. Do you think you will be able to offer that salary and attract a Ph.D.?
6. In the history of the college, she is the youngest person who ever received the B.A. degree.
7. The SEC is investigating the possibility of stock fraud in many Wall Street firms.
8. Why use *i.e.* when you can write its English equivalent, *that is*?
9. Acceleration due to gravity is 32 fpsps.
10. Which law school awarded that incompetent person a J.D.?

3.
1. The chilling phrase he used at the close of his speech to the Congress was "the threat of extinction."
2. In which great oration did Lincoln use the expression "A house divided against itself"?
3. To hell with his boring "Idylls of the King"!
4. The poor boy looked miserable as he struggled heroically with "Why Did I Laugh Tonight?"
5. We were all in the dark by the time Macbeth got around to exclaiming, "Out, out, brief candle!"
6. With a moment's hesitation the loyal minister replied, "The Queen is always right."
7. Are you certain that the witness said, "I was entirely to blame and will accept full responsibility"?
8. We are going to the auction next week to see whether we can purchase the manuscript of Dorothy Parker's "Big Blond."
9. In 1 Timothy, Paul wisely warns, "The love of money is the root of all evil."
10. Can you tell me the source of "A work that aspires, however humbly, to the condition of art should carry its justification in every line"?

4.
1. There was little left for the old Queen to do but die gracefully (Elizabeth Jenkins, *Elizabeth the Great*, (pages 322 to 324).
2. Many so-called underdeveloped nations (they are actually resource-rich nations that have not yet exploited their mineral riches) form a potent bloc within many United Nations organizations.
3. Now we will turn our attention to the career of Martin Luther (German theologian born in 1483).
4. Sen. Barry Goldwater (Republican of Arizona) retired from the Senate after many years of service to his country (and his party).
5. The last witness of the day took the stand and was sworn. (She was later to prove the most important witness the defense had in the case.)

6. Three types of dogs (collies, Weimaraners, and German shepherds) are not suitable pets for people living in small city apartments.

7. Many still remember Sam Rayburn with great affection for his firm performance in the chair at Democratic Party conventions (the Speaker was permanent chairman many times).

8. I hope to bring this matter to the floor (my health permitting) when the National Council on Women's Rights meets again.

9. Many students forget that there are several coordinate conjunctions besides *and* (for example *but, for, or,* and *nor*) and thus lose opportunities to write forcefully.

10. This approach to education has many of the virtues (and the faults) of all other systems I have studied. (I hope we have seen the last of such proposals for a while.) Also correct: This approach to education has many of the virtues (and the faults) of all other systems I have studied (I hope we have seen the last of such proposals for a while).

5. 1. Father Hans Gropius, S.J., has written a marvelous new book on ethics.

2. Whether you want to sit next to Ned, Jr., or not, you will be obliged to, since the dinner is being arranged by Mrs. Ned, Jr., and you know how insistent she is on having her own way.

3. He took his complaint to Francisco Ortiz, D.D., the one man in the entire seminary who would receive such a complaint.

4. Tamara Morgan, Ph.D., will never offer a course again in this department.

5. Mr. Barnum Jeffreys, Esq., will serve as Master of the Hunt.

6. 1. Can you help me find an inexpensive hotel room in Florence?

2. "The hardest knife ill-used doth lose his edge."—Shakespeare.

3. "Today I shall help you with your homework."
"Why today? Won't tomorrow do just as well?"

4. I shall ask Jane that question when I see her.

5. Questions, questions; nothing but questions.

6. Whom would you like to invite for dinner?

7. Can you find your way by yourself?

8. "Marine drill instructors never have been the kindliest of men."
"Never?" "Never."

9. What you call a mistake is what I call a deliberate evasion of duty.

10. "Is this your book?" he asked.

11. *Hamlet:* There's another. Why may not that be the skull of a lawyer? Where be his quiddities now, his quillities, his cases, his tenures, and his tricks? Why does he suffer this mad knave now to knock him about the sconce with a dirty shovel, and will not tell him of his action of battery? Hum!

12. *Hamlet:* Alas, poor Yorick! I knew him, Horatio, a fellow of infinite jest, of most excellent fancy. He hath borne me on his back a thousand times. And now how abhorred in my imagination it is! My gorge rises at it. Here hung those lips that I have kissed I know not how oft. Where be your gibes now? Your gambols, your songs, your flashes of merriment that were wont to set the table on a roar? Not one now to mock your own grinning? Quite chapfallen? Now get you to my lady's chamber, and tell her, let her paint an inch thick, to this favor she must come. Make her laugh at that. Prithee, Horatio, tell me one thing.
Horatio: What's that, my lord?
Hamlet: Dost thou think Alexander looked o' this fashion i' th'earth?

13. I ask you only one question: The petty amount of money this old man had in his pocket was enough to make you commit such a crime?

14. The attorney asked me whether I had any interest in the estate.

15. I wonder if you understand what a terrible act you committed.

7.
1. The policeman said once more, "Do you remember stopping at a bar on your way home from the party?"
2. I have repeatedly asked myself the most important question of all: Is this the man with whom I want to spend the rest of my life?
3. Jerome tormented himself with questions concerning the universality of temptation.
4. The director finally asked, "You are certain you want to take this position?"
5. I would like to know how much you care about my daughter.
6. Do you care for her enough to think of her happiness before yours?
7. Are you certain you followed all reasonable leads in your research?
8. You must make sure you ask the right questions of your witnesses.
9. Do you really know what you want to do with the rest of your life?
10. Has anyone ever asked you whether you know what you want to do with the rest of your life?

8.
1. May I hear from you soon.
2. Is there any chance you will be visiting our city sometime this year?
3. Will you please send me two pounds of your best coffee.
4. Will you please stop your bickering.
5. Is there any way I can convince you of my good intentions?
6. Can you please help me cross the street.
7. Is there any way out of this incredible mess?
8. May we show you the correct solution now.
9. Is there any cream for the coffee?
10. Will you please deliver the flowers I ordered.

9.
1. Why were they so interested in his locker? his school bag? his lunch box? his desk?
2. I cannot go on this way—do you understand?—because no good can come of so much deceit, lying, and treachery.
3. Can you repair washing machines? television sets? small appliances?
4. We are going to undertake a comprehensive study of American purchasing habits, voting patterns, and family structure.
5. Have you wondered why many city families now own dogs? why sales of locks and window bars have increased dramatically? why burglar alarm companies are mushrooming?

10.
1. Late in his term of office, the president still bored audiences with the same fumbling attempts at wit that had dulled his early years in office.
2. The unrealistic portrayal of life in Japan that marks Gilbert and Sullivan's *The Mikado* represented the only impression many Europeans of that time had of the Orient.
3. That certainly was more than a good brand of tobacco he had in his little cigarette.
4. Saint Wenceslaus, 903(?)–935 A.D., was duke of Bohemia in the last seven years of his life.
5. Shakespeare's earliest work as a dramatist, *Henry VI,* written in 1591(?), is not often acted today.

11.
1. Do you know that Anne's favorite story from *Dubliners* is "Araby"?
2. "Have you mailed the package yet, Jon?" his teacher asked.
3. The child kept pestering her mother with the one nagging question, "When will Daddy be home?" until she burst into tears.
4. Do they always say "please" every time they ask for something?
5. Can you remember his saying, "I will get what I want or you won't see me again"?
6. "Did the choir sing well?" the minister asked.
7. Is your mother the kind who always says, "Why do you want the car tonight?"

8. I am not sure he really said, "One more word like that, and I'll blow your head off. Do you understand?"

9. "Have you ever seen a more beautiful sunset in all your life?" the guide asked.

10. The worst news came at the end of the examination, when Dr. Alpert asked in his most innocent manner, "Have you ever had root canal therapy?"

12. 1. Please! Let the child explain what she means.

2. Gosh! That meal was the best I have ever eaten.

3. Lord! I've made a mistake.

4. Ah! That wine has such a delicate bouquet.

5. Ha! You are trapped and will never get away!

6. O! My offense is rank; it smells to heaven. (Shakespeare)

7. Lo! Thy dread empire Chaos is restored. (Pope)

8. Ouch! This needle really hurts!

9. Yes! I will do whatever you want.

10. No! You cannot have any more cake.

13. 1. What a mess I'm in!

2. What time is it?

3. I would say he was rich—he has much more than one million!—even by today's standards.

4. May the devil take them!

5. May I have a glass of water?

6. A fine husband you are!

7. Not another minute!

8. You marvelous child!

9. The greatest in all the world!

10. How she worried!

14. 1. Stop running through the halls!

2. Stop smoking if you want to live a long life.

3. Stand back!

4. Be quiet!

5. Have another glass of wine.

6. The little boy cried, "Run for your lives!"

7. Gather ye rosebuds while ye may,
   Old Time is still a-flying,
   And this same flower that smiles today
   Tomorrow will be dying.

8. Sell everything you own and run away with me.

9. Drink milk for health.

10. Get out as quickly as you can!

15. 1. Henry Baldridge—damn him!—shouted, "Help!"

2. How marvelous are the opening lines of "Tintern Abbey"!

3. "If you have nothing more to say," she answered, "get out of here!"

4. The bride's mother toasted the new couple: "May the new husband and wife live happily together! May their children enjoy a good family life! May the children's grandparents enjoy fifty more years!"

5. What a great song is "Happy Days Are Here Again"!

6.   The sergeant bellowed, "Rookie, get here P.D.Q.!"

7.   How I love Ernest Hemingway's story "Fifty Grand"!

8.   "How nice to see you again after all these years!" she exclaimed.

9.   Stop saying "England expects that every man will do his duty"!

10. All she could say was "Oh!"

Chapter 2

1. 1.   The size and effectiveness of your vocabulary affect your writing, speaking, and reading throughout your life.

2.   Norma has not yet decided whether she will continue in her present job, work only half-time, or give up work completely.

3.   Some of us are not aware of the expense, the anxiety, the inconvenience encountered in living outside great cities.

4.   Strauss found himself burdened by debt, seriously hampered by poor health, yet gloriously happy in his general acclaim.

5.   In our European travels we found ourselves received everywhere with warmth, hospitality, and generosity.

6.   Most of the merchandise the store offered for sale was shabby, overpriced, or old-fashioned.

7.   They were equally fond of swimming, dancing, hiking, and riding.

8.   The oldest daughter took up nursing, the next prepared for college teaching, but the youngest gave no thought to the future.

9.   Daisy was able to find her food, eat it, and hide the empty dish no matter how we tried to fool her.

10. Evergreen trees make a splendid hedge, are easy to maintain, and have long lives.

2. 1.   Wherever he went, Sam carried his tape recorder, typewriter, notebook, dictionary, and thesaurus.

2.   The angry landlord told my son to clean the apartment, pay the rent, and get out.

3.   "Coffee, tea, or milk?" was all I heard on the long trip across the country.

4.   Keats, Shelley, Byron, Coleridge, and Wordsworth are usually studied in a single college English course.

5.   During their long holidays together, Mickey and Margie concentrated on rest, good eating, and relaxed conversation.

6.   The children sat still all through the enforced recess and regretted their unruly behavior.

7.   The young bride took no interest in the conversation of her women neighbors, the men her husband invited home, or the daily telephone call from her doting mother.

8.   Unemployment statistics do not reflect accurately the number of people who are no longer looking for work, the underemployed, and all the unfortunate college graduates who have not yet found their first jobs.

9.   The tired author was still writing new material, correcting first drafts, and reading the initial galleys.

10. Many things adults do without thinking about them are difficult tasks for the young, the disabled, and the mentally handicapped.

3. 1.   The rebel army soon found itself without fuel and electricity, medical supplies, food and water, able-bodied troops and officers, and the will to fight.

2.   Nations of the world are now concerned with potential shortages of grain and fodder, vital minerals and fuels, and food for growing populations.

3.   Medical researchers maintain constant surveillance of epidemic and pandemic disease, new viral and bacterial strains, and water and air pollutants.

4.   Bread and jam, peanuts and popcorn, and candy bars and soft drinks cannot be counted on to nourish growing children.

5. Trick knees and athlete's foot are not the exclusive property of athletes.

6. The dancer moved rapidly across the stage, turned and leapt, and then dropped gracefully to her knees.

7. Communities often find that city administrators will usually listen patiently to complaints, promise attention and relief during elections, and continue to ignore people's needs.

8. He learned patience from his father and thrift from his mother.

9. Soldiers and sailors, school teachers and construction workers, and physicians and nurses marched together in the demonstration for better health care.

10. The building tilted dangerously during renovation, appeared to straighten and settle, and then suddenly collapsed completely.

4. 1. We have learned much about mistakes made throughout history, but our leaders do not seem to have profited much from those mistakes.

2. The islands still held strong attraction for Juan and José, and they could not become accustomed to life on the mainland.

3. Children are permitted to play baseball but football is forbidden.

4. One couple wanted to rent a large apartment, another wanted to rent a house, and the rest could not make up their minds.

5. A typewritten term paper makes a good impression, but the most important factor in earning good grades is the quality of thought and writing.

6. The cities are gradually facing up to the need for improving public housing, but sufficient funds are not easy to obtain in times of recession and inflation.

7. Sycamores shed much of their bark almost every summer, yet these shade trees do much to improve the appearance of streets in our neighborhood.

8. Prices of most commonly used foods seem to rise continually, and so frugal shoppers must select carefully when buying food for family meals.

9. Her laboratory assistant could find no reason for the death of the animals in the sterile room, nor could the consulting pathologist.

10. Roofing materials have not changed much over the years, but the average homeowner still has not mastered the art of putting a roof down perfectly.

11. Children were always welcomed by the lonely old couple, for they missed the sound of young voices in their home.

12. Drug users have little opportunity to find useful employment, and so they frequently resort to crime to gain the money needed to support their habits.

13. Inner-city problems will have to be solved by federal authorities, or municipal governments will soon find themselves bankrupt.

14. Graduate students in many universities find themselves unable to go on with their studies or embark on new careers.

15. They completed preparations for the trip and retired early.

5. 1. From middle age on, my aunt enjoyed far better health than ever before in her life.

2. Walking slowly through the park, she peered about constantly to see whether she could find the person who had snatched her purse.

3. In hope of eventual restoration of his pension, Joseph spent every penny he could find on lawyers.

4. In the end, Cynthia decided to return to her position on the faculty.

5. Escorted by her sons, the old woman walked proudly down the church aisle and took her place in the front pew.

6. With nothing left to lose, the gambler left the casino and walked slowly back to his lonely room.

7. Minus its tail, the old dog no longer looked the fierce fighter it once had been.

8.   In the aftermath of the cyclone, all the town could do was start the long clean-up operation and attempt to bring life back to normal.

9.   Unless more people volunteer, we will have too many supervisors and not enough workers.

10. As the clock began to strike, the entire crowd held its breath in anticipation of the impending announcement.

6. 1. With no money left to spend, the couple agreed it was time to return home.

2.   Improperly treated, even a minor illness can have serious consequences.

3.   Just as before, the injured ankle prevented full enjoyment of the afternoon's outing.

4.   In good times Hazel and Harry gave no thought to budgeting.

5.   Across the square the crowd gathered in angry protest against what seemed to have been an inequitable decision by the court.

6.   Straining to be heard, the street singer quickly wore himself out and left the neighborhood.

7.   To find the girl, all able-bodied people of the neighborhood banded together under the minister's leadership.

8.   In seeking to grasp the poet's meaning, the careful reader goes over and over every word of the poem in question.

9.   In the end there was nothing left to do but tear the building down and start all over again.

10. Before starting a fire, make certain that all the wood is dry.

11. Before lighting a candle, one might reflect for a moment on what the act of lighting the candle signifies.

12. According to our map the towns are at least twelve miles apart.

13. If you arrive early open the windows and sweep out the meeting room.

14. If you want to, you may take a place on the platform and have a few minutes to address the group.

15. Standing apart, the stranger made most of us uneasy.

16. From middle age on, my uncle saw his health decline gradually.

17. Walking slowly from the park, she peered about constantly to see whether she could find the men who had snatched her purse.

18. In hope of eventual restoration of his pension, Joseph spent every penny he could find on lawyers.

19. In the end Annette decided to return to her teaching position in the college.

20. Escorted by her sons, the old woman walked proudly down the church aisle and took her place in the first pew.

21. With nothing left to lose, the gambler quit the game and walked back to his lonely room.

22. Minus its tail the old dog no longer looked the fierce fighter it once had been.

23. In the aftermath of the cyclone, all the town could do was start the long clean-up operation and attempt to bring life back to normal.

24. Unless more people volunteer we will have too many supervisors and not enough workers.

25. As the clock began to strike, the crowd held its breath in anticipation of the impending announcement.

7. 1. The same bold spirit that took her through the life-threatening illness will see her through the present emergency.

2.   Decrepit, old Mrs. Lang no longer seems to get much pleasure from life.

3.   Blue denim slacks command a high price in countries that do not produce such clothing.

4.   Send me a dozen red roses and six white gardenias.

5.   Five long, hard years lie ahead for any newly elected President of the United States.

6.   Heavily grained red morocco cannot be genuine.

7.   Twelve interested jurors followed every word spoken by the impassioned young prosecutor.

8. That dusty, rutted road leads to the shack my friends rented in a rash moment.

9. A clean, well-lighted supermarket attracts shoppers eager to spend their few, hard-earned dollars.

10. Six happy minutes flew by during the transatlantic call.

11. Chinese red paint is now what I had in mind for my quiet, comfortable study.

12. New dormer windows are difficult to install without a strong aluminum or magnesium ladder.

13. Crisp, fresh salad greens are essential if you are going to tempt me to eat anything on a hot August night.

14. Beautiful Marilyn Monore died a tragic, premature death.

15. The exciting pennant race was not settled until the leaves had turned deep red.

8. 1. Margie especially admired graceful, controlled dancers who appeared to know and love music.

2. Rich, pungent tobaccos made his afternoons especially rewarding.

3. Some very old people are able to talk amusingly even with the extremely young.

4. We found his speech long-winded and boring, and so we left the committee meeting as soon as we could.

5. Henrietta played the long, demanding part as well as it could be played.

6. They seemed always to be searching for their long-lost youth.

7. Can you tell me where I can find a succulent, tomato-rich, dripping-with-cheese pizza in this neighborhood?

8. One inexpensive, excellent meal is worth sixty take-out Chinese deep-fat disappointments.

9. Young Prince Hamlet walked slowly about the darkened stage, reading from a small volume of poetry.

10. The long, cold Arctic nights do not bother David too much.

9. 1. Electrified, the audience arose as one person and applauded wildly for an orator who had treated important themes in clear and concise language.

2. Spent, the pony walked slowly behind the cowboy who had roped it so expertly.

3. Ironically, we are willing to entrust to our politicians sweeping powers we dare not employ ourselves.

4. Smiling broadly, the entertainer rose to her feet once more to accept the generous ovation given her final performance.

5. Awakened at last to the need for action, the legislature unanimously agreed to vote full power to the military junta.

6. Interestingly, there was little basic difference between their points of view.

7. Obviously, we must move to provide decent housing and health care for the underprivileged among us.

8. Saddled with so much responsibility at the age of fifteen, the young woman managed to make something of herself and go on to contribute remarkably to the good of the nation.

9. Finally, the family found a way to support all their relatives until economic recovery enabled them to stand on their own.

10. First, Alice and Bob decided to establish a self-sufficient life on a small farm.

10. 1. Ethel, who ordinarily is extremely quiet at parties, went about and talked with anyone who appeared interested in talking with an intelligent woman.

2. The ballplayer with the highest batting average in the league was not selected for the All-Star Game.

3. Plants that have finished bearing fruit should be cut back to save nutrients in the soil for plants that are still bearing.

4. Many imported wines that are heavily advertised are not nearly as good as domestic wines, which are usually the product of small vineyards.

5. My reliable automobile, which I bought second-hand three years ago, still takes me back and forth every day between my home and office.

6. The compositions Anne wrote as a child still give me pleasure.

7. A book as interesting as that one will always find readers among those who have a taste for fine literature.

8. Animals in our local zoo are perishing for lack of food and water, which are the responsibility of an overworked and underpaid staff.

9. Fruits and vegetables sold in supermarkets sometimes are not as high in quality as those sold by greengrocers.

10. Leaves that have turned yellow should be pruned and carted away to a compost heap, which will turn them into valuable sources of food for other plants.

11. We always donate all our old clothes to organizations that will repair them and see that deserving people receive them.

12. The Kennedy years, which saw the hopes of young Americans raised, came too quickly to an end.

13. Pictures in our family for years were lost when our house burned down.

14. The circus, which still gladdens the hearts of young and old, will be coming to town next week to give five performances under the big tent.

15. Most people who take pleasure in attending the theater like to live near a city that offers serious playgoers the chance to see good productions.

11. 1. *Incorrect.* The Vietnam War, shameful as it was in so many people's minds, is forgotten now by all except those who bear its wounds.

2. *Incorrect.* I received a telephone call that shook me thoroughly and sent me back to my study, unable to work for the rest of the day.

3. *Incorrect.* Our youngest son wants to settle in California, which is so far from home that we will not be able to see him except on summer holidays.

4. *Incorrect.* Infectious diseases, which often spread because of poor sanitation, are not easily controlled in countries that do not have adequate medical facilities.

5. *Incorrect.* Many women who have been elected to positions of major importance in their own countries still find themselves treated badly when they travel to other countries.

6. *Correct.*

7. *Incorrect.* Those of us who are willing to cooperate expect to be given some help by the others.

8. *Incorrect.* Some of the articles that appear in *Playboy* are worth reading.

9. *Incorrect.* Any man or woman who consults no one before undertaking a job as big as that one takes undue risks.

10. *Incorrect.* That metaphor, which I have read a dozen times, is as inappropriate now as it was the first time I read it.

11. *Incorrect.* Rather than try immediately to look up every word that troubles you, keep a list of such words and set some time aside for dictionary work each evening.

12. *Incorrect.* Universities that capitulate to every demand made by students will surely regret doing so.

13. *Incorrect.* Encyclopedias, which are expensive to buy and bulky to store, are valuable tools for families with several children in school.

14. *Incorrect.* The more time a man spends on himself, the less time he has for others.

15. *Correct.*

12. 1. Alexander Solzhenitsyn, poet and novelist, went into exile to protest conditions in the Soviet Union.

2. The book *All the President's Men* remained on the best-seller list for many months.

3. Her uncle Ralph always took her fishing when she was a child.

4. Vermont, the Green Mountain State, has a long history of independent thought and action.

5. Ms. Atkins, our school bus driver, can be relied on in bad weather as well as good.

6. Honey, a delicious and nutritious food, is produced by bees.

7. Jane's first choice, graduate study in English, proved an unwise selection for the job market of her day.

8. My earliest memory, seeing my grandfather sicken and die, affected me throughout my early life.

9. Arlene's career, dancer and singer, was cut short by her inability to face large audiences.

10. The feeling that something dreadful is about to happen is a common complaint of neurotics.

11. Rare earth elements, closely related metallic elements of atomic number 57 to 71, find many uses in high-technology applications.

12. Subway cars covered with graffiti, the artist decorations that express a yearning for recognition, used to be commonplace in New York.

13. The short story "A Little Cloud" remains one of my favorites.

14. *PM*, a newspaper that accepted no advertising, made a place for itself in journalistic history.

15. Her oldest brother, Fred, was unable to find work for three years after high school.

16. Anachronisms, or chronological errors, throughout the otherwise-serious film made most of the audience laugh and sickened the director.

17. College football no longer performs its primary function, raising enough money to finance the entire college physical education program.

18. Coniferous trees, or evergreens, supply most of the vast quantity of pulpwood needed for newspapers.

19. The most expensive office machine, the digital computer, creates enormous amounts of useless information while wasting paper and manpower.

20. *War and Peace*, Tolstoy's greatest novel, is read by every generation of lovers of literature.

13. 1. Doris managed to keep her wits about her when the man jumped in front of her and demanded her purse.

2. The City Council will meet twice next week, when the bill for revision of the charter comes up for its final vote.

3. Smoking is considered bad for the health, although pipe smoking is said to be less harmful than cigarette smoking.

4. The entire family decided to go to the movies together, although no film appealed to everybody equally.

5. I will not take a long airplane flight as long as you refuse to go along with me.

6. John asked to have a window fan installed in his office, because the hot weather was causing him to lose much time during the day.

7. The death of a family pet comes as a shock to everyone if it is not anticipated.

8. She walked down the street as if she owned everything she saw.

9. The Accounting Department will not send a representative to the meeting, since the meeting does not concern finances.

10. Ambiguity crops up wherever people gather, because no one is willing to take the time to think clearly or speak clearly.

11. He believed that things would turn out all right, since everyone in the group professed interest in the general welfare.

12. Candidates for public office will promise anything while having no intention to deliver on their promises, since promises are essential in winning elections.

13. Harriet would not say why she had made the decision, until most of us grew tired of wondering about her motives.

14. I promise that you will meet courteous people wherever you travel in the United States.

15. Wait until you are at least twenty-one, when maturity is a little closer.

14. 1. My business affairs, I tell you gladly, are in better condition today than they have been for fifteen years.

2. There is more than one way to deal with the problems of drugs and street crime, you know, and you must remain flexible.

3. They go on, nevertheless, dealing in marijuana and risking arrest despite their otherwise clean records.

4. Anne and Bob, as a matter of course, arrive late at every party they attend.

5. The child lay still and pretended to sleep all through the evening.

6. I must fight for my liberty, you will grant, above all other considerations if I am to remain true to my political convictions.

7. Most of the people in the company, furthermore, do so little work that one cannot understand how it remains a successful organization.

8. Air conditioners are accepted as a necessary item of office furniture by many who are willing to put up with high temperatures at home.

9. You will, please, think the matter over carefully before you make your decision.

10. Reference books, dictionaries included, are becoming so expensive that we must think a long time before deciding to purchase a volume we really need.

11. If we take much longer to pay the bill, you see, the company may decide to cut off our credit.

12. Taxes will never go down in our community as long as the taxable buildings keep disappearing and businesses maintain their resistance to staying in the inner city.

13. Rosa, acting against her better judgment, went along with the other girls that day and managed to get into serious trouble.

14. We cannot, as we have told you so many times, continue the present arrangement unless you agree to make important changes.

15. The lunch went badly, as I predicted it would, because both husbands insisted on dominating the conversation and totally ignoring their wives' interests.

16. I must, you understand, give my full attention to this report until I have finished it.

17. Will you finally, madam, cease interrupting until I have completed my full presentation of the evidence?

18. The opposing position will, therefore, not be supported unless a majority indicates sufficient interest to warrant a complete explanation.

19. Many members of the committee will, consequently, withhold their votes in deference to the wishes of the chair.

20. Oh, well, you cannot expect him to capitulate right after he has expressed himself so forcefully against the popular opinion.

15. 1. *Incorrect.* Anne's ability to diagnose rare diseases without relying on laboratory tests impresses all her teachers.

2. *Incorrect.* Those of us who wish to live productive lives should eat sensibly and drink only in moderation.

3. *Incorrect.* The citizen's group announced that there will be no further building on the street until the Landmark Commission reveals its decision.

4. *Incorrect.* The varsity soccer team is so pleased with attendance at its games that three additional games will be scheduled.

5. *Correct.*

6. *Incorrect.* What I find hard to accept is her unmatched obstinacy.

7. *Incorrect.* Omar's obvious popularity apparently made him the object of unremitting envy by many other men.

8. *Incorrect.* The woman with blond hair spent many hours each week at the beauty parlor.

9. *Correct.*

10. *Incorrect.* Have you never read *For Whom the Bell Tolls*?

11. *Incorrect.* The brave fire fighter carried two women and one child from the burning house.

12. *Correct.*

13. *Incorrect.* Those who gamble on their lives are admired only by the immature and the bloodthirsty.

14. *Incorrect.* The name I find hardest to remember is Myron.

15. *Correct.*

16. 1. Their best efforts entirely fruitless, the three sisters decided to abandon the idea of going into business.

2. Stockbrokers recall a certain day in November many years ago when the New York Stock Exchange experienced a tremendous drop in prices, the efforts of a few banks notwithstanding.

3. Sailors leaving port exult in the freedom of the seas, all cares and concerns of landlocked existence behind them.

4. The novels of Ernest Hemingway are universally admired, their freshness of language and innovations in style resembling nothing that went before.

5. All the oats and barley safely in the barn, farmers can turn their attention to much-needed repair of equipment and tools.

6. Taxi cabs are finding well-educated drivers these days, the time of great employment opportunities being past for college graduates.

7. All regular business being concluded, the party leader turned the attention of the faithful to the need for finding promising candidates for the next year's election.

8. Fred decided to return home, there being no chance to find full-time employment in the city.

9. Any chance for a reprieve ended, the unhappy prisoner turned his thoughts to making his peace with God.

10. The herd moved to lower pastures early, the upper fields having shown no sign of producing sufficient grass for its needs.

17. 1. They were cautioned against sailing out of the harbor that day and assured us they would not do so.

2. "Is this really the way it happened?" Mother asked. "Did you know that you were going to have to repair the car before starting out on the trip?"

3. My parents said they wanted to stay at home with us to celebrate our first wedding anniversary.

4. The child then added, "The man asked me to go to the movies with him to eat popcorn and have a good time."

5. Instead of advising us to relax and enjoy life, they keep telling us, "Exercise! Work! Eat less! Stop drinking! Stop smoking!" I answer, "Why bother with that routine? There is no point in living that way."

6. "Can you really take so much pleasure in misleading the gullible?" she asked me.

7. The conductor told the tuba player that sounds coming out of her instrument sounded more like bleats than music.

8. "Books are meant to be read," the librarian said; "they are not meant to be destroyed."

9. "Certain corrections are needed in the score," the composer said, "but I can accomplish them within the week."

10. "Can you imagine such behavior?" the old woman said. "In all my eighty-five years I have never seen anything like it."

11. "A horn was sounded to signal the arrival of a new shipment for auction," the historian wrote, "and all tobacco merchants in the town assembled on the waterfront."

12. Ms. Prentiss insisted she would get to the bottom of the mess before long and asked us to grant her a few more days.

13. "Are there any cookies in the house?" the child asked. "My friends are hungry."

14. The foreman said that no overtime would be needed until after Labor Day.

15. "You can be sure that I will do my best for you and you can bet I will get you the appointment you want," the instructor told the student.

18. 1. We have chosen June 21 as the best day on which to hold the dog show.

   2. Saturdays in August are all reserved for band concerts on the village green.

   3. It is difficult to believe she will be seventy years old on July 4, 1994.

   4. She was looking forward to Sunday, June 15, her wedding date.

   5. April 1 is April Fools' Day.

   6. I expect that January 1994 will be a good month for selling snow shovels.

   7. He was discharged from the Marine Corps on 12 July 1945.

   8. The fiscal year used to begin 1 July each year.

   9. New orders will not be taken at these prices after 6 September 1991.

  10. The new sales manager will take over on Monday, 10 March.

19. 1. He has written to the Director of Personnel, McGraw-Hill, Inc., 1221 Avenue of the Americas, New York, New York 10020.

   2. For a long time they lived in Branford, Connecticut.

   3. They have their offices at 795 Peachtree Street, N.E., Atlanta, Georgia 30308.

   4. I am looking forward to retiring to my parents' home in Siena, Italy.

   5. She has rented Post Office Box 56, Metis Beach, Quebec, Canada.

   6. You will be impressed by the Cathedral of Notre Dame in Paris, France.

   7. Palermo, Italy, was the scene of bloody fighting during World War II.

   8. For a long time he maintained an office at 502 Park Avenue, New York, New York 10022.

   9. The famous *Librarie Larousse* is located at 17 rue du Montparnasse, Paris VIe, France.

  10. Lawrence has decided to leave North Collins, New York, and try for a new life in Scarborough, Ontario, Canada.

20. 1. Chairman Godfrey Helms has appointed a committee that is expected to raise the profits of the factory.

   2. Ramses II reigned during the second millennium before the birth of Christ.

   3. The child was given the imposing name of Mark Eldridge Satterthwaite IV.

   4. One of the junior partners was appropriately named David Forsythe, Jr.

   5. Henri Lachaise, Chairman of the Department of French, holds two Ph.D. degrees.

   6. Adrian Longworth, Ph.D., has been Visiting Professor of Classical Languages at Smith College.

   7. Pharmacologists often hold the Ph.D. degree as well as the M.S. and B.S. degrees.

   8. The young man decided that an A.A. Degree would be sufficient for any job he had in mind.

   9. Robert Aldington, B.A., has been designated departmental expediter.

  10. Expo II was nowhere near as successful as Expo.

21. 1. Falling in love for the first time is like seeing the sun rise after the long Arctic night; falling out of love, like seeing your favorite team lose the seventh game of a World Series.

   2. In San Francisco a level street is an occasional treat; in Kansas City, a steady diet.

   3. A floppy hat suits the candidate best; a pillbox, not at all.

4. Bryan finds books his best companions and television his worst enemy, but Mary cannot find time for either.

5. We expect that Jon will be home in time for dinner, ready to eat as soon as he walks in the door; we are certain Henry will be late for dinner and ready to eat whenever he walks in.

6. Meeting her the first time was an experience unforgettable; seeing her the last time, an ordeal insupportable.

7. Barney's suit was a miracle of synthetic delight; his shirt and tie, crumpled visions of once-proud long-staple cotton.

8. Giving him the bad news that his employment with us was over was no problem for me; watching his reaction, a painful incident.

9. All of us decided to leave on Monday morning; the rest, on Monday night.

10. Jane began to forget she had ever known him; Charles, to remember how lovely their life together had been.

22. 1. Many of the workers appeared enthusiastic when interviewed on television, disgruntled when they spoke with friends.

2. Liberal arts students often speak openly against varsity sports, privately in favor of them.

3. I am willing to buy second-hand furniture, eager to purchase fine antiques.

4. Much of his time is spent in idleness, little in productive work.

5. Hunting for a job is difficult when times are good, impossible when times are bad.

6. How can a person keep calm when confronted with a situation so demanding, so confining?

7. Barbara told her sad story many times, told it even when no one could bear to hear it again.

8. She persisted in her search when others would have relaxed, would have abandoned their efforts.

9. Felice was an avid reader, an even more avid teller of stories.

10. Cities find themselves unable to provide desirable services for their citizens, unable even to provide essential services.

23. 1. Rather than Billy, let us try Bob again.

2. Once read, the book proved useful in all respects.

3. Most of the people lingered, for the afternoon showing was not ending on time.

4. Before leaving, the department store clerks had to process their full receipts.

5. Above all, apple trees must be carefully pruned.

6. Once we had eaten, the cat demanded its own food.

7. Because Luis could hit, his coach insisted on starting him.

8. To encourage the assistant manager to leave, the manager offered a two-week vacation instead of just one.

9. After she had eaten, the woman left without leaving a tip.

10. Several times in the past, weeks would go by without their exchanging a civil word.

11. Al thought his job was a great way of making a living, for his days on unemployment insurance had shown him the value of steady work.

12. Prompt payment of bills is essential, for good credit is built upon it.

13. Without exaggerating, thousands of errors are found each month in departmental calculations.

14. Terry couldn't tell the time, for his watch had been stolen.

15. They searched the entire forest, and the child still had not been found.

16. We can now forget about finding a good place to eat, for five dollars will buy only a bad meal.

17. Immediately after I fired, the superintendent of police came upon me.

18. If the band does not play, there is no chance anyone sober will be left at the party.

19. Even though Father spent many hours scraping and priming, Dick found plenty of painting left to do.

20. A poor job of finishing, Mother insists, will mean an entire job to do all over again.

21. All the corn kernels were golden, and green beans lent their bright color to the dish.

22. My sister is interested in decorating, and painting is a task my brothers detests.

23. Once you have studied Sam Johnson's interpretations of what words mean, Noah Webster can be appreciated more.

24. I was paid lower wages, for my sister-in-law was the store manager.

25. When you finally finish painting, Bill will give you other work to do.

26. June was pleased with her catch, for the tuna weighed more than one hundred pounds.

27. Everyone was there, but one of the team members was ill.

28. To shut the window, great strength is needed.

29. After this, one mistake will cost you dearly.

30. When old, cows give little milk.

31. Radio would be much more enjoyable if we could tune out noisy commercials and talkative disc jockeys.

32. Television can be as effective in influencing voters as strong-arm methods and chicanery once were.

33. The Boy Scout troop had difficulty in attracting new members that year and meeting its budget, and had to disband.

34. My sister is delighted with the new job she has found and with the additional income it brings.

35. The illness that ruined her final year of life made conditions difficult for the family in many ways and drained family resources.

36. Our community asks constantly for autonomy and lower tax rates.

37. Family medicine no longer is practiced by most physicians, in the belief that specialized services promote greater efficiency and better quality of medical care.

38. Clothbound books have the advantage of longer life compared with many paperbound books and pamphlets.

39. The child found himself faced with decisions and responsibilities too difficult for one so young with no adult to consult.

40. Many rulers in earlier centuries looked with disfavor on demands by their subjects for freedom and suffrage, and reacted with increased oppressiveness.

24. 1. "There's little to be done for those left homeless by the flood," the sheriff said.

2. O. Henry was at his satirical best when he wrote "The Man Higher Up."

3. He vowed to campaign in all the cities of the state as well as in the "tiniest hamlets you can name."

4. The old man sat back in his chair and calmly said, "I am ready to die."

5. First came an asthmatic wheeze and then his fateful words, "I am ready to die and want all efforts to save my life discontinued."

6. The client wanted her full legal rights and "any money I can collect," for the injury had left her completely disabled.

7. Golfers teeing off are advised to shout "Fore" just before they address the ball.

8. Arthur exclaimed, "Have you no mercy for one so young?"

9. Who can forget "'Twas brillig, and the slithy toves / Did gyre and gimble in the wabe"?

10. We cannot put up with "unintentional violence" and "unpremeditated assault" any longer.

Chapter 3

1. 1. Both candidates lacked the qualities that excite potential supporters; neither appeared to have solid support as the campaign drew to a close in November.

2. The many new nations of Africa find the United Nations an excellent platform for political propaganda; the older nations sense that the day is coming when they will be in the minority in that world forum.

3. The Representative from New York grew more and more disturbed; she could see that the problems of her beloved city were going to be ignored.

4. Many children have the advantage of a home life filled with love; too many others never experience the warmth and tenderness of parents who care for them.

5. The state of Ohio boasts a tradition of independent liberal arts colleges; students from all parts of the United States flock there to take advantage of the fine education offered.

6. I can remember a time when all politicians were admired by their constituents; almost nobody holds them in high regard today.

7. The collapse of the Teton Dam has caused many of us to wonder whether the public projects are planned carefully; it is no surprise that environmentalists are gaining new support.

8. At first colleges lacked adequate dormitory space for upper classmen and upper classwomen; the rapid building program of recent years has created the problem of excess capacity.

9. Corporate officers too often ignore the welfare of their employees; the result is that worker morale falls and absenteeism increases.

10. All applications for admission must be filed by the third week in November; late applications will be processed upon payment of a penalty fee.

2. 1. Shirley's first experience in graduate school was far from satisfactory; nevertheless, she returned for a second semester with her confidence unimpaired.

2. We were no longer welcome in Enrico's pizzeria; instead, for the next several weeks, we patronized his competitor across the street.

3. Our regular veterinarian was unable to board our old hound on short notice; consequently, we began to leave him at a kennel that had a poor reputation for cleanliness.

4. The closing date for applications had already passed; nevertheless, we decided to send in the papers and hope for the best.

5. Some attorneys manage to antagonize their clients; notwithstanding, when this happens, the attorneys have no option but to exert their best efforts in their clients' behalf.

6. The labor organizer compiled an excellent record during her first year in the field; indeed, she was declared the most successful negotiator in the union's history.

7. I shall return next week for another attempt at the record; meanwhile, I intend to spend all my spare time practicing turns and jumps.

8. This past season has been the worst in the orchestra's recent history; consequently, the budget deficit is at a dangerous level.

9. Margaret Mitchell found herself unable to sell *Gone with the Wind* to publisher after publisher; consequently, she felt that no one would ever publish the book that had consumed so many years of her life.

10. Katherine applied to several medical schools before finding one that would accept her; furthermore, many of them never even acknowledged receipt of her application.

3. 1. Students of language will find much valuable information in Wentworth and Flexner's *Dictionary of American Slang,* which is periodically revised; Partridge's *A Dictionary of Slang and Unconventional English,* a favorite of those who admire good writing; and Mencken's classic *The American Language.*

2. I enjoy several types of films: westerns, primarily because I love simple stories that always end happily; romances, which take me out of the real world for ninety minutes; and detective mysteries, because I never can guess who the guilty person is.

3. They all were gourmets: my mother, who never did learn how to cook properly; my father, who cared little about food; and my oldest brother, who would eat anything put in front of him.

4. My natural inclination to judge horses on the basis of beauty led me to lose all three races; the first, which had a beautiful but spavined little mare running against five fast geldings; the second, in which my roan dazzler never even left the starting gate; and the third, in which the ugliest seven-year old on the card won by nine lengths over a field of equine beauty contest winners.

5. The candidates this year include Jay Tolliver, a successful fast-food merchant; Irwin Gordon, a sometimes seller of worthless municipal bonds; Les Page, once a high school guidance counselor; and Mary McGraw, executive secretary to a traveling salesman.

4. 1. In her first visit to the leper colony, the young physician was appalled by the lack of care, sanitary facilities, and adequate diet; but on returning the next year, she was encouraged by the general improvement in health, morale, and living conditions of the afflicted people.

2. After many attempts to identify the gene, the researcher decided that he had overlooked the source of his materials, the temperature at which they had been stored before shipment, and the preparation of instruments for the delicate process; yet he was still far from solution of the problem, as it turned out, since there were many more variables to control in the demanding process.

3. Successful businesses require dedicated, capable employees who are willing to exert their best efforts in support of an enterprise that yields rewards only to the group that controls it, finances it, and establishes policy; but many people, accustomed to hard work under any conditions, do their best even when they see no chance, ultimately, of gaining adequate reward.

4. Plato suggested, according to some interpretations, that the loftiest occupation is the study of philosophy; but such a pursuit would not be possible for men and women forced by the demands of living to spend all their time seeking food, protecting themselves against attack by wild animals, and keeping warm in a harsh environment.

5. Once the convention was over, the delegates filed out, thoroughly confused, terribly disturbed by what they had seen, wondering whether they had really participated in a democratic process; and many of them still wondered about their roles when they went home the next day to be questioned by those who elected them, believing that every delegate would represent the people back home wisely, confidently, and carefully.

6. The individuals to watch as the events began to unfold, he said, were not Edwards, Pulham, and Godfrey; they were already too involved, by self-interest, by past actions, and by personal commitment to the goals of the organization.

7. On the economic question, to tell the truth, there was little to be done, little to be gained; and the harsh realities of the political situation, too long ignored, demanded either a policy of total and immediate commitment, since all parties were involved, or total absence of action.

8. Hazel intended, as well as she understood her intentions, to become a full participant in all activities of the program, including housing and public welfare, so that she could achieve what she had set out to achieve; Sam, for his part, had every intention of doing nothing, since he had become thoroughly disillusioned by what he had seen already.

9. By the middle of his second term, as a result of many months of hard work, Warren knew he would be unable to complete his thesis or his course work no matter how much time, effort, and dedication he put into his work; the only attitude he could adopt, therefore, was one of complete resignation to the failure that was on its way.

10. The committee, it appeared, credited him fully insofar as his research was concerned; but no one in the department, it was also clear, saw him as performing his teaching duties outstandingly, even acceptably.

5. 1. I am sending my applications to four schools: Williams, Cal Tech, Vanderbilt, and Case.

2. Bill can always get work as a nurse, social worker, or teacher.

3. Our club has four standing committees: Budget, Ceremonies, Personnel, and Awards.

4. The Chamber of Commerce represents the interests of all the businesses in our area, including companies in the following industries:

        metallurgy
        chemicals
        aerospace
        office equipment

5. My favorite authors are Dos Passos, Dreiser, Mann, and Galsworthy.

6. Leading companies in the United States automobile industry are General Motors, Ford, and Chrysler.

7. Lincoln Center, in the heart of New York City, each year produces excellent ballet, drama, and music for the general public.

8. The New England states include Maine, New Hampshire, Vermont, and Massachusetts; Rhode Island is so small that we are inclined to overlook it.

9. Some of the following are suspected of containing carcinogenic substances:
        tobacco
        fish
        pork
        beef
        chicken
Can you identify the suspect substances?

10. Emma soon became known for the quality of her work in the following media: needlepoint, batik, tie-dye, and macramé.

6. 1. The departmental chairman rose to his feet and began: "Not one of the distinguished members of this university has addressed the root question even though we all have heard opinions on every aspect of our peripheral functions. What I ask is whether we do ourselves more harm than good by refusing to face what is really troubling all of us."

2. The child's nurse answered, "I have always done my level best to raise the boy the way a boy should be raised."

3. At the conclusion of the service, the minister left the pulpit and walked to the floor of the church: "I must speak on the matter of your responsibilities as citizens in deciding which of the two candidates for President you prefer. For my own part I say that no one in the clergy has any right to instruct you in such temporal matters."

4. Their position was stated plainly by their leader in these unforgettable words: "I am going to make you an offer you cannot refuse. Either you return the cash immediately and see your family again or you die right now."

5. Nietzsche said of the mind of the vain man: "It resembles a well stocked and ever renewed store that attracts buyers of every class. They can find almost everything, have almost everything, provided they bring with them the right kind of money—admiration."

6. The old man looked at his wife and said, "I shall not live much longer, I know, but I do not want to make out a will just yet."

7. Thomas Mann, in *The Magic Mountain,* had this to say of time: "Time has no divisions to mark its passage; there is never a thunderstorm or blare of trumpets to announce the beginning of a new month or year. Even when a new century begins, it is only we mortals who ring bells and fire pistols."

8. Helen replied, "There is no reason for buying a house just yet, since we are getting along well enough in this apartment."

9. I still recall words spoken by Elmer Davis after World War II: "Atomic warfare is bad enough; biological warfare would be worse; but there is something that is worse than either. The French can tell you what it is, or the Czechs, or the Greeks, or the Norwegians, or the Filipinos; it is subjection to an alien oppressor."

10. Let us all consider this thought: If we do not ensure a decent life for all our people, then none of us will rest easy again.

7. 1. The war in Vietnam had an impact on the people at home unlike that of any other recent American war: people seemed torn between a deeply engrained patriotism and a suspicion that a terrible mistake had been made.

2. World War I ended for the United States in a little over a year; World War II lasted almost four full years.

3. Familiarity breeds contempt: if peoples everywhere got to know one another better, the world would be torn apart.

4. The pleasures of marriage are not understood by the unmarried; they think only of emotions and passions remote from the contentment of the happily married state.

5. The museums of New York City are rich in art treasures; the night life is unsurpassed anywhere.

6. The dying man said he would not want even one extra hour of life: how could he pretend that his life had been enjoyable?

7. Without great art, life would be less human: the work of the masters dignifies and enriches our existence.

8. Thoughts of suicide console the desperate: they help many of us get through especially bad nights.

9. A good critic tries to see the world through the eyes of the playwright whose work he evaluates: can it really be this way, are people capable of such actions, is life really that good or that bad?

10. Fear of being caught prevents many honest people from committing crime; desire to be caught prevents many criminals from living honest lives.

8. 1. Several counties were severely affected by the recent hurricane: Westchester, Suffolk, Putnam, and Nassau.

2. Our group will meet on Monday night if a quorum is present; otherwise, the next meeting will be delayed one month.

3. When the store reopens for business, certain managers will no longer be working there: Ms. Chadwick, Mrs. Taylor, and Mr. Forsythe.

4. I would be pleased to have your comments regarding Arlene, who led the chorus last week; my supervisor is considering her for promotion to leader of the combined chorus and has asked me to collect whatever information is available on her musicianship, leadership qualities, and reliability.

5. The prospectus left many questions unanswered: Are the archives complete? Are the documents well preserved? Are scholars encouraged to use the facility?

6. Kentucky and Tennessee burley tobaccos were carefully cultivated, harvested, selected, and aged to give the smoothest smoke possible; yet, despite the best efforts of the company to control all aspects of distribution, careless packaging ruined thousands of pounds of the prize mixture.

7. We are interested in obtaining one copy of each of the following:
    John T. Gause, *The Complete Word Hunter*
    Alfred H. Holt, *Phrase and Word Origins*
    C. C. Bombaugh, *Oddities and Curiosities of Words and Literature*

8. Can you define the following terms: feminine rhyme, masculine rhyme, double rhyme, triple rhyme, end rhyme, and internal rhyme?

9. Chiasmus is defined as the use of phrases that are syntactically parallel but have their elements reversed, as in this line from Pope: "Works without show, and without pomp presides."

10. We all admire her wizardry with words; her difficulty in dealing with people destroys whatever effectiveness she otherwise has.

Chapter 4

1. 1. Hemingway's novels have delighted generations of readers (promoters of bullfights appreciate them too) since 1926, when *The Sun Also Rises* was published.

2. In *haiku* the poet writes in three lines totaling seventeen or nineteen syllables (what would the great

sonneteers have done with so little room in which to work?); *haiku* employs allusions and comparisons primarily.

3. Chapman once remarked that readers in years to come would not be able to tell (Hawthorne is the obvious exception here) that people in America were of two sexes.

4. Modern critics are not always masters of English prose (I am not speaking of Hugh Kenner and Edmund Wilson); we can say the same of earlier critics as well.

5. Earlier works in accounting pointed out erroneously that capital gains were to be treated as ordinary income (what a tax liability the unwary incurred!), but later works corrected this error.

6. The student writer is always passionate, whether intending to be so or not, in presenting ideas to readers (can a student writer really be said to have more than one reader?); the seasoned professional reserves passion for the occasional story or essay.

7. Many other stones are quite large (the heaviest ones weigh fifty tons and more) and are the remains of a cap of sandstone that once covered the entire area.

8. According to Leon D. Adams, writing in a popular magazine, road signs create hazards for drivers (are you one of them?) rather than advance the cause of traffic safety.

9. Stephen Dedalus (*A Portrait of the Artist as a Young Man*) moves from childhood through boyhood into maturity (Salinger's protagonists never quite make it). [This sentence can also be punctuated as two sentences: Stephen Dedalus (*A Portrait of the Artist as a Young Man*) moves from childhood through boyhood into maturity. (Salinger's protagonists never quite make it.)]

10. I remember well the lessons my father tried to teach me. (His favorite text was thoroughness in work, a lesson I never learned too well.) What I remember best of all was not the subject of any particular lesson, but the manner in which the teaching proceeded. I had first to stand before him while he slowly took off his awesome leather belt. While I waited in full anticipation of that dreadful first blow, he would sit down and—holding the strap in both his hands—would stare hard at me until I could return his gaze no longer. Finally he would say (and how I loved that moment), "Well?" I quickly responded, "I'll never do it again, Pa." "Never?" "I'm sure I'll never do it again, Pa." To my knowledge (I don't tell my own children this), he never once hit me with his strap. I am certain I would remember if he had.

2. 1. Nuclear energy has not yet fulfilled its promise: (a) nuclear power plants are often shut for repairs, (b) nuclear fuel is far more expensive than fossil fuel, and (c) nuclear plants cost much more to construct than we originally were led to believe.

2. A Rembrandt painting was auctioned off for ten million dollars ($10,000,000.00) and promptly resold for half again as much.

3. The Department of Welfare cut off funds from the family because (1) the father managed to find a part-time job, (2) two of the children left home, and (3) the couple could produce no marriage certificate.

4. To gain a liberal arts degree at our college, students must take at least one elective course in (a) mathematics, (b) science, (c) history, and (d) Latin, in addition to fulfilling elective requirements in a major field.

5. The terminal marks of punctuation are (1) the period, (2) the question mark, and (3) the exclamation point.

3. 1. "Can you imagine a better use for it [water] than saving the life of a child?"

2. Can you find it (I assume you want to) without disturbing everything else in the room?

3. "I'm a Noo Yawkuh [*sic*] and willing to suffer the consequences," he wrote in a letter to his mother.

4. "That book [*The Great Gatsby*] showed Fitzgerald at the top of his form."

5. Willa Cather's great novel (*My Antonia*) continues to fascinate readers.

6. In replying to the two women, Lincoln wrote: "*The religion that sets men to rebel and fight against their Government,* because, as they think, that Government does not sufficiently help some men to

eat their bread in the sweat of other men's faces, is not the sort of religion upon which people can get to heaven.'' [Author's emphasis.]

7. ''Empathy is the projection of one's feelings into a perceived situation, an *Einfühlung* [literally a feeling into—Ed.], in which the viewer merges his own emotion with the situation.''

8. A trope (also known as a figure of speech) must be highly evocative to be effective; a trope that is not significant or moving is commonplace, not worthy of the name.

9. Irony of fate (Fowler says this phrase is hackneyed) describes the view that God finds amusement in manipulating human beings.

10. ''Gothic novels still find readers today [the first was Walpole's *Castle of Otranto,* 1764], and many writers earn a good living by turning such romances out as rapidly as they can to satisfy a growing audience for paperback tales designed to chill the willingly chillable.

Chapter 5

1.   1. ''How will I ever get through graduate school now that tuition has been increased again?'' Grace asked.

2. The police officers all demanded pay increases, claiming that they could not pay their living expenses on what they were then earning.

3. I ask you once more, ''Do you really intend to return the money I lent you?''

4. Rebecca prefers the Compact Oxford, although I don't know why. As Harry said yesterday, ''That damned compact majority dictionary has done more to ruin eyesight than all the movies in town.''

5. ''When are you going to mow the lawn, John?'' Mother asked.

6. ''I cannot help recalling the ugly incident every time I see Mike,'' I said. ''He doesn't seem at all contrite.''

7. ''Of all the many types of trees in the woods near our house,'' he said, ''the copper beeches are the most spectacular.''

8. ''If you must disagree with me constantly,'' Hazel said, ''would you please just ignore me from now on.''

9. I told you that I was surely not going to be with you last evening.

10. ''Is there any point in continuing this conversation,'' she said, ''if we still are going to end up fighting?''

11. She insisted that she was sorry about the trouble she had caused.

12. ''If that teacher gives us one more assignment, I think I'll do something desperate to get out of it,'' Annette said.

13. The headwaiter looked at us the way headwaiters always look at us and said, ''I'm sorry. I cannot seat anyone who is not dressed properly.'' He paused and then went on, ''You wouldn't want me to offend our other patrons, would you?''

14. ''Please stop that lawnmower for a while,'' I begged. ''The noise is killing me.''

15. ''Can you find your way by yourself,'' I asked, ''or should someone go with you for part of the way?''

16. ''Your mortgage payments have been at least one month late in each month of the past year,'' the bank president said; ''therefore, I shall have to ask you now to pay the rest of your mortgage in full.''

17. ''Does it hurt very much?''
''More than I can say. I've never felt worse pain.''
''Let me stop now and give you another injection before I complete the extraction.''

18. ''Were you in the room when the defendant said that?'' the attorney asked.

19. ''Are you certain the child asked for another chance?'' the principal said.

20. Are you willing to testify that the prisoner said, ''If I don't get my parole this time, I'll break out of this prison''?

2. 1. In a poem written in 1892, William Butler Yeats commented on the brevity of human life: "From our birthday until we die, Is but the twinkling of an eye."

2. Mark Twain, in *Life on the Mississippi,* described the childhood ambition he shared with all his friends:

> When I was a boy, there was but one permanent ambition among my comrades in our village on the west bank of the Mississippi River. That was, to be a steamboatman. We had transient ambitions of other sorts, but they were only transient. When a circus came and went, it left us all burning to become clowns; the first negro minstrel show that ever came to our section left us all suffering to try that kind of life; now and then we had a hope that, if we lived and were good, God would permit us to become pirates. These ambitions faded out, each in its turn; but the ambition to be a steamboatman always remained.

3. What did Thoreau think of the way men and women spend their lives? "Our life," he wrote, "is frittered away in detail."

4. Why did Thoreau retreat to Walden?

> I wanted to live deep and suck out all the marrow of life, to cut a broad swath and shave close, to drive life into a corner and reduce it to its lowest terms, and, if it proved to be mean, why then to get the whole and genuine meanness of it, and publish its meanness to the world; or if it were sublime, to know it by experience, and be able to give a true account of it in my next excursion.

5. The old ballad goes on:

> John he made a steel-driving man,
> They took him to a tunnel to drive,
> He drove so hard he broke his heart,
> He laid down his hammer and he died, my babe,
> He laid down his hammer and he died.

6. Brutus continues: "Not that I loved Caesar less, but that I loved Rome more."

7. Milton referred to "Jonson's learned sock," meaning his ability to write drama.

8. The Superintendent of the Census in 1890, commenting on the status of the American frontier, wrote: "Up to and including 1880 the country had a frontier of settlement, but at present the unsettled area has been so broken into by isolated bodies of settlement that there can hardly be said to be a frontier line."

9. Who can surpass Carl Sandburg's characterization of Chicago as "Hog-butcher for the world, Tool-maker, Stacker of Wheat"? Yes, this "Player with Railroads and the nation's Freight-handler" even today is "Stormy, husky, brawling," indeed the "City of the Big Shoulders."

10. In the fourth edition of *The American Language,* Mencken declared that "the pull of America has become so powerful that it has begun to drag English with it," and today many British scholars abhor the Americanisms that have become commonplace in British speech, just as the French inveigh against *franglais.*

11. In his poem "Locksley Hall Sixty Years After," Tennyson cautions writers and thinkers against careless expression: "Authors—essayist, atheist, novelist, realist, rhymester, play your part,/Paint the mortal shame of nature with the living hues of art."

12. Franklin D. Roosevelt closed his first inaugural address with a call for the assistance of divinity: "In this dedication of a Nation we humbly ask the blessing of God. May He protect each and every one of us. May He guide me in the days to come." He then proceeded to the reviewing stand to watch the inaugural parade.

13. The record of Franklin D. Roosevelt's press conferences reveals the ability of the man to engage in give-and-take with members of the press, always with humor when appropriate. For example, a reporter once asked him whether a ban on highway use during a parade included "parking shoulders." He replied:

"Parking shoulders?"

"Yes, widening out on the edge, supposedly to let the civilians park as the military goes by."

"You don't mean necking places?"

14. Herbert Hoover once said, "Corporations are not a thing apart from the people, for they are owned by somewhere between six and ten million families."

15. And what did businessmen think of American civilization? "If you destroy the leisure class," J. P. Morgan once told a Senate committee, "you destroy civilization."

3. 1. The pompous man went on at great length: "Have you considered, dear friends, whether you can, to quote the Old Testament, 'in the day of prosperity be joyful, but in the day of adversity consider,' or have you so wasted your inner resources that you no longer can be anything but joyful and 'in the day of adversity' stop trying completely?"

2. The exact words I used in the examination were: "Conrad manages to focus on moments of decision, moments when men must make difficult choices. This is why Conrad has been called 'a historian of fine consciences.' "

3. "In conclusion," the speaker said, "I want only to quote Kipling on the evils of tobacco: 'A woman is only a woman, but a good cigar is a smoke.' "

4. In *The Autobiography of Benjamin Franklin,* we find the following: "We have an English proverb that says, 'He that would thrive, must ask his wife.' It was lucky for me that I had one as much disposed to industry and frugality as myself."

5. Our biology teacher opened her lecture by saying, "I want to speak today of mosquitoes, described once as flying insects with a 'damnably poisonous bite, which everyone except hotel managers has seen, heard, or suffered from.' "

4. 1. I was fortunate enough to be present at the Oberlin College commencement exercise in May 1938, when Robert Frost delivered an address entitled "What Became of New England?"

2. Have you read Norman Mailer's "Nixon in Miami," which is included in his *Miami and the Siege of Chicago*?

3. He specialized in such Gilbert and Sullivan songs as "I've Got a Little List" and "My Object So Sublime."

4. He cited as one of his principal sources Chalmers Roberts' article on the decision not to intervene in Indochina in 1954, "The Day We Didn't Go to War," *The Reporter,* September 14, 1956.

5. They published a brief portion of the article "Telling the Employees," which appeared in *Time* in 1955.

6. When we saw *Madame Butterfly,* we were so late that we did not take our seats until the soprano was ready to sing "One Fine Day."

7. *The New York Times* published the article "Which Way America?" during the year before the United States bicentennial.

8. Frances Perkins, long a member of the cabinet in President Roosevelt's administrations, published "The Builder of Roosevelt's Presidency" in *The New Republic* in 1954.

9. Matthew Arnold's poem "Dover Beach" is often quoted.

10. Joseph Brodsky's poem "A Halt in the Desert" appears in his *Selected Poems,* published in the United States by HarperCollins.

5. 1. Do you know that "normalcy" was coined by Warren G. Harding?

2. We owe "ecdysiast" to the fertile mind of H. L. Mencken.

3. The ecdysiast walked slowly across the stage, shedding articles of clothing as she went.

4. If you are going to study rhetoric, you will have to learn such terms as "chiasmus," "diacope," and "periphrasis."

5. The old slang expression "twenty-three skiddoo" is rarely heard these days.

6. Do you know anyone who uses "amanuensis" for "secretary"?

7. He was not above using such clichés as "stone-cold dead," "gift of gab," and "rotten to the core."

8. Few people today make a distinction between "disinterested" and "uninterested" in their speech or writing.

9. Once she started her analysis, all we heard from Emma was Freudian jargon: "libido," "ego," "superego," and the rest.

10. High school teachers of English have prejudiced generations of students against starting sentences with "and" or "but."

6. 1. *Correct*

2. *Correct*

3. *Correct*

4. *Correct*

5. Paul was one of the good guys, but Sam was always a bad guy.

6. "Get off your duffs and get out there and win," the coach said.

7. *Correct*

8. Do you remember when boys wore knickers and girls wore bloomers?

9. He told me he was a psychoanalyst, but I didn't believe him.

10. "Have you read 'In Memoriam' in your English class? Our class really dug it even though we thought it was pretty heavy stuff," George said.

11. Every third word the girl said was "hell," but I can't repeat the dirty words she threw around.

12. A really fine person just does not try to push you around like that.

13. They were willing to pay for first-class seats, but only tourist accommodations were available.

14. The late Alexander Calder made his reputation by creating mobiles out of sheet metal and wire.

15. A book bound in morocco is more expensive than one bound in cloth.

7. 1. "So," he said, "you have written another so-called masterpiece that will go unnoticed by the world."

2. "Did he actually say, 'I'm going to conquer the world,' or is that another one of your embellishments?"

3. In his poem "Il Penseroso" Milton described the pleasures of the contemplative life.

4. Her skin was as smooth as velvet and her eyes deep pools of mystery and promise.

5. He always promised more than he could deliver and never seemed at all embarrassed by his failures.

6. "I want to caution you," she said, "against hasty actions."

7. That cheese was riper than you can imagine.

8. You have been booked for the late train.

9. He always attempted to appear charming, but his charm was that of a dead fish sitting in the hot sun for six hours.

10. His term paper was as dull as most of them are.

11. Louise is a hard worker, isn't she? (Louise is a poor worker, isn't she?)

12. His pretense at a democratic manner made me sick to my stomach.

13. When we had finished eating Bob's sad attempt at a gourmet meal, we went to the drug store to buy something for our stomachs.

14. They buy only the finest food and then ruin it.

15. I see you have been out stealing a few odds and ends.

8. 1. "Let the music and dancing begin!" the pompous host said.

2. As we left the stadium, Jon said, "What a baseball game that was!" I replied, "Bring on the Cincinnati Reds!"

3. Can you remember Herman's tone when he said, "I have changed my life completely"?

4. How ridiculous we found Alice's claim that her teaching was "unsurpassed in the department."

5. "I shall be going to St. Louis in a few weeks to see whether I can hire a new administrative assistant," she said, "to replace my present assistant. Wish me luck."

6. "Why can't the English learn to speak?" Rex Harrison sang.

7. "I have twice had the good fortune to see Da Vinci's 'Mona Lisa,' " my cousin said as we walked in the garden, "and don't care whether I never again have the chance to see another painting."

8. "Sylvia cares enough about her sisters, brother, and father," I suggested; "I want to know why she does not care about herself." (A period can also be used in place of the semicolon.)

9. Kenyon quickly said, "Unless the city plays a more active role, our neighborhoods will sicken and die."

10. "When you have a chance to read 'Sports of the Times' in this morning's *Times*, you will know why professional football no longer is a sport," he said.

11. I replied, "You have only to hear him read 'To be or not to be' to understand why he is called the finest young Shakespearean actor now performing."

12. "A friend of mine who fought in Germany during World War II says there is considerable doubt over whether General McAuliffe was the one who replied 'Nuts!' when the Germans demanded surrender of the 101st Airborne Division," she said. "What's more, there's even greater doubt that the actual reply was 'Nuts!' "

13. "I quote Noel Coward on 'mad dogs and Englishmen' whenever my friends ask me to spend a day on the beach," her letter said. "Why turn your skin to leather by the time you reach forty, when it does not take much strength to resist a chance to loll about half-naked in front of a gallery of gawking young men eager to exhibit their rippling biceps and hairy chests?"

14. The first question on the test really stumped me: "If Moby Dick is the symbol of evil, what does Captain Ahab symbolize? What does Queequeg symbolize?"

15. All of us agreed that Selma gave the best reading of "Ode to the West Wind"; she gave each line its full poetic impact, modulated her voice beautifully, and appeared to understand and experience all the lines, from "O wild West Wind, thou breath of Autumn's being" through "If Winter comes, can Spring be far behind?"

Chapter 6

1. 1. Everything was turning out just the way I wanted it: I was rich and famous and sought after—but my alarm clock ruined everything.

2. Just when the crops were ready for harvesting, a storm flattened our fields—how can one predict the weather?

3. Catherine had planned for every contingency she had foreseen—how could she have done more?

4. The feeble voice of the electorate spoke once again—slightly less than half of the eligible voters went to the polls.

5. I called to him again and again, "Please, John, don't go. Please, John, don't go. Please, John—" but I could not get him back.

6. What she really meant was—you know what she meant.

7. We all were concerned—you know how much we cared—that the brothers were getting in too deep.

8. I think we overfed the poor thing—you know how pups look at you with those sad eyes.

9. These are not hard times—if only you had lived during the Great Depression.

10. A new threat has arisen—you may not understand it now.

2. 1. The neighborhood insists on all its rights—proper housing, hot lunches for schoolchildren, safe streets, fire protection—and gets them too.

2. The young couple wanted so few things—a small house, a faithful dog, and decent air to breathe—and couldn't get any of them.

3. Alice is looking for a job in either of her fields, editing or teaching.

4. The suit he was wearing—a four-button yellow velvet—achieved its purpose fully when he entered the theater lobby.

5. His old car, a battered Studebaker, is now up on blocks.

6. Their favorite drinks, coffee and tea, were becoming too expensive for their budget.

7. Three dogs—an Irish setter, a Russian wolfhound, and a German shepherd—were the scourge of the neighborhood.

8. His degree, Master of Arts in Social Work, will enable Robert to gain useful employment among the hill people of South Carolina.

9. Anne's achievement—a Doctor of Medicine degree *cum laude*—made her entire family happy.

10. The promised reforms—improved city planning, provision for open space in the city center, and rent allowances for the indigent—became important issues in that year's elections.

3. 1. Popular conceptions of political morality—one must use that word, no matter how far-fetched it seems—do not speak well of our practicing politicians.

   2. John Milton (1608–1674) is considered one of the three greatest English poets.

   3. Zircon, a common mineral, is frequently used in inexpensive jewelry.

   4. The Rocky Mountains—I last saw them in 1970—are one of the great tourist attractions in the United States.

   5. Rockville, Maryland, is one of the finest suburbs of Washington, D.C.

   6. By the time we had finished talking—Joseph later told me we had talked for three hours—both of us were so tired we fell asleep in our chairs.

   7. I don't mind spending a good deal of money for a word processor—how would I pursue my writing if I did not have one?—yet $2,600 is a great deal more than I can justify for even the finest machine.

   8. Once a furnace wears out—they all must wear out eventually—the homeowner can do nothing but buy a new one.

   9. We overlook the tremendous variety of beautiful terrain one can see in just a few hours' drive from New York City—we overlook other advantages as well—and miss the chance for a relatively inexpensive camping vacation.

   10. Cemeteries—would God we could do without them!—charge so much for their services that only the grief of bereaved families and the awkwardness of death without burial preclude a consumers' boycott.

4. 1. A dictionary, thesaurus, word processor, and paper—these tools of the trade are the mainstays of a modern writer's life.

   2. Police officers, fire officers, and sanitation workers—no municipality can do without these men and women.

   3. Beagles, coon hounds, and spaniels—these breeds often serve the hunter well.

   4. *Finnegans Wake, Alice's Adventures in Wonderland, Looking Backward,* and *Pilgrim's Progress*—all are concerned with dreams.

   5. Sloops, schooners, yawls—such ships are commonly seen in coastal waters.

   6. Joseph Conrad, Herman Melville, and William Faulkner—these and other fine novelists are studied in her English class.

   7. The young boys frequently set fires in vacant buildings; they robbed vagrants, old women, and helpless children; they burglarized neighborhood shops—there was nothing they wouldn't do.

   8. Lithographs, prints, and etchings—you will find them all for sale in most art galleries.

   9. A walk in the park, a Sunday stroll on Fifth Avenue, a trip to the Cloisters—these were the things we missed when we left New York.

   10. Theater, concerts, libraries, and museums—these are the attractions of a great city.

5. 1. How I wish—can you understand why?—I were closer to death!

   2. Eloise insisted on remaining behind when the group left base camp—what a mistake that was!

   3. The entire play—what a fiasco!—took four and a half hours to run through during dress rehearsal.

4. The basic problem—how can we pay for the new car?—will not be solved by sitting here and worrying.

5. Everyone in the family—what a crowd!—squeezed into the camper for the trip to the lake.

6. Once you have determined what the roofing repairs will cost—I hope you are still listening.

7. The mountains are so beautiful in autumn—how I wish we were still there!

8. Some politicians can never manage to maintain a discreet silence on sensitive matters when questioned by the press—they refer to reporters as interrogators—and do themselves more harm by speaking than they would by respectfully declining to answer.

9. The tired old champion—what a runner she was in her prime!—sat in the dressing room for almost an hour without looking up.

10. Norman Mailer—will anyone ever write a better first novel?—is a marvelous stylist and an engaging public personality.

6. 1. one hundred 2. six hundred 3. five-ninths 4. seven-sixteenths 5. twenty-six
6. eleven 7. twenty-four 8. two million 9. five-eighths 10. eighty-eight

7. 1. all-American 2. ex-wife 3. self-fulfillment 4. *ex cathedra* 5. exophthalmic
6. self-worshipping 7. self-winding 8. selfless 9. self-incriminating 10. self-starters

8. 1. first cousin 2. father-in-law 3. stepson 4. stepfather 5. daughter-in-law 6. son-in-law 7. grandfather 8. great-grandfather 9. great-grandson 10. granddaughter

9. 1. semi-industrialized 2. semifinalist 3. antilogarithm 4. antigravity 5. anti-intellectual
6. full-length portraits 7. still life 8. fire-resistant 9. ice-free winters 10. trash can

10. 1. That man's rule can surely be termed iron-fisted government.

2. The long-term outlook for the economy is sound.

3. Our medical-school faculty includes two Nobel laureates.

4. A five-foot-three shortstop is as unusual as a left-handed catcher.

5. Early blooming roses can be damaged by late frosts.

6. Dave and Dina are a poorly matched pair.

7. The 1976 New York Yankees and Cincinnati Reds were unevenly matched.

8. A well-suited couple can expect a happy life together.

9. Fast-moving films always attract large audiences even if their casts are poorly chosen.

10. He felt bright eyed and bushy tailed that morning, ready for the rapid-fire discussion his advisers predicted.

11. Down-at-the-heels salesmen cannot expect to achieve sure-fire results.

12. The so-called teacher addressed his students in a quavering, pity-me voice that revealed his insecurity.

13. Open-minded students can learn a great deal from such a teacher.

14. She was open minded, but her associates could not bring themselves to treat her as anything but a stereotype.

15. Third-rate scholars produce third-rate scholarship.

11. 1. transcontinental 2. trans-Canadian 3. extraterritorial 4. Pan-American 5. Pan-Germanism 6. transpacific 7. Trans-Adriatic 8. mid-July 9. pre-Roosevelt
10. anti-Islamic

12. 1. My fourth- and fifth-grade teachers were especially valuable in teaching me essential study skills.

2. They stood second and third in their classes.

3. Much of the great literature of the eighteenth and nineteenth centuries goes unread today.

4. We were fortunate to win red and blue ribbons at the dog show.

5. A cat we had for many years was neither a blue- nor a red-ribbon winner yet managed to bear almost twenty prize-winning kittens.

6. Next year, according to our landlord, all second-, third-, and fourth-floor rooms will be completely redecorated.

7. First-, second-, and third-ranked pupils will be eligible for the final competition.

8. Did you know that the Titan missile had first- and second-stage rockets?

9. Entering students will be assigned by time of receipt of applications to pre-, mid-, and post-July classes.

10. First- and second-semester students register last in our school.

13.
1. Under the city statutes then in existence, he was entitled to two 6-month delays.

2. The judge gave her a suspended 30-day sentence.

3. A champion weightlifter cannot be bothered with 50-pound weights unless they are added to barbells already loaded with a few hundred pounds.

4. H-hour instructions were as precise as the company commander could write; the G-2 had made sure of that.

5. We have lived through development and deployment of the A-bomb and the H-bomb, but we have yet to see the latter used in anger.

6. The F-15 aircraft has not been without its failures.

7. The battalion S-3 developed plans for the attack.

8. We will have to buy seven 6-inch boards in order to make that bookcase.

9. The designer decided to use three 5-inch rules on each page of the magazine.

10. We bought a dozen 14-ounce mugs to prepare for the party.

Chapter 7

1. 1. Alice's 2. city's 3. hour's 4. Aristophanes' 5. Luis's 6. Lois's, company's 7. moment's 8. Harris's 9. Hawes's 10. Timer's

2. 1. Thomases' 2. children's 3. mothers', children's 4. hours' 5. alumnae's 6. workers' 7. weeks' 8. years' 9. Physicians', patients' 10. guards'

3. 1. anybody's 2. no one's 3. Somebody's 4. Everybody's 5. Each one's

4. 1. one another's 2. each other's 3. brother-in-law's 4. sergeant-at-arms's 5. Chief Justice's

5. 1. Wodehouse, Clark, and Peal's 2. Puerto Rico and Haiti's 3. Colgate and Skidmore's 4. Wentworth and Flexner's 5. Maria and José's

6. 1. Janet's and John's 2. Frank's and Anne's 3. Pooch's, Willy's, and Louie's 4. Plato's and Socrates' 5. April's, July's, and October's (*also acceptable as* April, July, and October)

7. 1. haven't 2. We'd have 3. can't, they've 4. '92, '91 5. shan't

8. 1. its 2. It's 3. its 4. its 5. its 6. its 7. its 8. it's 9. it's 10. it's

9. 1. x's, y's 2. A's 3. rpm's 4. BTU's 5. '90's (this ugly expression can be improved by dropping the second apostrophe: '90s)

Chapter 8

1. 1. Wallace Stegner's most successful novel was *Remembering Laughter*, which appeared in 1937.

2. They were fortunate enough to find a copy of the *Nation* that carried the article they wanted to read.

3. "The Return of a Private" is one of Hamlin Garland's best stories in his volume *Main-Traveled Roads*.

4. Hemingway's story "The Three-Day Blow" appeared in his *In Our Time*, which was published in 1925.

5. Charles Lindbergh's name is inseparable from his companion on the long journey to Le Bourget, *The Spirit of St. Louis*.

6. If you know only *The Great God Brown* and *Ah Wilderness!*, you know only half of Eugene O'Neill's greatness.

7. Many statues of Aphrodite had been attributed to Praxiteles (fourth century B.C.), but none more lovely than the *Aphrodite from Arles*.

8. The Archaeological Museum in Salonika has a mosaic signed "Gnosis" that is entitled *Stag Hunt*.

9. Have you ever seen *La Traviata* or *The Barber of Seville*? If you have not, you have not seen Italian opera at its best.

10. Have you read "Annabel Lee," "Ulalume," or "Lenore"—three of Poe's most frequently quoted poems?

2. 1. The sculptor lived circa 460 A.D.

2. Many students in my classes have chutzpa to a degree seldom approached in people my own age.

3. Greek tragedy relates the failure of heroes to ignore warnings from the gods; the hubris of these tragic figures leads inevitably to catastrophe.

4. We had a dozen *escargots* before going to *escalope de veau* with plenty of *vin ordinaire*.

5. He never failed to complete his poems with a brief *envoi* that restated the principal theme.

6. The cadets of Company A showed sufficient esprit de corps to win the prize month after month.

7. As far as I am concerned, Saul Bellow's novels are *ne plus ultra*.

8. Who can forget the *Schrecklichkeit* of Nazi concentration camps?

9. Their summers were perfect examples of *dolce far niente* that more than made up for winters of intense activity.

10. As far as I can tell, the voters were more interested in *via trita, via tuta* (the beaten path, the safe path) than in taking a chance on an unknown candidate who promised much but never explained how he could carry out his ambitious programs.

3. 1. "But the Airedale . . . was the worst of all my dogs."

2. "When you sit by a pond or winding stream . . . from the corners of the mind thoughts come out and sun themselves."

3. "People who owned closed models . . . bought ball grip handles for opening doors, window anti-rattlers, and deluxe flower vases of the cut-glass anti-splash type."

4. "He fell into the habit of stealing out at night and engaging in long drinking bouts. . . ."

5. "Whether Thurber's drawing requires psychiatry or not, a great many people . . . cannot get enough of it."

Chapter 9

1. 1. Nothing 2. Can 3. Haying 4. The 5. Everyone

2. 1. For 2. In 3. They 4. Which 5. And 6. And

3. 1. Be 2. There, You 3. Something 4. correct 5. correct 6. correct 7. Stop
       8. Go 9. Gather 10. The

4. 1. O 2. O, I 3. I, I 4. correct 5. correct

5. 1. Freudian 2. Native Americans, Southwest 3. Ireland, England, Wales 4. Truman 5. Newtonian 6. British, Americanisms 7. Law Olmsted, New York's, Central Park 8. correct 9. Anglican Church 10. Aberdeen Angus 11. Winston Churchill 12. Roosevelt, American 13. Shakespearean, Petrarchan 14. Francophile, French, Gauguin, Mallarmé 15. Chippendale, New York, London

6. 1. Van 2. Von 3. Du 4. Von 5. Van 6. Van 7. van 8. van, van 9. de, de 10. di

7. 1. Caspian Sea, Europe 2. Pike's Peak 3. correct 4. Little Egg Harbor, New Jersey 5. Salt Lake 6. County Cork, Cuyahoga County 7. correct 8. Strait of Macassar 9. Lebanon, Pennsylvania, Pittsburgh 10. Lingayen Gulf, Luzon

8. 1. correct 2. West 3. East 4. Midwest 5. West New York, New Jersey 6. Southeast Asia 7. Western Michigan 8. United States, Far West 9. South, United States 10. South Carolina

9. 1. Jersey, Middle Atlantic States 2. Bay State 3. Old South, New South 4. Black Forest, Germany 5. Ireland, Emerald Isle 6. Rocky Mountains, Great Plains 7. Salton Sea, Salton Sink8 . California, Golden State 9. Nutmeg State 10. Athens of the Midwest

10. 1. Empire State Building, New York 2. Pennsylvania Avenue, Washington, D.C. 3. Bureau of Media Services, Florida Department of Commerce, W. Gaines Street, Tallahassee, Florida 4. Arizona's, North Central Street, Phoenix 5. John Hancock Tower, Chicago, United States 6. Italy's Paestum 7. Marks Cathedral, Venice 8. Royal Dutch Petroleum Company 9. World Trade Center 10. Pennsylvania Academy of the Fine Arts, American

11. 1. United States Senate 2. Commonwealth of Massachusetts, Senate, House of Representatives 3. Church of Christ, Scientist, Christianity 4. National League, American League 5. Commonwealth of Nations, Governor-General, Queen, Canadian 6. Toastmaster's Club 7. correct 8. Chairman of the English Department, University of Pennsylvania, Provost of the University, Dean of the Graduate School of Fine Arts 9. Brotherhood Award, Rotary Club 10. Bridgeport Gas and Electric Works, Connecticut Utilities Companies

12. 1. Deuteronomy, Numbers 2. Jesus, His, His, God 3. Veda, Hindu 4. Hebrew, *Adonai*, Orthodox Jews, God 5. *Missa Solemnis,* Christmas 6. Messiah 7. Ten Commandments, Israel8 . Almighty 9. Virgin Mary, Her 10. Ramadan, Islam

13. 1. United States, Nobel Prize for Economics 2. North Atlantic Treaty, July, North Atlantic Treaty Organization 3. Mason-Dixon Line, Pennsylvania, Maryland 4. Magna Carta, American, Bicentennial Year, United States 5. Catholic Church, First Vatican Council, Second Vatican Council 6. Germany and Italy, Rome-Berlin Axis, Japan 7. Versailles Treaty, World War 8. Casablanca Conference, Prime Minister Churchill, President Roosevelt 9. American Civil War, Appomattox, General Lee 10. William the Conqueror, England, Battle of Hastings 11. Middle Ages, European, Italian Renaissance 12. Lutherans, Augsburg Confession, Melanchthon, Lutheran, Diet of Augsburg 13 . correct 14. Gerald Ford, Waterloo 15. July, Korean War, North Korea, South Korea

14. 1. Sir, Prime Minister 2. correct 3. Sergeant 4. Professor 5. correct 6. President 7. Chancellor 8. Ambassador to the Court of St. James 9. correct 10. University Professor

15. 1. Litt.B., Litt.D. 2. Ph.D. 3. Ph.D., French Department of Middleford College 4. D.D.S. 5. D.Ch.E.

16. 1. *Collier's, The Saturday Evening Post* 2. *Saturday Review of Literature* 3. *Vermont Life* 4. "The Fall of the House of Usher" 5. "The Wife of Bath's Tale" 6. "Women in the Literature of the Middle Ages," *Proceedings of the Modern Language Association* 7. *Rolling Stone* 8. *The Mayor of Casterbridge* 9. *Two Gentlemen of Verona* 10. *Wall Street Journal,* "Prices of Commodities and Their Effect on Food Prices"

Chapter 10

1. 1. stabbed 2. slipping 3. appearing 4. tearing 5. deference 6. pestered 7. scrapped 8. scrapping 9. committed 10. commitment 11. conferred, conference 12. beginning 13. widening, deepening 14. running 15. barring, unveiling 16. sunning 17. spanned 18. controlled 19. concurrence, allotted 20. preferential

2. 1. dissect 2. bisect 3. glowworm 4. outtalk 5. pen name 6. whosoever 7. drunkenness 8. bath towel 9. bathhouse 10. meanness 11. meanest 12. formerly 13. formally 14. uncommonness 15. commonality 16. disappearance 17. summons 18. beach house 19. illiterate 20. overrule 21. overreact 22. unnecessary 23. regardless 24. irrefutable 25. misshaped 26. cutthroat 27. reemphasize 28. connect 29. connubial 30. coincidentally

3. 1. tracing 2. hinging 3. singing 4. outrageous 5. bracing 6. Embraceable 7. likable 8. changeable 9. serviceable 10. advisement 11. collapsing 12. charging 13. Suffragettes 14. dying 15. dyeing, dyeing 16. impinging 17. singeing 18. vengeance 19. arrangements 20. hoeing

4. 1. freight, unwieldy 2. weird 3. conceit, receipt 4. brief, siege, thieves 5. Pierced, relief 6. shriek, priests 7. believe 8. relieved, chief, neighbors 9. thieves, sieve 10. reign 11. vein 12. field 13. heinous, neighborhood 14. deceive 15. fiercest 16. yield, niece 17. believe, brief 18. achieve 19. ceiling 20. Seize, grieve

5. 1. Goodbodys 2. attorneys 3. counties 4. quays 5. barflies 6. spies, counterspies 7. convoys 8. Terrys 9. sulkies 10. parties

6. 1. sorrier 2. wispiness 3. daily 4. allays 5. tawdrier 6. drier *or* dryer 7. happiness 8. Cattiness 9. slier *or* slyer 10. grimier

7. 1. tornadoes 2. avocados 3. patios 4. radios 5. silos 6. torpedoes 7. echoes 8. studios 9. barrios 10. potatoes

8. 1. medium 2. alumnus 3. index 4. criterion 5. automaton 6. curriculum 7. synthesis 8. erratum 9. parenthesis 10. ovum

9. 1. costly 2. ghoulish 3. goalie 4. balmy 5. condemnation 6. disciplinary 7. goulash 8. subtlety 9. doubtless 10. gout 11. debt-ridden 12. knowledge 13. solemnity 14. temperament 15. February 16. pneumonia 17. laboratory 18. muscle 19. mussel 20. psychological

10. 1. there, too, here 2. personal 3. tiers 4. stationery 5. waiting, overweight 6. prophesy 7. pried, boards, loose, upstairs 8. wry, principal 9. locale 10. Their, morale 11. Mussel, muscles 12. knead, rye 13. Maybe, may be 14. loan, local 15. wholly 16. it's 17. too, hopping 18. eminent 19. needed, dessert 20. decent 21. There, dissent 22. disparate 23. dual 24. excess 25. access 26. feinted, threw 27. dungeon, their 28. allusions 29. Except 30. affect 31. already 32. altogether, way 33. fore 34. fowl 35. formerly 36. flue, desperate 37. statues, extant 38. Accept 39. its, ordinances 40. naval 41. breathe 42. bore 43. beets 44. banned 45. anecdotes 46. bidding 47. bridle 48. bred 49. butt 50. garrot 51. fare 52. gait 53. guerilla 54. cues 55. currants 56. clothes 57. serials 58. complement 59. coarse 60. cite 61. discreet 62. sighted, deer 63. die, threw 64. devise 65. for 66. elude 67. diary 68. current 69. except, cymbals 70. lye 71. elicit 72. hale 73. censures 74. soared 75. propose 76. peered 77. preyed 78. quiet, quite, too, to 79. role 80. wrapped, mailed 81. rote 82. root 83. route 84. haul 85. its, paws 86. pique, threw 87. statutes, than 88. slight 89. stake 90. sale 91. steel 92. pedaled 93. sewing 94. scene 95. site 96. site 97. shone 98. staid 99. wiles 100. plane, courses

11. 1. mimicking 2. exceed, inadmissible 3. formidable, incomparable 4. contemptible, practicable 5. peaceably 6. panicked 7. supersede 8. unchangeable 9. accede
10. incredible 11. inaudible 12. undamageable 13. measureable 14. lovable
15. incomparably

Index

ORDER CODE	TITLE		QUANTITY	$ AMOUNT
_____	_____		_____	_____
_____	_____		_____	_____
_____	_____		_____	_____
		LOCAL SALES TAX		_____
		$1.25 SHIPPING/HANDLING		_____
		TOTAL		_____

NAME _____
(please print)

ADDRESS _____
(no P.O. boxes please)

CITY _____ STATE _____ ZIP _____

ENCLOSED IS ❑ A CHECK ❑ MASTERCARD ❑ VISA ❑ AMEX (✓ one)

ACCOUNT # _____ EXP. DATE _____

SIGNATURE _____

PRICES SUBJECT TO CHANGE WITHOUT NOTICE AND MAY VARY OUTSIDE U.S.
FOR THIS INFORMATION, WRITE TO THE ADDRESS ABOVE OR CALL THE **800** NUMBER.

Make checks payable to
McGraw-Hill, Inc.

Mail with coupon to:
McGraw-Hill, Inc.
Order Processing S-1
Princeton Road
Hightstown, NJ 08520

or call 1-800-338-3987